*Using Formative Assessment
to Differentiate*
Middle School
Literacy Instruction

Using Formative Assessment to Differentiate

Middle School Literacy Instruction

7 Practices to Maximize Learning

Leslie Laud
Pooja Patel

CORWIN
A SAGE Company

CORWIN
A SAGE Company

FOR INFORMATION:

Corwin

A SAGE Company

2455 Teller Road

Thousand Oaks, California 91320

(800) 233-9936

www.corwin.com

SAGE Publications Ltd.

1 Oliver's Yard

55 City Road

London EC1Y 1SP

United Kingdom

SAGE Publications India Pvt. Ltd.

B 1/I 1 Mohan Cooperative Industrial Area

Mathura Road, New Delhi 110 044

India

SAGE Publications Asia-Pacific Pte. Ltd.

3 Church Street

#10-04 Samsung Hub

Singapore 049483

Publisher: Lisa Luedeke

Acquisitions Editor: Carol Chambers Collins

Associate Editor: Megan Bedell

Editorial Assistant: Sarah Bartlett

Production Editor: Amy Schroller

Copy Editor: Rachel Keith

Typesetter: C&M Digitals (P) Ltd.

Proofreader: Jennifer Thompson

Indexer: Scott Smiley

Cover Designer: Anupama Krishnan

Permissions Editor: Karen Ehrmann

Printed in the United States of America

Library of Congress Cataloging-in-Publication Data

Laud, Leslie.

Using formative assessment to differentiate middle school literacy instruction : seven practices to maximize learning / Leslie Laud, Pooja Patel.

p. cm.

Includes bibliographical references and index.

ISBN 978-1-4522-2621-7 (paperback)

1. Language arts (Middle school)—Evaluation. 2. Academic achievement. I. Patel, Pooja. II. Title.

LB1631.L267 2013

428.2′4—dc23   2012035557

This book is printed on acid-free paper.

12 13 14 15 16 10 9 8 7 6 5 4 3 2 1

Contents

List of Figures

Preface

Over the past two decades, both of us have worked as middle school English teachers and as learning specialists in urban and suburban schools in public and independent school systems. As teachers committed to differentiating middle school literacy instruction, we sought guidance on practical issues and tried to put together a coherent description of what using formative assessment to differentiate literacy instruction looks like. After compiling and developing resources and formulating a framework for how to differentiate literacy instruction, we began presenting at conferences and teaching others. We found an overwhelming demand among literacy teachers to learn more about how they can effectively differentiate literacy instruction in their classrooms.

As we began to use more formative assessment practices regularly, we quickly saw a transformation in students. Struggling, passive students became active, competent learners. Students who excelled but perhaps didn't work as hard as they could were suddenly stretched to achieve beyond what even they thought they could accomplish. Using formative assessment to differentiate literacy instruction provided us and our students with a tool kit for regularly experiencing this kind of eagerness and engagement in learning.

Research shows that instruction is most effective when differentiated so that students are taught at their individual instructional levels (Huebner, 2010). When instruction is either too difficult or too easy, students become frustrated or bored and learning declines. Teachers recognize this intuitively, yet they often find it challenging to differentiate instruction in ways that will challenge each student. Differentiation is facilitated first and foremost when teachers use formative assessments to understand where students are at and then to modify instruction. As a colleague recently put it, "Differentiation and formative assessment are inseparable, like the music of Gladys Knight and the Pips—their music can only result from their combined work together." Formative assessment is effective only when used to differentiate instruction, and differentiating instruction can effectively take place only when following useful, targeted formative assessment.

So what is formative assessment? Formative assessment differs from midunit or end-of-unit (summative) assessments that are used to summarize learning. Formative assessment is collected before and during learning, then used in partnership with students to enable them to know where they stand in mastering unit goals. Teachers use formative assessment data to inform their instruction, and students use it to chart and direct their course of learning. Formative assessment data, when used collaboratively, shift the dynamic to a partnership in which teachers and students work together to ensure students achieve their personal best, whether this involves finally mastering a basic proficiency or further enhancing already advanced skills. In addition, formative assessment is the key objective of the assessment standards of the National Council of Teachers of English (NCTE) and an integral part of instruction to help students master the Common Core State Standards.

Although substantial research on the effectiveness of differentiating instruction is growing, few large-scale studies exist. However, Black and Wiliam (1998) collected over 250 articles and book chapters showing the effectiveness of formative assessment (and the resulting differentiation) in raising student achievement. This research shows that formative assessment can double student gains, and that it may result in the highest gains for students who struggle. Due to the scarcity of large-scale research and legislation such as No Child Left Behind and Response to Intervention that mandates research-based methods, schools have begun to turn to formative assessment and differentiating instruction methods to improve teaching, particularly given the strength of the research base on formative assessment.

This book specifically shows how using formative assessment to differentiate literacy instruction offers the most promising framework for equipping students to use spoken, written, and visual language to accomplish their own purposes with regard to learning, enjoyment, persuasion, and exchange of information (NCTE, 2009, Standard 12), particularly enjoyment. The assessment practices in this book have been shown in our experience and in research cited throughout this book to raise not only achievement but also student motivation. Raising student motivation is a key focus of Standard 1 in NCTE's *Standards for the Assessment of Reading and Writing*. These standards recognize the teacher as "the most important agent of assessment" (NCTE, 2009, Standard 2), although this book argues that students also play a critical role as agents of assessment.

This book presents this information through a framework of seven practices we have developed based on research and classroom experiences. These practices, which we detail in Chapter 1, provide teachers with a snapshot of what a differentiated class looks like as well as concise directions on how to achieve one. Woven throughout the book are practical suggestions, real-world examples, reproducible activities, and connections to NCTE standards and Common Core State Standards. We include this information to illustrate how teachers can use assessment to cultivate the kinds of "centers of inquiry" in their classrooms "where students and teachers investigate and improve their own learning and teaching practices, both individually and as learning communities" (NCTE, 2009, Standard 3).

Chapter 1 offers a framework for formative assessment as well as a purpose for using it. It gives an overview of seven practices that will help teachers start using formative assessment to differentiate instruction, and it highlights ways to create a successful classroom climate in which students accept that individuals will often do different work and feel safe acknowledging areas in which they would like to improve.

Chapter 2 provides an overview of how to specify and convey standards. It also begins the discussion of how to design, administer, and score standards-based assessments, which allow teachers to determine what to teach and how to teach it. It then offers instruction in how to measure what is being learned along the way, and these data provide invaluable feedback that recursively informs next steps to be taken.

Chapters 3 and 4 focus on differentiated instruction. Chapter 3 defines and describes it, whereas Chapter 4 delves into various ways to differentiate and tier lesson plans and tasks. Chapter 4 also offers practical strategies for running a differentiated classroom, including planning units, overseeing tasks, grouping students, dealing with homework, and grading.

Chapter 5 focuses on time management. Since most teachers may be responsible for up to more than a hundred students by middle school, this chapter suggests the most practical and time-efficient ways to create, adapt, collect, and analyze assessments.

We wrote Chapter 6, which addresses specific strategies to support students who struggle, with Shira M. Cohen-Goldberg. This chapter offers a broad framework for fine-tuning differentiation supports to address foundational and higher-order thinking skills.

Chapter 7 offers techniques to challenge students who show strength in the subject. It provides a brief overview of traits that define students who show giftedness or are high achieving and then offers multiple suggestions for ways to enhance their learning.

This book is a result of the journey that we have taken in our efforts to best serve our students. We consider ourselves fortunate to have discovered the value of formative assessment. In the following chapters we share our learnings, and we invite you to share in the journey and keep in touch with us (Leslie@hillforliteracy.org or Pooja979@gmail.com) so that we all can continue to move forward as we learn from one another and help our students continually grow.

Acknowledgments

We would like to thank our many colleagues, whom we have learned so much from over our careers. In particular we owe gratitude to the English teachers at UNIS, especially Gina Voskov, Elaine Kelly, Dan Love, Sheema Karp, Linda Miglierina, Julia Ferguson, Debra MacRae, and Geoff Van Kirk, with whom we have planned countless lessons and engaged in many heartwarming and informative discussions. Leslie also expresses gratitude to her HILL colleagues. Together we have made our lessons more meaningful and effective for our students. Several of the ideas that we have brainstormed, contemplated, or created have found their way into this book.

We would also like to thank the many present and past administrators at UNIS and beyond, including our principals Chris Muller, Anthony Brown, and Lisa Arrastia, whom we have had the honor to work with. We have been lucky to have leaders that have inspired, motivated, and challenged us to do even better. We thank the countless researchers, writers, and conference speakers to whom we owe an enormous debt for all that they have taught us. Karen Harris and Steven Graham, we would not have realized the researchers that were within us without your constant guidance and feedback. Wiley Schubert Reed, your inner poet truly shines and has helped us tremendously. We love your creativity and enthusiasm.

The students we have worked with are forever in our minds. Thank you for working with us, speaking your mind, and embracing our ideas wholeheartedly. Above all, thank you for having faith in your teachers and working to reach your true potential— even when the journey was bumpy.

Finally, we would like to thank our editor and the staff at Corwin for helping us through the process of completing this book.

Pooja thanks Leslie for her tremendous belief in her as an educator, as well as for her breadth of knowledge and information and for the way she always listens to any ideas presented. Pooja learns something from Leslie every time they work together, and without her, she could not have accomplished what she has. Pooja would also like to express her deepest gratitude for the other cheerleaders in her life who truly understand, support, and believe in her passions: her dad; her mom; her brother, Paras; her husband, Mihir; and Gus Uncle.

Leslie thanks Pooja for bringing new spirit and ideas that continuously renew, reenergize, and improve the lives of all of us, who are constantly learning from her, as well as of all of the students lucky enough to have her as a teacher. Leslie also thanks her family members: Kishor, Arjun, and Ravi.

About the Authors

Leslie Laud, EdD, is a facilitator at Hill for Literacy, where she works with school systems to implement literary reforms. She has differentiated instruction in her own classroom, and in co-teaching with her colleagues, for almost two decades. She teaches the online course Evidence Based Writing Strategies Instruction at Bank Street College of Education. She has presented at many conferences both nationally and internationally and has also published many articles in leading journals such as *Educational Leadership* and *Teaching Exceptional Children*. She currently leads staff development groups with teachers in school systems in the Boston area. She received both her doctorate in curriculum and instruction and her master's in special education from Teachers College at Columbia University.

Pooja Patel is a learning specialist who is currently working as a middle school English and humanities teacher at the United Nations International School. She has taught a class at Bank Street College of Education and has presented at national conferences. Additionally, she has published articles in peer-reviewed journals such as *Preventing School Failure* and *Teaching Exceptional Children*. She is also the director of Teachers 4 Student Success (t4ss.org), a nonprofit organization dedicated to providing research-validated literacy instruction to all students regardless of age, disability, and socioeconomic status. She received a master's degree from the reading specialist program at Teachers College at Columbia University.

About the Contributor

Shira M. Cohen-Goldberg is a lead facilitator at Hill for Literacy, Inc., where she works with schools to improve systems for teaching literacy in the realms of curriculum, assessment, and professional development. She has formerly been a literacy coach in Chelsea, Massachusetts; a Reading First Implementation Facilitator for the Massachusetts Department of Elementary and Secondary Education; and a classroom teacher in New York City and California. She received a master's degree in language and literacy from the Harvard Graduate School of Education.

Leslie Laud: To my parents
Pooja Patel: To my mom, my dad, Mihir,
Paras, and Gus Uncle

1

Getting Started With Formative Assessment

When we first read about formative assessment, the compelling research sparked our immediate interest. In a nutshell, formative assessment involves collecting and using ongoing assessment data regularly *to inform teaching and learning*, rather than merely to assign grades. Research shows that formative assessment can double student learning, and it can result in even greater gains for students who struggle (Black & Wiliam, 1998). The more formative assessment is used, the greater the gains. Students given one formative assessment per 15-week period scored 13% higher on final achievement measures. Students receiving 20 assessments scored 26% higher, and those who received 30 assessments scored almost 30% higher (Bangert-Drowns, Kulik, Kulik, & Morgan, 1991).

After using formative assessment regularly, we found this research even more compelling. We witnessed this accelerated growth as our students in special education were mainstreamed back into regular education at rates we had never seen before. Even more gratifying, we watched students beam with pride at what they could now accomplish. Our most disengaged students came alive as they systematically took charge of their own learning and saw their efforts pay off. Moreover, our students unanimously told us how much they liked formative assessments. While the research piqued our interest, our experience secured our buy-in.

In this first chapter you will find:

- An introduction to the formative assessment framework
- An overview of the purpose of formative assessment

- Three ways to begin using formative assessment, with vignettes that illustrate the three paths teachers typically follow
- A self-assessment tool to help you determine how much formative assessment you already use in your own classroom
- Steps to establishing a classroom culture that supports formative assessment practices

AN INTRODUCTION TO THE FORMATIVE ASSESSMENT FRAMEWORK

Formative assessment provides a framework of practices in which both you and your students use assessment data to shift the mindset away from gauging "What has been taught?" toward "What has been learned?" You and your students then use the information gained to guide what you teach and what they focus on learning.

So what exactly is a "formative assessment framework," and where did this framework originate? Formative assessment is a framework of related practices originally proposed by Sadler (1989) and perpetuated by other researchers and practitioners. This framework includes not only the collection of assessment data to inform instruction and learning, but also several related practices that guide which data to collect and how to use these data. Wiliam (2010) formally defined the formative assessment framework as how teachers or students use assessment data to make decisions about next steps—decisions that are better founded with these data than those made without these data.

The research of Black and Wiliam (1998) references and builds on Sadler's (1989) framework. In their view, for assessment to qualify as formative assessment, it must:

- Be based on and directly convey criteria or standards
- Be followed by detailed, clear, and specific feedback
- Involve students in self-assessment, using feedback and goal-directed behavior
- Use the data gathered to inform next steps and adjust teaching practices
- Recognize the enormous impact of assessment on students' confidence and motivation

Therefore, the process of formative assessment involves (1) specifying and conveying standards, (2) collecting assessment data on where students are in relation to these standards, and (3) sharing the data with students via detailed feedback. It is essential to ensure that students are actively involved; their participation is a critical piece of the formative assessment framework. Students will often score their own formative assessments and determine how they can use the results to inform what they focus on learning.

It is also critical for you to use the assessment data "to inform next steps and adjust teaching practices," or to differentiate instruction. Tomlinson (1999) defines differentiating instruction as an organized, flexible, proactive approach to adjusting instruction so that it best meets the needs of all learners and promotes maximum growth for all.

As discussed in the Preface, we developed our own formative assessment framework based on research and classroom experiences (see Figure 1.1). Our framework presents seven practices, or steps, for practitioners; each practice is followed by research that validates its effectiveness.

We suggest that you approach the list of practices as you would a buffet. Do not expect to engage in all of these practices at once or within a short time frame. Teachers we have worked with have repeatedly recommended that we emphasize this. Fortunately, choosing and using only a few practices will still increase student achievement. For the most part, the teachers we worked with tested the practices by selecting only a few of the strategies; in some cases, they used even the ones they chose only partially. Yet they quickly discovered that student achievement rose in notable and exciting ways. This finding is confirmed by larger-scale research (Ruiz-Primo & Furtak, 2006).

Figure 1.1   Seven formative assessment practices.

1. Establish supportive and self-directive class climate norms (Andrade, 2010).

2. Specify measurable standards to be mastered and convey them to students (Black & Wiliam, 2005).

3. List extensions and interventions before collecting data (Wylie & Wiliam, 2006).

4. Preassess before each unit and continuously assess throughout the unit (Black & Wiliam, 2005; Reeves, 2003).

5. Involve students in using assessment data and teacher feedback to inform next steps they will take in their learning (Black & Wiliam, 1998).

6. Use assessment data to support and challenge students with tiered activities and scaffolded extensions (Hmelo-Silver, Duncan, & Chinn, 2007).

7. Differentiate homework and graded assessments to meet instructional levels (Bryan & Burstein, 2004).

The first column of Figure 1.2 shows classroom characteristics and practices that exemplify these formative assessment practices; the second column shows those that do not.

Figure 1.2 Comparison of formative assessment–based and performance-based classrooms.

Formative Assessment–Based Classroom	Performance-Based Classroom
Practice 1:	
• The teacher proactively sets and manages classroom climate	• A competitive climate flourishes
Practice 2:	
• Unit targets are specified and conveyed up front	• Targets are not conveyed, or are conveyed only just before tests
Practice 3:	
• Learning outcomes and interventions are preestablished	• Learning outcomes may be unclear until assessments are crafted at the end of the unit • Interventions are considered after problems surface
Practice 4:	
• Preassessment precedes each unit, and frequent check-ins take place during units	• Only summative tests are used
Practice 5:	
• Teachers and students review assessment data to design individualized supports and challenges • Both teachers and students use data to set next steps	• The same work is given to all • Students follow the teacher's lead
Practice 6:	
• Lessons break off into tiers • The teacher makes use of frequent and flexible student groupings	• The whole class is usually instructed together • The curriculum or text drives what is taught
Practice 7:	
• Homework, tests, and grading systems are differentiated	• The same homework and unit tests are given to all

These practices can seem daunting. As one teacher joked, "Being expected to do all seven of these practices now there's an argument for merit pay!" But again, you can pursue these individually. First, use the self-assessment at the end of this chapter to note which ones you already do. Then consider each carefully, weighing which benefits would help the most in your current situation. We suggest you prioritize and select two or three to focus on each year.

THE PURPOSE OF FORMATIVE ASSESSMENT

As we have noted, the ultimate role of formative assessment in the classroom is twofold:

1. You will use the results of the assessments to alter your teaching practices.

2. Your students will use the results to set goals and focus their learning efforts.

The fundamental purpose must be to increase student learning, not to collect data. Let us take a brief look at that purpose in more detail here.

A colleague recently asked, "What is formative assessment, and what is the purpose?" Almost any assessment can be used summatively or formatively. Traditionally, schools have focused on summative assessments, which summarize learning and are used to compare students' achievements to one another for the purpose of assigning grades or ranking students. In contrast, formative assessments actually inform next steps taken by students and teachers in ways that enhance achievement. Essentially, formative assessment looks forward to how the information we gain from looking at student work can inform future instructional decisions, much like how information gained from a physical exam might inform future health choices we make.

Moreover, formative assessment is often conceptualized as "assessment *for* learning" rather than "assessment *of* learning." Summative assessment takes time away from learning for assessment *of* learning. But with formative assessment, you can use assessment purposefully *for* learning, as an integral contribution to learning. You can integrate assessment with learning so that it becomes a powerfully effective learning activity itself. Formative assessment is not about giving assessments; it is about using the results to teach differently (Reeves, 2005).

Formative assessment offers a paradigmatic shift concerning some of the deepest purposes of education. Until recently, schools functioned to sort students (Wiggins, 2005). School practices, including assessment, separated those who knew from those who did not. Assessment results were often used to determine who could continue in academic tracks and who would be placed in vocational tracks. Now schools must ensure that all students strive to meet certain standards. Organizations such as the National Council of Teachers of English (NCTE) have called for a shift in the purpose of education, with the primary role of assessment no longer being to "*prove* [emphasis added] whether teaching or learning has taken place, but to *improve* [emphasis added] the quality of teaching and learning and thereby increase the likelihood that all members of the society will acquire a full and critical literacy" (NCTE, 2009, Standard 3).

So the role and purpose of assessment, along with many school practices, has become to maximize learning for *all* rather than *some* students. The formative assessment framework enables you and your students to identify standards and to assess where students are in terms of mastering all of those standards. The formative assessment practices offer a research-validated route for the steps that will then need to be taken to close any gap.

THREE WAYS TO BEGIN USING FORMATIVE ASSESSMENT

Given the definition, framework, and purpose of formative assessment, where and how should you get started? The vignettes in the following sections illustrate three paths that we have observed teachers, including ourselves, take as they get started:

1. Preassessments before a new unit

2. Midunit concept check-ins

3. Specific skill probes

Following these vignettes is a self-assessment tool you can use to identify where you are in using the seven practices that make up our framework—and next steps you can take.

Keep in mind that the teachers in the vignettes began in different places and pursued individually designed goals. Additionally, each teacher used a combination of formative assessment practices, but not all seven.

Preassessments Before a New Unit

Preassessments are a central practice used frequently in high-performing, high-need districts (Reeves, 2003). Ms. Yang, an eighth-grade teacher in a suburban district, decided early in the year to start using preassessments to enhance how she differentiated instruction. (We discuss differentiated instruction in great detail in Chapter 3.) She based that decision on the following research:

- *Students typically already know 40% to 50% of what teachers expect them to learn from an activity (Nuthall, 2007).*
- *Preassessments help teachers determine instructional levels and avoid reteaching known material.*
- *When students self-correct, they focus on what they need to work on, set goals, and become motivated to improve.*
- *Although teachers often believe they can predict students' performance, research has shown time and again that their judgments are often inaccurate (Begeny, Krouse, Groce, & Mann, 2011; Eckert, Dunn, Codding, Begeny, & Kleinmann, 2006).*

To begin, Ms. Yang identified practices she already used. She regularly offered differentiated classwork, homework, and tests so that students would spend more time working at their respective instructional levels. She decided her next step would be to give formal diagnostic preassessments before units.

As a trial, Ms. Yang gave a preassessment performance task that measured sentence variety in essay writing. To her surprise, one typically high-achieving student used far fewer types of sentences than most of his peers. His preassessment revealed strong vocabulary, solid organization, and clearly stated ideas, yet little sentence variation. In fact, his efforts came in well below the district's benchmark expectations. Yet based on the limited writing samples Ms. Yang had seen from him, she had assumed he had already mastered this skill.

The student was also surprised by these results, which helped him learn what to focus on next. In fact, after he had scored his preassessment, Ms. Yang was thrilled to hear him say, "I thought I used varied sentences, but now I know I need to work on these. I found a sentence-combining website where I can practice this."

The preassessment helped her change her differentiation plan for this student. Originally, she had planned to work on an enrichment task with him and a few other students. Instead, based on the results of the preassessment, she had him work on sentence-combining exercises, an activity that increases sentence variety and further enhances overall writing quality (Saddler, 2005).

At the end of the day, Ms. Yang felt that her decision to try preassessment was beneficial to her class. In this case, it helped her identify where to focus her teaching, and her student also knew exactly where he needed to focus his learning.

Midunit Concept Check-Ins

Mr. Klein, a sixth-grade teacher who worked in an independent school located near a major city, decided to begin with midunit concept check-ins. He was curious about whether or not students were learning the material, and he felt a midunit check-in would leave him enough time before the end-of-unit assessment to address gaps if needed. He also wanted to give students a chance to work on enrichment tasks if they showed mastery of the material or concepts at a faster pace.

Through read-alouds and interactive discussions (Fisher, Frey, & Lapp, 2008), Mr. Klein had modeled how to identify characters' points of view. In these lessons, he had worked to gradually release responsibility to his students. One night, when he was reviewing the class's homework, he had found two persistent misconceptions that students made when identifying point of view on their own. As a result, he designed a quick check-in to confirm what he had seen in their homework.

In class the next day, Mr. Klein helped students self-correct their check-ins. First, he explained which point of view each passage had conveyed. Then, as students corrected their responses, he provided more general feedback on the two misconceptions he had noticed and helped each student identify which misconception he or she had made.

Research shows that this kind of feedback is a two-way street, benefiting both students and teachers (Hattie, 2009). The feedback from the check-ins helped the students understand what they needed to learn, and it also helped Mr. Klein recognize that he needed to ramp up his teaching efforts. Following the check-in, he chose to use skits (Meltzer, Cook Smith, & Clark, 2002) to reteach the lessons on point of view.

The initial check-ins had provided relevant information for Mr. Klein to best match his students' needs to specific tasks. For instance, some students had struggled to identify when the narrator was being sarcastic, so Mr. Klein had them work on scenes in which they acted out different points of view that they pretended to hold (but did not actually hold).

Students who had shown a mastery of point of view in the check-in wrote and acted out brief new passages that portrayed more subtle perspectives. Then they practiced identifying point of view in each other's passages. They took delight in seeing who could write in the most difficult-to-discern point of view.

As this occurred, Mr. Klein worked with two students who were having the most pronounced difficulties. He explicitly showed them how to write skits from varied perspectives. He also had them practice making personal connections to events in the story; this helped them make the specific kinds of inferences needed to identify point of view. They then wrote and acted scenes out.

As an exit ticket from class, Mr. Klein had each student read a two-sentence passage and identify point of view. This validated for him and his students that the activities were a success.

Specific Skill Probes

Ms. Lee, a fifth-grade teacher in an urban high-need district, wanted to enhance how she formed writing groups based on students' initial skill levels. She recognized that skill level measures of specific areas such as fluency, comprehension, and writing were probably the best-researched formative assessment measures and offered the greatest promise of lifting student achievement (Stecker, Fuchs, & Fuchs, 2005).

Ms. Lee's district used AIMSweb probes, including the writing measures, to monitor student skill levels. In these writing probes, teachers count how many correct word sequences students write within three minutes. Yet, as Gansle, Noell, VanDerHeyden, Naquin, and Slider (2002) have noted, there are concerns about the quality of feedback these probes offer. Ms. Lee shared these concerns; she suspected that the probes mostly reported writing mechanics errors, and she found that they did not provide much useful instructional guidance.

In the past she had often used the data from these probes and observations she had made in class to create three groups based on whether students had shown full, partial, or emerging mastery in writing. Now she wanted to augment her data by doing a deeper analysis of underlying skills. She believed this would allow her to group students according to more clearly targeted skill areas, informed by multiple sources of data.

Ms. Lee's class norm was "We all learn differently." Consequently, she wanted to move beyond grouping by global readiness levels so that she could move students away from regularly comparing each other hierarchically.

To do this, she redesigned her open response preassessment rubric to better capture the different skill elements, and she adopted an additional Quick Writes assessment format. Quick Writes is an emerging supplemental writing measure that uses a more rubric-oriented scoring method. Initial research is finding this method to be sensitive to instruction (Green, Smith, & Brown, 2007; Mason, Kubina, & Taft, 2009).

First, Ms. Lee had her students self-correct their open responses with her redesigned rubric. She also asked them to complete a more substantial self-reflective evaluation to more closely analyze the areas they found challenging. This included a framework for using the data from their preassessments to set learning goals.

Her students proved to be adept and thoughtful in their post-preassessment analyses. She then asked them to decide which skill areas they felt they should address. She instructed students to put their heads down. Then she called out various areas to work on. Students raised their hands when she called out their area. This allowed her to group them by genuine area of need, because it prevented them from raising a hand just so they could work with a friend. The students were surprised that the groups were mixed up more than they had been before (when they had been grouped by levels based on whether they had shown full, partial, or emerging mastery in writing). In fact, they thought that Ms. Lee had randomly selected groups.

Once the students were grouped, they began working on their specific skill areas as they revised their pieces, referencing models Ms. Lee provided that exemplified how to address each skill area. Tasks included identifying more details in the passage and citing them, using clearer topic sentences, making more connections between ideas, and using sharper vocabulary.

> *Ms. Lee recognized that peer editing effectively raises writing achievement (Diab, 2010; Yang, Ko, & Chung, 2005), so she then had her students peer edit the work of those from other groups. This allowed students with different strengths to provide feedback to one another.*
>
> *Pleased with the outcome, Ms. Lee also knew that the students would not be able to rank the groups hierarchically. This helped her create a classroom climate where students focused on learning the skills they had not mastered, rather than on peer comparison.*

SELF-ASSESSMENT: DETERMINING HOW MUCH FORMATIVE ASSESSMENT YOU ALREADY USE IN YOUR CLASSROOM

The teachers in the previous vignettes understood that achieving a comprehensive vision of using formative assessment to differentiate instruction occurs over time, and that the path to doing so is unique. Fortunately, research has found that many teachers already use some basic formative assessment practices as a natural part of their work. And when they do, the more practices they use and the more frequently they use them, the greater their students' achievement (Ruiz-Primo & Furtak, 2006). To begin, complete the self-assessment in Figure 1.3 to identify the formative assessment practices you already have in place. Your results can help you decide your next steps. *For a downloadable version of the "Differentiating Practices Rubric,"* *go to* http://www.corwin.com/books/Book237623.

Figure 1.3	Differentiating practices rubric.

Differentiating Practices Rubric

We all begin in different places and pursue different goals as we grow as teachers. This self-assessment provides an overview of practices that can enhance how you use formative assessment.

On a scale of 1–4, rate how frequently you do each practice:

1—I do this often, 2—I do this occasionally, 3—I've tried this, 4—I haven't tried this yet

Practice 1: Establish a Supportive Climate				
I foster self-directed, independent approaches to learning.	1	2	3	4
Students recognize that doing different work helps each student get what she or he needs.	1	2	3	4

Practice 2: Specify and Convey Standards				
I clearly convey objectives (targets) before beginning each unit.	1	2	3	4
Practice 3: List Extensions and Interventions				
I list potential extensions and supports before designing and then collecting formative assessments.	1	2	3	4
Practice 4: Preassess and Continually Assess				
I use diagnostic preassessment tasks before beginning each unit.	1	2	3	4
I systematically collect formal and informal assessment data all along.	1	2	3	4
Practice 5: Involve Students in Next Steps				
I use assessment data to tier homework, class activities, and assessments.	1	2	3	4
I have students self-score assessments and use the results to decide next steps to take.	1	2	3	4
I stress the importance of self-initiated learning that is based on teacher feedback and self-scored assessments.	1	2	3	4
Practice 6: Use Data to Challenge and/or Support				
I regularly use flexible groupings for differentiated tasks.	1	2	3	4
When reviewing homework or class participation during teaching, I enable students who "get it" to move on as I assist others.	1	2	3	4
I use an extensive bank of supplemental resources.	1	2	3	4
I have a bank of strategies for challenging students (e.g., open-ended tasks, higher-order questions, abstract projects, compacting contracts, and extension resources).	1	2	3	4
Practice 7: Differentiate Homework and Assessments				
I differentiate homework and hold students accountable for the different work they do.	1	2	3	4
I differentiate class assessments.	1	2	3	4

The rest of the chapters in this book are "keyed" so that you can see which sections highlight and model each practice:

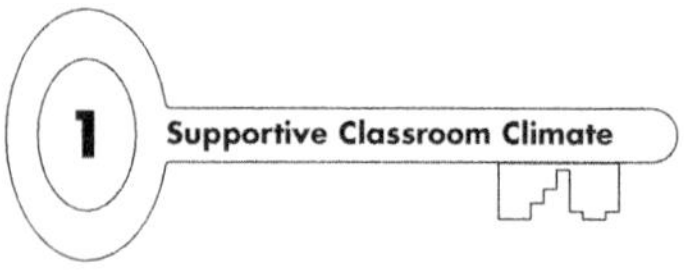

1 Supportive Classroom Climate — Practice 1: Establish a supportive climate—Chapter 1, last section

2 Conveyed Standards — Practice 2: Specify and convey standards—Chapter 2

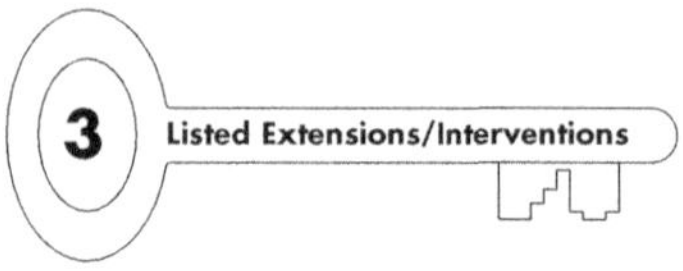

3 Listed Extensions/Interventions — Practice 3: List extensions and interventions—most chapters, particularly Chapters 4, 6, and 7

4 Continuous Assessment — Practice 4: Preassess and continually assess—most chapters, particularly Chapter 2

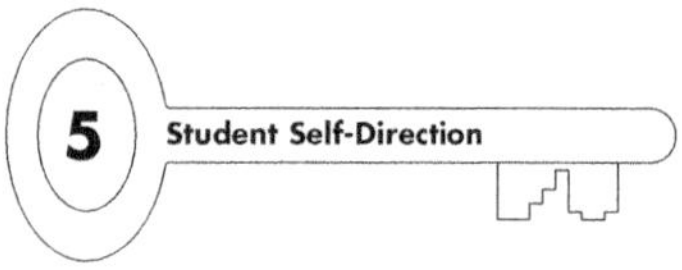

5 Student Self-Direction — Practice 5: Involve students in next steps—most chapters, particularly Chapter 3

6 Data-Informed Instruction — Practice 6: Use data to challenge and/or support—all chapters

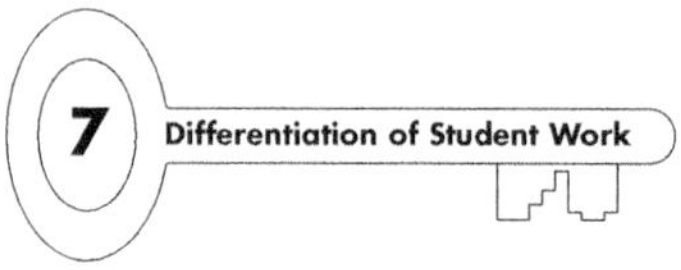

7 Differentiation of Student Work — Practice 7: Differentiate homework and assessments—Chapter 6

STEPS TO ESTABLISHING A CLASSROOM CULTURE THAT SUPPORTS FORMATIVE ASSESSMENT PRACTICES

The next section gives an overview of how to establish a supportive classroom climate, a key element in getting started with using formative assessment to differentiate instruction.

A supportive climate needs to be in place before the potential gains of formative assessment can grow wings. ♀ In one of the most extensive reviews ever conducted on the power of feedback, a core component of formative

1 Supportive Classroom Climate

assessment, researchers concluded that climate is "critical" if students (and teachers) are to welcome and use corrective feedback (Hattie & Timperley, 2007). According to Andrade (2010), one of the leading researchers on formative assessment, students must perceive the major factors that underlie formative assessment to be both valued and valuable. Moreover, the NCTE *Standards for the Assessment of Reading and Writing* emphasize how important it is for teachers to consider how "the climate produced by assessment practice" can facilitate or impede learning (NCTE, 2009, Standard 3).

The following vignette highlights the various ways in which Mr. Miles, a seventh-grade English teacher working at a public school in a suburban setting, establishes climate. His classes consist of 25 students varying in ability from those identified as having a learning disability to those who are high achieving. An analysis of each of his actions and how they develop climate follows the vignette.

From day one, Mr. Miles lays the foundation. He explains that students will need to work on different tasks according to regular formative assessment data that show where they are in their skills and understandings. He models respect for the fact that learning happens at different paces and in different ways and conveys the expectation that all students will also respect this reality. He emphasizes how important it is to ensure that all students feel safe and comfortable no matter how they learn. When students work on tasks from different angles or on entirely different work he says, "Since we all learn differently, different learning experiences are fair." He often makes the analogy to a sports team: "Each player brings a different skill set, but all skill sets are needed for the team to perform optimally together."

Since self-assessment is a basis for becoming self-directed, a core norm Mr. Miles cultivates, he carefully designs repeated opportunities to coach students in developing accurate self-assessment skills through frequent practice, feedback, and guidance of their efforts. As they determine where they are in their understanding of a topic, he is careful to remain nonjudgmental. He also avoids complimenting students who do well, because he has realized that privileging students who perform well sets a model and sends a message that can undermine the establishment of a climate in which all levels of performance are respected.

One week, as he prepares to launch a new unit, Mr. Miles decides to preassess the extent to which his students know the elements of an action-adventure story. First, he asks his students to select and read an action-adventure story from a list he provides. Then, as a preassessment, he asks them to demonstrate their knowledge of the essential elements of the genre by completing one of the following assignments:

- *Write a series of paragraphs.*
- *Create a multiple-scene diorama with a keyed explanation of each part.*
- *Write a magazine exposé.*
- *Create a trailer that gives an overview of the major elements.*
- *Write a first-person narrative monologue that conveys the major elements.*

The skill assessed here will not be the presentation but whether the student can convey an understanding of the key elements of an action-adventure story. By varying the assignment, Mr. Miles allows students to have an opportunity to complete the work in the medium that they are most comfortable with. Students who might otherwise be hampered by unrelated skill challenges, such as written expression difficulties, can now choose an alternate route to show what they know about action-adventure genre elements. Mr. Miles also recognizes that student motivation and achievement rise when they are given choices (Hattie, 2009).

After students complete this work, Mr. Miles reviews the key elements of an action-adventure story and lists them on the board. Students self-correct their work and list any elements they have not identified. The next day, Mr. Miles reads a brief story at the start of class and then asks students to identify the action-adventure traits exemplified in it. They self-correct their work with a key that indicates whether they "get it," "need more practice," or "have questions" about the elements of an action-adventure story.

In the past, Mr. Miles has found that when he asks students about their level of understanding, many will state they "get it" but then fail to pass the quiz. This is particularly the case with struggling students, who notoriously have difficulty with accurate self-assessment (Stone & May, 2002). Now Mr. Miles is able to use the key to help students self-evaluate accurately, as well as to encourage them to use the data from their evaluation to make a homework choice that offers the amount of practice appropriate to their needs.

As students ask clarifying questions about the differentiated homework tasks he has assigned for that evening, Mr. Miles quickly checks to ensure they have chosen the homework that will best match their needs. He agrees with a few who have chosen to skip the basic comprehension questions and do only the extra extension question, which involves comparing a similar event from the last few stories to this story and noting why there are similarities. These students have shown they have fully mastered identifying elements of action-adventure stories. He is careful not to convey a congratulatory tone as he agrees to their homework selection. In this way, he is careful to avoid making others, who do require the extra practice, feel any less than those who are ready to move on to the extension.

Mr. Miles recommends that one student complete a graphic organizer of the chapter's text structure before doing the comprehension questions. As usual, he is careful to focus on the task and not on her as a person, since research has shown that this approach is important to increasing achievement (Hattie & Timperley, 2007).

"We all should seek ways to get what we need," he reminds the entire class. "Whether you choose to do the comprehension questions or the extension is not the central issue. What matters is whether, in the end, you master the targets for the unit."

In this snapshot, Mr. Miles works to establish a climate in which students feel supported, safe, and comfortable with differences. Additionally, he carefully cultivates independent work habits and a self-directed approach to learning, which is necessary if students will be working on differentiated tasks during the year and will not have direct teacher guidance at all times. This also helps students who are passive learners to become more active and self-driven learners.

Establish a Climate of Respect

In the previous vignette, Mr. Miles modeled respect for all students. As you work to establish a climate of respect, you may wish to follow his approach:

- Purposefully distribute praise among all students, even when aspects of the task do not come easily to them.
- Be careful not to overvalue verbal intelligence in your praise. Instead, carefully compliment students on factors that are more easily within their control, such as effort level. Do not compliment the student with "Good job"; instead, focus on giving feedback on the task, such as, "I saw you do several extra practice exercises, and then you remembered all the elements of the genre on the quiz we took the next day."

In his many years of teaching, Mr. Miles has seen plenty of struggling students make tremendous leaps with the right coaching and practice. As a result, he has come to question how narrow the band of capability really is. He believes most students can excel in the right conditions, which further fuels his endeavor to reserve praise for ability and instead give praise for effort.

Furthermore, in his classroom, Mr. Miles cultivates respect for all. He sets a climate in which it is expected that all students will demonstrate respect for peers' unique learning profiles in ways that make everyone feel safe and supported. Here are some of the ways you can also achieve this:

- Rather than working to make differences invisible, celebrate them from the start.
- Point out how some students may instantly "see" a concept but struggle with articulating it. Others can easily make lists that enable them to explain a concept. Emphasize that both types of students "get it."
- Create tasks that offer choice and allow students with different strengths to shine.
- Be careful with the language that students use when they are correcting their work or when they are unsure about a concept. Discourage "I don't know this." Instead, encourage students to say, "I haven't learned this yet" or "I have questions."

- Emphasize that since all students are different, giving the same work to all would unfairly privilege one learning profile over another. Note that *different* sets the stage for *differentiation*, which is actually fairer.

In terms of grouping, Mr. Miles recognizes that middle school students are highly adept at quickly determining "high" and "low" groups and that this tendency cannot be easily minimized. Consequently, he often places students in "mixed" groups, offering different levels of challenge to different students within the wider groups so that all have the chance to attain a similar level of mastery of the standards. He is more casual now when he announces groups, confident that he is taking the right measures to give all students what they need individually to come up to the standard level. He has also become more capable of designing preassessments that reveal more nuanced learning profile differences that he can use to form groups, rather than forming them only on readiness levels.

Cultivate Self-Directed Learning

Self-directed learners learn more and are more successful in school (Andrade, 2010). Self-assessment practices in particular have powerful learning potential. In the vignette, students benefited from scoring their own work with the answer key after hearing the action-adventure short story and listing genre elements.

The first step to cultivating self-directed learning involves using formative assessments that students self-score and then use to design plans for how they will master concepts they have yet to learn. Such assessments, which are described in detail in Chapter 2, can help you place students in charge of understanding and managing how they will learn. With this approach, you can take the role of the facilitator or the collaborator and not the instructor.

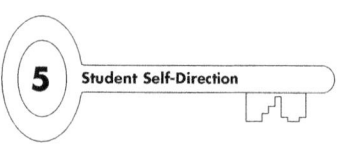

In his classroom, Mr. Miles repeatedly asks students to self-evaluate their learning of each topic with carefully selected phrases such as "Got it," "Need more practice," or "Have questions." ♀ In addition, he expects his students to make a plan for what they should do next to move ahead in their learning. In the vignette, this occurs when he allows them to select from a variety of homework options.

Mr. Miles often approaches his students' questions with questions of his own. In this way, he allows them to realize that (1) they already understand much of the concept, and (2) sometimes they can answer their own questions with the right support. With this approach, he encourages perseverance and avoids being seen as the sole authority, which could diminish students' belief in their own skills and abilities.

In these ways, Mr. Miles builds a climate in his classroom in which students feel supported, safe, and comfortable and become self-directed in how they approach learning. Building such a climate is the first and arguably most important step in using formative assessment practices to differentiate instruction.

2 Standards, Feedback, and Assessment Options

Chapter 1 illustrated ways teachers can get started with using formative assessment practices. This chapter:

- Addresses how to specify and convey the standards that the formative assessments measure
- Recommends practices for giving feedback on mastery of standards in ways most likely to raise student achievement
- Offers specific suggestions and models for designing, introducing, and scoring standards-based formative assessments, particularly preassessments

HOW TO SPECIFY AND CONVEY STANDARDS

One of the first priorities of the formative assessment framework is to enable students to use the data collected to determine where they stand in relation to existing standards. ♀ Therefore, you must first specify and convey unit standards in measurable terms so you and your students can use assessment data to reveal where they stand in mastering them. In a sense, this tells students what the "finish line" looks like and where it is so they can chart their course accordingly. For basic

Conveyed Standards **2**

skills such as reading speed or decoding accuracy, sharing and measuring this information is straightforward—for example, a sixth-grade student should read roughly 120 words per minute.

But what about standards that are complex and not easily defined? For complex concepts such as critical literacy, you first need to break down standards carefully and specify gradations of understanding clearly. You then need to convey these standards to students. Furthermore, you should provide samples of student work that meet these standards and show gradations of understanding. The goal is for students to fully understand the standards, see that their peers have achieved them, and believe that they can attain mastery as well (Stiggins, 2005).

Learning progressions offer a valuable way to identify for students the more nuanced substeps that occur along the way to mastering a standard. Essentially, learning progressions can be thought of as progressively more sophisticated levels of understanding of a standard. Research has formally defined learning progressions as describing the path students often follow as they learn (Masters & Forster, 1996), and more recently as describing successively more sophisticated ways to think about ideas (Wilson & Bertenthal, 2005).

For example, learning progressions can break a global standard such as point of view or author bias into smaller degrees of understanding. When these standards have been broken down and specified, it will be easier for you to define subtle differences in how students think about these concepts. Specifically, formative assessments can help you identify where a student is in a learning progression of conceptual understandings that underlie and make up a standard.

Take the theme of power in the science fiction genre, for instance. Science fiction uses many concrete elements such as technological advances and futuristic setting details; however, the element of power and who has control is a sophisticated concept woven into the story. This more abstract concept requires that students understand the story details, big picture, and larger societal implications. Generally, science fiction stories have an obvious authority figure, but the element of power and control tends to run much deeper than just the person in control. Students can show nuanced degrees of understanding of power. If students are asked to write about the theme of power in a science fiction story, their grasp of the concept may fall somewhere in the progression from more simplistic notions to increasingly more sophisticated understandings (see Figure 2.1).

As you work to identify where a student is in such a learning progression, the concept becomes less black-or-white. That is, instead of trying to determine whether a student does or does not "get it," you can

| Figure 2.1 | Learning progression for the concept of power in science fiction. |

Emerging

- Identifies who has power in a story
- One person (or group) tells another what to do
- Leader has all the power

Developing

- Power is a pervasive and driving force in all societies (and relates to present times)
- All humans experience varying degrees of being in control of their lives

Advanced

- All people have power to varying degrees, depending on how they wield it
- Power can shift based on perception and the way people make decisions and manipulate the events that are happening.
- Power is based in perception and can be lost if people choose not to allow the person to have the power

use formative assessments that identify where a student is in the learning progression to help you and the student plan for more nuanced next steps to take. Teachers and students often find it reassuring to see that data from formative assessments frequently reveal that a student has moved toward mastering a concept, even if the concept is not *fully* mastered.

As another example, at the heart of science fiction is the question "What if?" When many students begin to study science fiction, they look for stories with UFOs or green Martians. Yet as students move beyond such simplistic, surface notions, they can learn that science fiction stories use highly imaginative advancements in science as one of their core elements.

Recently, we asked a group of students who were reading science fiction to identify the "What if?" question for each story. For example, *Robot Dreams* by Isaac Asimov (1986) poses the question, "What if robots had free will and/or thought?" We knew that for students to successfully identify this question as the basis for Asimov's stories, they would need to be able to do the following:

- Comprehend the story
- Find the most relevant elements
- Synthesize this information

We chose a formative preassessment to determine where students were in understanding these concepts as well as their ability to identify and synthesize them.

Many students were able to answer the question, "What is the 'What if?' question in Asimov's story?" at a basic level but included too many concrete, simple details from the story, such as, "What if robots could think and then would come back and kill humans?" Although that is correct, it does not accurately synthesize the story and get to the crux of the (deeper, larger) question about the essence of free will and what it means to have it.

This preassessment helped us identify students who understood the story and were able to comprehend and synthesize the information and extrapolate deeper understandings. As shown, it also identified those who could understand the story yet had difficulty synthesizing. This preassessment also identified those who had difficulty understanding the story altogether.

This is just one example of the different types of formative assessment you might try in your classroom. Since science fiction stories often have similar underlying themes, you could preassess students with one story and then postassess after the unit with a story that has similar challenges so that you can see the growth in students' understandings.

Finding learning progressions and categories of predictable misconceptions need not consume much time. For instance, we generated the emerging, developing, and advanced categories in Figure 2.1 after skimming student responses and doing a quick Internet search.

When you identify your students' learning progressions, you can specify clear gradations along the way to mastering a standard. This will help you better craft formative assessments that can inform instruction. We suggest that you follow these steps:

- Brainstorm and research learning progressions before you decide what kind of data you will need to collect to gain insights into where students fall on such continua of understandings.
- List potential interventions and differentiations you will use.
- Design the formative assessment.
- Collect the data from students using the formative assessment.
- Analyze the data and refine or expand these learning progressions.

Standards are sometimes best specified and clarified interactively. After collecting work samples, you can analyze the content and use this to further specify levels of understanding that lead up to mastering the full standard.

You will want to ensure that the preassessment is designed to go beyond a merely diagnostic level of revealing what students know. ♀ The aim is to uncover continua about how students think. You can then use this information to determine not only *what* you will teach but *how* you will teach it. Figure 2.2 is an example of a preassessment designed to uncover what students might know about the role of conflict in stories.

Teachers can use a list like this to convey to students the standards that they are expected to master.

Figure 2.2	Conflict preassessment.

Circle Y (yes) or N (no).

Do you feel familiar with any of the following core learning goals?		
1. Identify a conflict in a story	Y	N
2. Identify the major events that led up to it	Y	N
3. Synthesize the causes of the conflict	Y	N
4. Determine the impact of the conflict	Y	N
5. Determine the wider implications of the conflict	Y	N
6. Explain how another character would react differently	Y	N
Read the story just assigned Write responses to each. As we correct them, check off which you could do.		
1. Identify the conflict in the story	Y	N
2. Identify the major events that led up to it	Y	N
3. Synthesize the causes of the conflict	Y	N
4. Determine the impact of the conflict	Y	N
5. Determine wider implications of the conflict	Y	N
6. Explain how another character would react differently	Y	N

I will work on these core learning goals:

1.

2.

As you consider which standards to focus on, remember that the standards of the National Council of Teachers of English (NCTE, 2009) have asked teachers to place greater emphasis on developing student thinking along lines such as:

- Building an understanding of the human experience through philosophical, ethical, and aesthetic dimensions
- Using a wide variety of strategies for writing with different purposes
- Using research to answer student-generated questions and developing an understanding of and respect for diversity in languages and cultures

Conveying standards for conceptual mastery is challenging. However, specific and detailed rubrics that show continua of understandings offer one way to do this.

Before you begin a new unit, clarify for yourself what the end-of-unit criteria will be. This type of "backward design model" will ensure that you can convey these criteria to students through rubrics such as the learning progressions shown in Figure 2.2. Always keep in mind the aim of using formative assessments, including learning progressions, in your classroom. Once students clearly understand the standards, they can:

1. Determine where they are going

2. Identify what they have mastered

3. Identify what they still need to master

Again, through formative assessment, you have identified the finish line for students—and together you can begin to take the steps needed to get them there.

RECOMMENDATIONS FOR FEEDBACK ON MASTERY OF STANDARDS

As you clarify standards and use them to design assessments, it is also invaluable to plan for how you will give feedback on mastery of these standards. You should do this planning at the same time as you specify standards; this will ensure that you do not omit the step of providing feedback.

5 Student Self-Direction

Students constantly derive feedback from self-assessment. ⚲ One of the best ways to foster students' deep processing of the standards is to ask them to use answer keys that convey those standards. Students begin to internalize the standards as they:

1. Take assessments that list the standards

2. Score them with the keys that convey the standards

3. Note which standards they have mastered and which ones they still need to work on

Teachers can also provide feedback that shows where students are in relation to standards when they review tests, quizzes, projects, class activities, discussions, or other student work.

It is important to note that feedback that advises students on next steps to be taken is far more effective than feedback that evaluates (Hattie & Timperley, 2007). Summative feedback, such as grades or scores based on the number of answers that are correct, is far less effective than clear, specific advice, which often results in far greater future achievement. Feedback that has the least value focuses on the child as a "great student" (Hattie & Timperley, 2007).

In 1985, Elwar and Corno reported on how homework feedback affected mastery of standards. They found that positive feedback that provided specific directives had far greater impact than feedback that simply noted whether responses were correct or incorrect.

Supportive and guiding feedback conveys a sense of hope that students can and will improve. As a result of such feedback, students are more likely to sink their teeth into their learning. For example, one of our students never appreciated vacuous praise, but she devoured specific suggestions for how she could improve, and then she took tremendous pride in her improvement. As you make lesson plans, be sure to provide students with opportunities to use the feedback they receive on preassessments and assignments; this will give them the satisfaction of seeing improvements on postassessments and other work at the end of the unit. Like our student, your students will be able to take pride in their own progress.

One way to convey instant feedback is to make use of task checklists like the ones in Figure 2.2. As students go over the list, they will instantly know where they stand in relation to where they should ultimately be. Alternately, when you correct assignments, you can include recommendations to use specific alternative strategies or explain ways to work more effectively. Here is an example of a child's response to a comprehension question:

In a quote from Chapter 6 of *To Kill a Mockingbird*, the children think that the shadow is Boo Radley. They call him a shadow because they can't really see him.

And here is the teacher's response:

Shanti, you remembered to write in full sentences and you correctly identified the topic and the main point. Next time, you can try to analyze the quote some more with specific detail about how the characters feel and why they feel that way. Think about why the author has used the words. The word *shadow* has been used because shadows are mysterious and unclear. In this chapter, Boo Radley is also unknown and mysterious to the children. So you might want to be even more specific in explaining word choices the author makes. Good luck on the next quiz! Looks like you are well ready.

—Ms. Sue

As you can see, the feedback starts with a positive, gives specific guidance, and then concludes with more positives.

Feedback like this is time consuming, so you will need to generate time-efficient ways to provide it, such as using a structured format like the one shown in Figure 2.2 or limiting the feedback. For example, you might write a note like Ms. Sue's on each child's work on an occasional basis but not regularly. Given how time consuming this feedback is, you should also ask students to respond with a note that confirms that they understand the feedback and explains when they will use it.

Feedback on More Than Accuracy

As you provide feedback, make sure that it is:

- Timely
- Specific
- Detailed
- Understandable to the learner

As Hattie and Timperley (2007) note, it is essential to provide at least as much feedback on processes that students use as feedback on task accuracy.

You should also find that providing feedback and advice on how students self-regulate their thinking as they work will yield greater gains than providing feedback on accuracy (Hattie & Timperley, 2007). For instance, you might note that a student used excellent self-checking strategies by outlining ideas in the margin but then did not use appropriate fix-up strategies when she found that parts were missing.

To develop a formative assessment tool for exploring what processes students use when they write responses, you might design a questionnaire that asks them to identify the steps they complete before they create a final written product. To further support this questionnaire, you might ask students to complete the process and create a first draft of the written product for homework.

Feedback to Foster Self-Direction

As we noted earlier, when you provide students with clear, specific feedback that provides advice on how they can better achieve mastery of unit standards, you kindle their natural motivation. Students overcome passivity, become self-directed, and work harder to meet expectations. You can fan the flames even further by ensuring that the goals students pursue are measurable, detailed, and achievable (Patel & Laud, 2009). For example, following preassessments, you can coach students to set the goal of getting 20% more correct.

Often students believe it is the responsibility of teachers to take the lead in providing guidance on next steps to take. However the strongest students do this regularly, detecting errors in their work and mentally planning how to correct them and avoid them in the future. Coach your students to write feedback for themselves after self-scoring their work. Check their feedback quickly, sign off if you agree, or help students revise the feedback as appropriate.

Again, as we mentioned earlier, it is essential for students to habitually act on all feedback. Consequently, as part of their next assignment, ask them to demonstrate in a note how they used prior feedback in this assignment, whether it was teacher feedback or feedback and next steps they had generated themselves.

SUGGESTIONS AND MODELS FOR DESIGNING, INTRODUCING, AND SCORING STANDARDS-BASED FORMATIVE ASSESSMENTS

Once standards have been specified, they inform the entire process of how teachers design, introduce, and score preassessments. The following vignette dives more directly into the next element of formative assessment: preassessments. The vignette involves a unit on poetry, a genre the

Common Core State Standards Initiative (n.d.) recommends be taught in middle school (Standard R.L. 6.10).

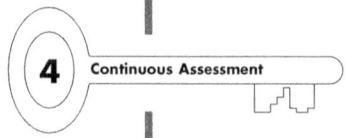

Ms. Sue is an eighth-grade teacher at an urban public school. Her classes consist of 25 to 27 students varying in ability from those who have been identified as having a learning disability to those who are high achieving.

Ms. Sue is deeply committed to NCTE's stance on teaching critical literacy, and she agrees that it is important to use assessments to measure NCTE's critical literacy skills so that they will not be marginalized or deemphasized in the curriculum (NCTE, 2009, Standard 7). ♀ *Consequently, Ms. Sue actively avoids designing assessments that measure only a narrow range of literacy skills.*

Before beginning a poetry unit, Ms. Sue designed a diagnostic preassessment to look at students' nuanced understandings of poetry (Figure 2.3). Essentially, the results of the preassessment would enable individual students to determine what next steps they would need to take and allow Ms. Sue to see what differentiated adjustments she would need to make in her instruction. The preassessment would accomplish this by:

1. Clearly listing the unit's standards

2. Providing tasks to assess students' understanding of each standard

3. Offering self-scoring, which would guide students in identifying which elements they had mastered and which they would need to work on during the unit

Since grades can actually hamper learning (Black & Wiliam, 2005), Ms. Sue intentionally presented this task to her students as a learning opportunity rather than as an evaluation, and she assured them that the preassessment would not be graded. Instead, she explained that it was an opportunity for them to discover which standards they had mastered and which ones might require additional learning and practice. The feedback they received from their self-scoring and from Ms. Sue's comments would be used only to help clarify what they would need to work on in the upcoming unit.

To externalize the task, Ms. Sue explained to her students that the preassessment would merely uncover the poetry understandings that they had not already "been taught"; she said it was not intended to measure how "skilled" they were at poetry analysis. She told them that they would use this information to decide which areas might need review and which ones they had not learned yet. Then she passed out the preassessment and asked them to begin. (For a free, downloadable version of the poetry preassessment, go to http://www.corwin.com/books/Book237623.)

Figure 2.3   Poetry preassessment.

Unit Standards

Rate how well you feel you know how to do each of the following on a scale of 1 to 4 (1 = not so well, 4 = very well).

Summarize what's happening	1	2	3	4
Describe the mood/atmosphere	1	2	3	4
Identify poetic elements	1	2	3	4
Determine the message	1	2	3	4
Defend your opinion	1	2	3	4

Light
Wiley Schubert Reed
Why does a light go out so quickly?
Why doesn't it stay lit forever?
It lasts for its lifetime, then melts away as a candle would,
Until it's gone, like it was never.

It flickers, deciding whether it wants to go,
And once it decides to cower,
It's dim, and seemingly not there, until it's really gone,
But it's still warm, like its last hour.

Eventually it should be replaced,
So there is no more gaping hole, in the space
Where it used to be before, when I'd never thought
it would shine no more,
And yet still there is no light, that glows to me,
that's warm and bright.

But maybe that *is* for the best,
Maybe it left to give me a rest,
But still, I want another light,
To make me *really* feel right.

And one day the hole is gone,
And where it was, the loneliness undone,

(Continued)

(Continued)

But this new light is a little bit different,
It's smaller, brighter, it's not the old light, just its crescent.

It feels different, it smells different, and it looks different too,
But again, it isn't the old light, it's bound to be different to you.

And as the light has been there, for a little while,
it begins to feel like it's right,
And on my face it paints a smile.

For this light is no replacement at all,
It's not the same light, refurnished on the wall,
For this light has a different warmth to give,
For this light has a different life to live.

Task Questions

What is happening?
What is the mood/atmosphere like?
What poetic elements are used? Why are they effective?
What is the message?
What is your opinion of the poem?
Stop here and wait for directions on self-correcting the preassessment.

Corrections

For each question, place a check mark in either the "Achieved" or "Needs practice" column.

	Achieved	Needs Practice
Summarized the poem's action		
Described the mood/atmosphere		
Identified at least two poetic elements		
Determined the message		
Defended my opinion		

After 20 minutes, Ms. Sue posted exemplary responses on the Smart Board. Because she knew that research shows that exposure to models raises achievement (Graham & Perin, 2007) and that students benefit from seeing what typical peers can accomplish (Schunck & Zimmerman, 2007), she used models written by peers from prior years. Each exemplary response also included a justification for the answer, which is essential with more complex literacy tasks when many different responses can be correct. Wiggins (2005) notes that, as an essential component of formative assessment, students must understand the standards they are expected to master and be able to fully articulate characteristics of strong models of these standards.

Ms. Sue then asked her students to stop their work and put their pencils away. She called their attention to the Smart Board and asked them to make a list of the attributes of a strong justification. She then presented students with a checklist of elements of a strong justification and had them identify which elements from the list they had come up with. This process ensured that students would actively engage in and think deeply about the standards for a strong justification.

Students then self-scored the assessment with colored pencils, using the models and the checklist Ms. Sue had circulated. As noted, self-scoring has been found to dramatically raise achievement (Joseph & Eveleigh, 2011). Conveniently, self-scoring also saves teacher time.

After scoring their justifications, the students used evidence (data) from their preassessments to check off which areas of poetry analysis they had already learned and those they had not yet mastered (and thus would need to learn).

Having students select what they need to work on helps them develop confidence and thus enables them to embrace active learning goals. These are not the same as performance goals, which rest in the belief that tasks require an innate ability that one either does or does not possess. As we have noticed, when preassessments are followed by feedback, additional practice, and further opportunities to show that the material is now mastered, this lays the foundation for fostering active learning goals. Embracing active learning goals, a core feature of typical formative assessment models, also lifts achievement, particularly in the face of challenge (Grant & Dweck, 2003). Therefore, Ms. Sue offered students the option of selecting their own homework (see Figure 2.4) based on their preassessment scores.

Figure 2.4   Preassessment homework choices.

Preassessment Homework Choices

Choice 1

If you achieved the five objectives, select an activity from the extension bank.

Choice 2

If you missed summarizing the poem's action or identifying poetic elements, complete Activity 1.

Choice 3

If you missed describing the mood/atmosphere, determining the message, or defending your opinion, complete Activity 2.
*If you like, you may also do the extension in Choice 1, no matter what choice you make.

For class the next day, Ms. Sue planned several activities to support different areas of learning. At the start of the lesson, she asked students to look at the data they had gathered from scoring their preassessments before determining which task to do. She specifically referred them back to the preassessments because she knew that students often struggle with accurate self-assessments (Stone & May, 2002) and that data can better equip them to do this. She then asked her students to put their heads down and raise their hand when she called out an area in which they needed work. She assigned students a group number based on which task they chose. As we noted in Chapter 1, this process ensures that students do not select the same work (and group) as their friends; rather, they select the work that best matches their needs.

In this case, all students made appropriate choices, but if that had not occurred, Ms. Sue would have offered guidance in the form of a brief, informal chat as she walked around the room. Students then moved into groups based on their number, and each group worked on a separate activity.

Each day, Ms. Sue opened with a poem that students analyzed. Then, based on the preassessment and subsequent work in class, Ms. Sue had them spend part of each lesson working on differentiated extensions or additional practice assessments.

At the end of the unit, as a postassessment, students completed an assessment having the same format as the preassessment. It included a similar poem and covered the same concepts but asked for slightly different responses. At that point, when the students had to assess how well they knew each of the responses in the opening of the quiz, almost the entire class gave themselves the highest rating. When they corrected the postassessment, they all beamed at their gains. After this activity, Ms. Sue returned the preassessments to students. One student, who had really struggled throughout the unit, was thrilled with his improvement.

When students receive differentiated instruction, as they did when Ms. Sue assigned different tasks to different groups, assessment becomes a celebration rather than a comparative evaluation. In Ms. Sue's class, students were able to celebrate their individual achievements rather than compare their final outcome to that of peers. Ms. Sue's students actually looked forward to and were motivated by the postassessment so they could see how far they had come. This situation certainly differs from traditional scoring, in which only a few students excel in comparison to their peers. It also builds tremendous buy-in as students see they are fully capable of making gains and mastering standards.

These students also recognized that even with their different choices, they all had made improvements and fully mastered analysis of the poem and/or identification of key poetic elements. Ms. Sue pointed out that they had all "chosen well, no matter what choice was made" because they chose what they needed to master the material and they did all master it.

Now that Ms. Sue has learned to use formative assessments regularly, she often remarks on the change in her own approach to lesson and unit planning. Before using formative assessment data to regularly check student learning, she relied on "philosophies" or "beliefs" about how students learn to guide her instructional planning and decision making. Today, in sharp contrast, she lets herself be guided by data that she collects on what her students are actually learning. These data often surprise her when they contradict her personal beliefs about what "should" work best instructionally. After an activity, she no longer vaguely says, "We found doing this helpful." Instead, she cites specific class assessment scores and shows exactly how much they rose or fell with different teaching techniques. No longer does she say, "I like that," when she hears a teaching idea. Now she asks if there are data to support it.

Figure 2.5 Determining next steps.

Student Self-Direction **5**

Keep this form and attach it to your next poetry analysis assignment. Following the assignment, reflect on how you applied what you learned from this first task, including feedback you received, to your next assignment to improve your skills.

Describe what you did well on the preassessment.

Describe some areas where you can improve.

Describe some next steps that you can take.

List your goals for mastering these objectives.

What evidence will you provide that shows you took these steps?

Preassessment Options

Often teachers feel that they know where students are in terms of their learning, so they omit the preassessment. However, this is a big mistake. Teachers are frequently inaccurate in their judgments of where students are at, particularly with students who are low achieving (Begeny, Krouse, Groce, & Mann, 2011), and they are often surprised by what is found during the preassessment. This has been our experience whenever even the most expert teachers we know have given preassessments. And as we have shown here, preassessments directly benefit students. ♀ They offer students a valuable opportunity to activate prior knowledge and connect new information to what they already know about the topic. Also, as they self-score the preassessment, they gain a realistic sense of what they know.

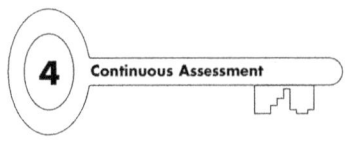

If you are not ready to design your own diagnostic preassessment, then you might consider some of the premade preassessments currently available from a variety of sources. For example, you need look no further than online state testing preparation sites, such as the one created for the Massachusetts Comprehensive Assessment System (www.doe.mass.edu/mcas). These sites offer well-constructed potential preassessments, and alternate-year tests can be used as postassessments so students can see gains in their skills.

Figure 2.6 offers an example of a point-of-view preassessment rubric. Using such a rubric, you might pull a quote from a reading that students have completed for homework and ask them to identify the speaker, the context, and the significance of the quote and what it reveals about the point of view of the speaker. Before giving this preassessment, you could map out extra supports for students who are struggling with mastering point of view, as well as extension exercises.

Figure 2.6   Point-of-view preassessment rubric.

Developing Knowledge

Identifies the section of the story that the quote refers to

Adequate Knowledge

Identifies the speaker and context correctly

Advanced Knowledge

Identifies the speaker, context, speaker's motivation, and insight into the nature of the speaker

Here are other preassessment activities to try:

• Use K-W-L (Know, Want to learn, Learned) charts before units, asking students to write what they already know about a topic or concept and what they want to learn. These can serve as instant "preassessment" and feedback on learning. Students can later revisit them and add what they have learned. This format is also a good introduction to preassessments for students because it allows them to acknowledge and feel good about what they already know.

• Ask for a show of hands to see what percentage of the class already knows certain points, and then adjust the lesson accordingly.

If you establish an honor code, ♀ and students understand that the purpose of the assessment is not to evaluate them but to understand them (and to use the information to differentiate instruction to best meet their needs), then you can also give preassessments as home-

Supportive Classroom Climate **1**

work. Clearly mark on them that students should not receive assistance with them. When you establish the ground rules, students are less inclined to use supports that might skew the assessment. It is also helpful to discuss this with parents via e-mail or letter, or in person at back-to-school night, so they are informed about the process and do not step in to help their children.

Eventually, the class will become accustomed to the process and will expect preassessments and other formative assessment routines. Teachers will even find that students comment when they have not taken a preassessment for an extended amount of time.

Tips for Preassessments

• *Emphasize to students that this is a chance to show what they have been taught.* Stating it this way externalizes the assessment so that it is an assessment of what they have been *taught* rather than of how *smart* they are.
• *Introduce preassessments sensitively.* Students can feel unnerved when they see a preassessment that has information they do not know. Some teachers tell students, "Sometimes even the students who usually do quite well in most English class tasks are not familiar with the content on a preassessment. This means nothing more than the fact that they haven't seen the material before. What matters is determining what you know and what you don't yet know, and the preassessment helps you do this. Once you have this information, you can better focus your learning and effort and use your time more efficiently." Others reassure their students by stating,

"Preassessments are a roadmap for *me*. They help to show us what route we need to take to get you to the final destination. It is primarily to help me."

- *Keep preassessments as brief as possible.* They should not take up much class time, because students are sometimes unfamiliar with the concepts or skills included in them. Briefer preassessments may also be less stressful for students.

- *Construct preassessments so that they offer a valuable learning experience as well.* This ensures that teaching time is not actually lost. Teachers we know who vigilantly guard their time find that at a minimum they can do one preassessment and one formal formative assessment check-in per unit, which studies have shown is more than enough to prompt noteworthy gains in achievement (Bangert-Drowns, Kulik, Kulik, & Morgan, 1991).

- *Introduce positive language.* When students do not know something on a preassessment, encourage them to write *HLY* ("Haven't learned yet") rather than *DK* ("Don't know"). This supports the idea that you are looking at what they have been *taught* rather than how *intelligent* they are.

- *Remind students that they themselves will correct the preassessments.* Then they will not worry about what you will think.

- *Let students know that they will have an opportunity to take the assessment again at the end of the unit (not with the same content, but with a similar format and the same concepts).* This can motivate them to self-direct their learning during the unit and to maximize how much they learn. It can also reduce their stress level.

- *Design preassessments to activate background knowledge.* For example, when you ask students to create a list of the poetic elements or devices they have learned and to provide examples of these elements, you help them activate background knowledge. Even if students have not learned the names of elements or devices, they may describe attributes such as "same consonant sound at the beginning of words next to each other." This information can help you jump-start instruction.

- *Include final challenge questions.* This allows you to test outward until you find areas that even high-achieving students can benefit from learning. For example, for a poetry unit, you might include a question about interpretation of a poem or analysis of an implied metaphor.

Continuous Formative Assessment

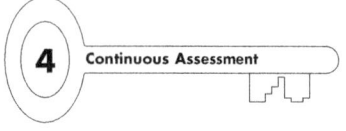

After taking the first and most basic step—diagnostic preassessment—you can then use continuous formative assessment concurrently with instruction throughout the unit. ♀ You probably regularly score homework and classwork already, which offers some sense of where students are. Formative assessment requires you to do this more systematically. It also extends out to urge students to self-assess their own work more systematically and set goals to improve. As we have noted, teachers often do not have time to analyze all student work, so emphasizing students' self-scoring is also practical. Furthermore, adolescents—particularly those who are low achieving often believe they have mastered concepts when in reality their grasp is still shaky (Sung, Chang, Chang, & Yu, 2010). Continuous formative assessments give them a stronger, more realistic sense of where they are, and do so more frequently.

Students can regularly self-assess their classwork, assessments, and homework for accuracy by self-checking. 🔑 As mentioned, there are often several acceptable responses (although there is usually a core reply required), so they can also self-assess their work's  accuracy with answer keys that provide models or rubrics. Having students generate their own rubrics for scoring their work is a research-based practice as well. Andrade, Du, and Mycek (2010) discovered that when students read a model, generate criteria for what makes it high quality, and then use a rubric based on these traits to self-score their work, they write more effectively than students who do not use models and rubrics. You can also teach students that while they are completing tasks, they can "outline out" (make a brief outline in the margin that lists major points made) and check off each element they are certain is correct.

Essentially, students should develop the habit of self-assessing their work with answer keys and rubrics so frequently that they become linked in students' minds. Work should not feel complete to students until they have checked it. Ideal self-scoring enables students to receive timely, specific, understandable feedback that focuses on next steps—all qualities of effective feedback (Wiggins, 1998). Moreover, doing so facilitates self-monitoring.

In addition to following these embedded approaches to continuous formative assessment, students can complete semiformal check-ins. Figure 2.7 shows a minor conceptual check-in that can replace a major preassessment. It provides practice with and assessment of identifying point of view. For this type of check-in, you can select quotes from texts and have students identify the speaker and significance of the quote. As enrichment, students can create new quotes, create a new character, and then give that person a unique sense of "voice" in the mix.

A key tenet of formative assessment is regular "retakes" (Stiggins, 2007); that is, students can retake assessments as often as needed until they master the topic. Since point of view is an essential standard, all students would be expected to show mastery of this skill. Therefore, they would repeatedly work on it with each new work (story, novel) until mastered.

Figure 2.7	Point-of-view check-in.

Correctly Identified Point of View	Point-of-View Error	The defining "voice" trait was:
1.	I thought it was another character because . . .	
2. √		
3. √		
4. √		
5.	I thought it was . . .	

We have had students complete such assessments daily during the start of class over several days until all showed mastery. For other topics, of course, retakes may be optional.

Students can also engage in simple ongoing formative assessment by regularly writing reflections on how well they understand the work. They can do this:

- At the end of class in an "exit slip" that they turn in as they leave
- On their homework
- On assessments
- On projects (essentially on anything that they submit)

Post the following questions to remind students to jot down their reflections regularly:

How is my understanding of the current topic?

- Needs more learning
- Seems okay
- Great! I'm ready for a challenge
- Other _____

Based on today's work, a question I have is:

_____

_____

_____

Students can also indicate their responses by standing/sitting, using thumbs up/thumbs down, using whiteboards, lifting a red/green stick or cup they have on their desk, or using technology mechanisms (if available).

Although students can initially answer the question "Where am I?" with self-scoring global diagnostic preassessments, you should continue to prompt them to ask this question throughout the unit as they self-score class work and homework. At that point, they can use methods as simple as putting a check mark next to responses they are confident about or using answer keys. All in all, students should habitually pause and discover where they stand in mastering each element of each new unit. You can set this up by using a backward design model (Wiggins & McTighe, 2005) in which they constantly assess their progress toward mastering a list of clearly stated unit standards.

Potential Preassessment Pitfall

A classic difficulty with formative assessment occurs when teachers give a preassessment, look it over, and then teach the unit after making minimal adjustments. This will not achieve the positive effects on student learning that the formative assessment research base has found. Teachers and students must both actively use the data from preassessments to make instructional adjustments and to determine next steps for learning, and the more data driven and structured those adjustments and steps are, the better.

Teachers who use preassessments and formative assessment feedback should keep in mind a few cautions:

- As we have noted, feedback about the person yields the smallest and possibly a negative impact. Instead, feedback should advise students on next steps.
- Preassessments can initially lead to problems in self-esteem if students are not used to them. In particular, students who have traditionally been placed in high-level groups may become disheartened when occasional preassessment scores suggest that they need to shore up foundational skills for certain units. To alleviate this issue, you can remind these students that learning is a journey, not a destination. (More ideas for working with gifted and high-achieving students appear in Chapter 7.)

As we have shown, formative assessment shifts the focus for students away from comparison to peers and toward their own gains and mastery of clear standards. One of our students, Joanna, had struggled with writing since day one. Despite being conscientious, she often failed assessments. By sixth grade, she had come to expect this, but it still hurt every time. When she took her first formative assessment preassessment, she was thrilled that it did not count and excited to know that she would get a chance to retake it after the unit and thus had a chance to improve her score. She worked diligently all through the unit, requesting extra practice for task elements she knew she still needed to master. When she went from a 40% to an 85%, she felt on top of the world. She never asked how she scored in comparison to her peers; she just celebrated her own improvement and how much she had learned. As you begin to use more formative assessments in your own classroom, you will ensure that your own students have cause for celebration, too.

3

What Is Differentiated Instruction?

As we noted toward the end of Chapter 2, formative assessment on its own, even practice with using it, does not lift achievement (Parr & Timperley, 2008) *unless you use the assessment data to make informed, evidence-based changes to teaching* (Stecker, Fuchs, & Fuchs, 2005). This chapter focuses largely on how you can use these data to inform instructional changes through differentiation and tiered instruction.

Differentiated instruction systematically varies instruction and curriculum for diverse learners. It prioritizes considering *how* we teach in addition to *what* we teach (Tomlinson & Eidson, 2003). *Differentiation* refers to the broader picture of the entire lesson where different tasks are used to provide varied and effective experiences that result in fuller learning in the classroom. You make informed decisions about differentiation based on the unit and students' needs.

Of course, differentiated instruction does not mean that you need to provide separate lessons for every child or every group of children. It also does not mean that you need to differentiate every lesson. Similarly, when formative assessments indicate that all students have little knowledge of a new topic, whole-class teaching is appropriate until subsequent formative assessments show that some students are moving at a faster pace, have mastered the material, and require more challenge. Then differentiated instruction may be introduced.

In this chapter, we will explore two bases for differentiated lessons:

1. Student characteristics (readiness and interest)

2. Instructional characteristics (content, process, and product)

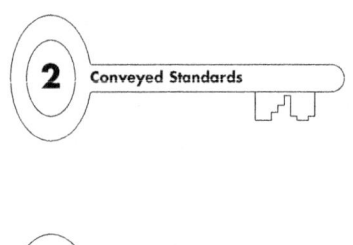

In most cases, you will begin the instruction with the same lesson to introduce the objectives for the whole class. ♀ Then you will offer multiple routes for students to pursue. Ideally, these routes will have variations to address the needs of all students, but they will address the same larger opening concept within the same lesson.

Activities based on tiered instruction fall under the differentiation umbrella. ♀ Specifically, *tiered instruction* refers to the leveled activities that you match to student readiness levels. Considerable research on using differentiation to raise student achievement centers on the effectiveness of tiered activities (Richards & Omdal, 2007; Coyne, Konold, Maynard, Pullen, & Tuckwiller, 2010; Vaughn, Childs, Maschinski, Paul Niño, & Ellsworth, 2010). Here are some of the steps you will take as you begin to use tiered instruction:

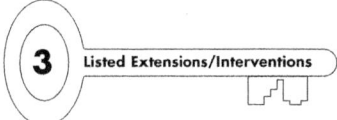

1. Determine lesson objectives. ♀

2. Identify potential varied assignments. ♀ Lessons can be differentiated by:
   o Readiness—what students know at that moment
   o Interests—what motivates and inspires the students
   o Content—information students should understand, which is typically mandated by the department, school, or local or state government
   o Processes—methods students use to gain knowledge
   o Products—methods student use to show understanding.

3. Collect targeted formative assessment data. ♀

4. Use the data to assess the level of understanding each student brings to the lesson. ♀

5. Begin tiering instruction slowly.

Some teachers begin by tiering just one or two lessons in each unit. Then they increase this number over time.

This chapter provides research-based practices for using data to differentiate instruction to facilitate learning gains. We recognize that at first, differentiating instruction can be overwhelming. It requires thoughtful planning and, in some cases, additional time to initially locate or create varied resources. However, as you accumulate the kinds of banks of differentiated resources we describe, you will find that your preparation time decreases.

When you first start working with differentiated instruction in your classroom, you will probably want to concentrate on the following two areas:

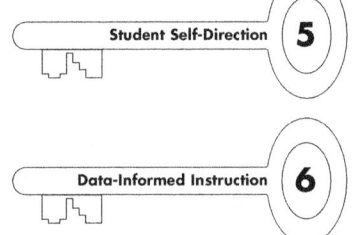

1. Make continual adjustments to the lessons based on student feedback. ♀

2. Incorporate differentiated follow-up tasks, which are also referred to as *exit points* (Heacox, 2002). ♀

For the most part, the process of making adjustments based on student feedback becomes easier over time. It primarily involves making trade-offs, so further planning time is not usually required.

You will use exit points to change the focus on instruction when a student has mastered the concept being taught or would benefit from instruction provided in a different method. For example, if your class is learning about figurative language, you would use exit points to encourage those students who have mastered identifying similes to move on to another skill rather than continuing to practice activities with similes. You will use these exit points during the practice time that follows the introduction to the lesson.

DIFFERENTIATING LESSONS BY STUDENT CHARACTERISTICS

Now that you have seen an overview, let us take a look at the first framework for differentiated lessons: student characteristics (readiness and interest).

Differentiating Lessons by Readiness

Readiness refers to a student's current instructional level with regard to knowledge, understanding, and skill level. ♀ It does not measure ability but what the student understands and can do at a specific point in time (Tomlinson & Eidson, 2003). Preassessments or formative assessments can measure readiness. One model for thinking about how to tier by readiness

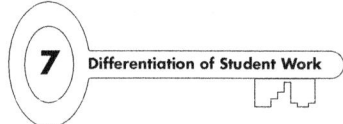

7 | Differentiation of Student Work

is Carol Ann Tomlinson's "Equalizer" (Tomlinson, 1999). ϙ In this model, you view attributes of the lesson as knobs on a stereo that can be adjusted one way or another to increase or decrease the challenge level of a task, depending on student readiness. Students who demonstrate, through formative assessments, mastery of the categories on the left (which represent earlier stages of readiness) would be given tasks aligned with the categories on the right.

The Task-Planning "Equalizer"

Foundational	_____	Transformational
Concrete	_____	Abstract
Simple	_____	Complex
Single Facet	_____	Multifaceted
Structured	_____	Open
Slower Pace	_____	Quicker Pace

Let us look at each component of the task-planning "equalizer" in more detail.

Foundational tasks strengthen the building blocks (fluency, decoding, vocabulary, writing mechanics, reading comprehension strategies, basic elements of a genre) for students to then do more *transformational* tasks in which information is reorganized, manipulated, or thought about in a new way. Here are some specific examples.

- *Foundational.* Students learn to identify common narrative text structures (Williams et al., 2002), with a focus on identifying conflicts in stories. You then support them in discovering and defining one of the three types of conflict a book may have.
- *Transformational.* Students explore questions such as: What is the value of conflict? How can conflict fuel progress and create new understandings? How do conflicts in stories we have read illustrate the concept that a crisis may also be an opportunity? You encourage collaborative discourse in which students build on one another's thinking and pose increasingly challenging questions to one another. This discourse supports the effectiveness of these tasks in helping students transform knowledge (Hmelo-Silver & Barrows, 2008).

Concrete tasks are literal tasks that have clearly defined correct responses. *Abstract* tasks are theoretical tasks that require deeper generalizations, levels of engagement, or insights. As an example of a concrete task, students can count out the syllables in a multisyllabic word, separating each syllable in each word with a slash. A more abstract task might ask students to find the core similar concepts in words with related Latin or Greek roots, such as *captain* and *capital.* (The Latin definition of *cap* is "head," and both words are abstractly defined as "heads.") Again, let's look at a few more specific examples.

- *Concrete.* Students learn and accurately apply the mechanical and grammatical rules for using dialogue, through studying models and practicing this embedded process in writing rather than through isolated drills (Graham & Perin, 2007).
- *Abstract.* Students reflect on and experiment with dialogue in terms of its effect on the reader, writing several versions of an exchange that use dialogue differently to create intentionally varied effects.

Simple tasks require a straightforward solution, whereas *complex* tasks require grasping a more challenging concept. Using story grammar (Morris & Mather, 2008) to support students in answering basic questions on plot would be a simple task. Identifying critical points that signify changes in the evolution of a character arc would be more a more complex task. Here are a few more examples:

- *Simple.* Students learn and apply the steps for paraphrasing a nonfiction piece (Hagaman & Reid, 2008).
- *Complex.* Students write a persuasive paragraph using information from a nonfiction piece to defend or oppose their viewpoint.

Single-facet tasks involve one step, such as answering a basic factual comprehension question or describing the setting of a story. In contrast, *multifaceted* tasks require more steps and connections, such as writing an open response analytical paragraph that explains the moral dimensions of a problematic action committed by a character, including how other characters in the story might respond differently if faced with the same dilemma. Here are a few more examples:

- *Single facet.* Students define in their own words vocabulary words found in texts (Marzano, 2009) or identify specific morphological roots in the words (Bowers, Kirby, & Deacon, 2010).
- *Multifaceted.* Students provide multiple definitions of vocabulary words found in texts, and then they explain how different meanings

might impact the meaning of the text. They also find examples in which authors purposely use a word with multiple meanings.

With *structured* tasks, all steps are fully explained and the solution has one defined answer. In contrast, with *open* tasks, students can make more choices, research alternatives, and evaluate options. To be effective, open tasks should be carefully scaffolded (Hmelo-Silver, Duncan, & Chinn, 2007). Here are specific examples:

- *Structured task.* Students listen to a story read by the teacher and map out the story grammar elements (Stetter & Hughes, 2010).
- *Open task.* Students select a book series and invent a new story for the series, mapping elements of this next story with story grammar strategies.

Finally, tasks can be adjusted for the *pace* at which they are to be completed. For example, if your class is working on a narrative writing unit, you can plan extension activities that focus on writing style in which some students move through the planning and outlining processes at a faster pace (or skip steps) while the rest of the class moves at a slower rate, engaging in multiple planning and brainstorming stages to include the essential elements of a story. Here are a few more examples:

- *Slower pace:* Students who struggle with fluency read fewer chapters of a novel and answer similar strategy-based comprehension questions.
- *Quicker pace:* Students who read fluently read multiple chapters of a novel and answer strategy-based comprehension questions.

Differentiating Lessons by Interests

Lessons can also be differentiated by student interests. To begin, you can allow students to make choices based on their interests and gather data on these interests. ♀ Research shows that when you provide choices based on interests, you will also increase students' motivation, effort, and academic performance (Brooks, Freiburger, & Grotheer, 1998; Hattie, 2009; Irvin, Meltzer, & Dukes, 2007). In particular, when middle school students are motivated by what they are reading, achievement increases (Kamil, 2003).

For example, we decided to differentiate our seventh-grade students' final poetry project based on student interests. The students selected poems to read and used these as models as they created an anthology of self-written poems. During drafting periods, students showed high levels of engagement as they read, analyzed, and provided feedback on each other's poems—all activities found to strengthen comprehension skills (Hadaway, Vardell, & Young, 2001). As Hattie (2009) notes, peer feedback is another formative assessment practice that can significantly raise achievement, and it helped keep students engaged in our example. At the end of the unit, our students enthusiastically shared their poems with their peers. Overall, we concluded that as we allowed students to choose their poetry, we bolstered excitement and engagement, and we potentially strengthened the typical gains expected from these activities.

Student Self-Direction 5

Figure 3.1 shows an interest survey you can use to gather information for planning lessons. To prevent losing valuable instructional time, you could ask students to complete the survey for homework. It can also serve as a meaningful "getting to know you" activity at the beginning of the year. Keep the surveys on file and then refer to them regularly throughout the year as you look for ideas to help students tap into their interests. Alternatively, you can take quick polls of students' interests at the beginning, middle, or end of units to make informed decisions about activities around student interests.

Figure 3.1 Interest profile.

List your specific interests in the following categories:

Hobbies, passions, or activities: What are your favorites?

Music: What are your favorite songs, artists, groups, instruments, or genres (e.g., rock, jazz, hip-hop)?

Sports: What sports do you like to watch and/or play?

Entertainment: What do you like to do for fun or on a free day?

Community service projects: What community service projects have you completed? Are there any community projects that you are interested in?

Favorite books, movies, and TV shows: What are your favorite books, TV shows, and movies?

Genre of movies and books you enjoy: What genre of movies/TV shows/books do you like to watch/read the most?

List any other interests.

DIFFERENTIATING LESSONS BY INSTRUCTIONAL CHARACTERISTICS

Lessons can also be differentiated according to instructional characteristics. These include content, processes, and products (Tomlinson, 2001; Tomlinson & Eidson, 2003).

Differentiating Lessons by Content

Content is the information that students should understand as a result of instruction. It is what the learner will know and be able to do as a result of the lessons. ♀ As a guide to determine what content should be taught, teachers typically use curricula, resources, and national, state, and local standards such as those of the National Council of Teachers of English (NCTE, 2009) or the Common Core State Standards Initiative (n.d.). Before planning lessons, you should decide on the important knowledge, understanding, and skills that are critical for most learners to gain, as well as the tools they will use to access the information (Tomlinson & Eidson, 2003). Collect formative assessment data to help you decide what to teach and how to teach it. ♀ For example, you might decide to differentiate content by:

- Providing texts at varied levels (Burns, 2007)
- Supplementing information with audio recordings (Stone-Harris, 2008) or videos
- Facilitating comprehension through drama activities
- Using increasingly higher levels of explicit and systematic strategy instruction (Archer & Hughes, 2010)
- Providing a bank of key words and definitions to be explicitly taught (Kamil et al., 2008)

The following vignettes highlight the various ways in which Ms. Rodriguez differentiated instruction by content. Ms. Rodriguez was a sixth- and seventh-grade English teacher at a private school in an urban setting. Her classes consisted of 22 to 24 students varying in ability from those who were identified as having a learning disability to those who were high achieving.

As students in Ms. Rodriguez's sixth-grade class analyzed the structure of a story, they each completed a visual poster project in which they highlighted the evolution of a character. Based on the recommendations of the National Read Panel, Ms. Rodriguez knew that analyzing story structure and using graphic organizers were two effective strategies for improving comprehension (National Institute of Child Health and Human Development, 2000). ⚲ Therefore, she made sure to clearly articulate these standards and ways that students could demonstrate mastery of these standards.

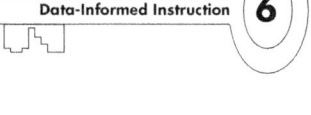

For the poster, the students created a series of images that represented changes in the character, addressing the Common Core State Standard in which students analyze the interaction of particular story elements (Common Core State Standards Initiative, n.d., R.L. 6/7/8.3). Further, they provided written explanations for the character's evolution using literal and inferential examples from the plot of events, emotions, and characteristic traits. ⚲

Based on the data from a preassessment and other observations made in class, Ms. Rodriguez assigned more obscure characters to students who showed sophisticated understanding of the plot and character development. She also prompted them to include more inferential elements, which can be too challenging for students who have difficulty understanding the general plot (Johnston, Barnes, & Desrochers, 2008). For students who needed more support, she provided scaffolding with graphic organizers and a list of suggested chapters to refer to. Ms. Rodriguez had recognized that a few students needed even more support, so she gave them mini lessons in which they explicitly reviewed the plot of the story and completed the scaffolds together. In the end, all of the students created projects that appeared similar. Upon closer examination, however, Ms. Rodriguez discovered that some of the projects had more complex characters, events, and characteristic traits; her differentiation tasks had successfully kept all students appropriately motivated and challenged, eliminating feelings of superiority or inadequacy among peers. ⚲

As mentioned, an effective way to differentiate instruction using content is to provide students with texts of varying difficulty (Burns, 2007). In the next example, Ms. Rodriguez differentiated by using a variety of chapters from the same novel. The task remained the same for all the students, but the level of explicit or implicit action-packed events differed vastly from chapter to chapter for each of the chosen chapters. In this class, sixth-grade students were asked to identify and plot fast-paced events from two chapters of the action-adventure novel *Gregor the Overlander, Book One* by Suzanne Collins (2004).

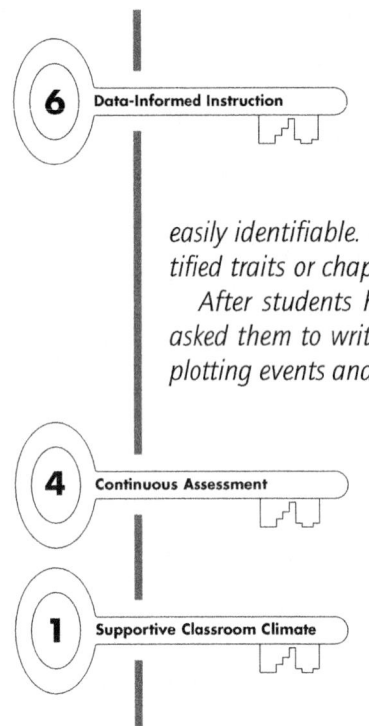

As she planned the unit, Ms. Rodriguez decided that she would assign one chapter to students and then let them choose an additional chapter. ♀ She deliberately assigned chapters based on the students' skills. Students who had mastered identifying events received either more complicated chapters with limited events or chapters with many events that were not discrete or easily identifiable. Other students received either chapters that included easily identified traits or chapters that were action packed.

After students had charted the events of the assigned chapter, Ms. Rodriguez asked them to write a one-page summary highlighting the actions. She knew that plotting events and overall text structure facilitates comprehension (Williams & Pau, 2011) and so would serve as an organizational tool that would help the students craft in-depth summaries with relevant information. ♀ Depending on how well students did with the assigned chapter, Ms. Rodriguez made personalized suggestions to some, recommending that they choose an additional chapter that had more explicit plot structures and, therefore, better matched the readiness levels they had demonstrated. ♀ However, she also ensured that she provided students with choices among the chapters. This allowed them to make a case for selecting other chapters if they felt strongly about doing so.

Varying the readability level of material seems to be one of the most accessible ways to differentiate by content. You can easily modify lessons by providing resources at different levels. Although it can seem daunting to locate resources at different levels, even with the surge of leveled readers, certain units such as those that focus on a specific genre may allow you to vary readability levels quite easily.

For example, during a poetry unit, Ms. Rodriguez wanted her seventh-grade students to identify poetic elements in different poems. The assignment required each group to analyze its assigned poem for poetic elements, interpret the poem's meaning, and present its findings to the class. ♀

To begin, Ms. Rodriguez used data from a preassessment to identify students' current level of ability. The task asked students to identify and analyze poetic elements and interpret the meaning of a poem. Ms. Rodriguez was surprised as she reviewed the assessment data, because even though there is a relationship between fluency and comprehension (Daane, Campbell, Grigg, Goodman, & Oranje, 2005), her results showed that some of the students who typically struggled with decoding longer words and often faltered with comprehension in class were actually some of the most sophisticated at analyzing poems. She suspected that since most of the poems were shorter than other readings, these students were able to focus less on decoding, engage in multiple readings (Ardoin, McCall, & Klubnik, 2007) in a short amount of time, and consequently make more meaning. These results further confirmed Ms. Rodriguez's experience of the power and importance of using formative assessment as feedback to plan lessons (Black, Harrison, Lee, Marshall, & Wiliam, 2004).♀ ♀

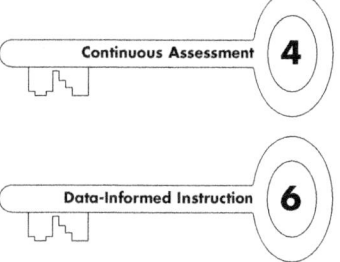

Based on the preassessment data, Ms. Rodriguez grouped the students by current level of ability and then introduced the activity by assigning each group a poem. All the poems were similar in font and size, but both the poem and poetic elements had different levels of difficulty. She instructed each group to identify a specific number of poetic elements from the poem and then provide their peers with directions on becoming "experts" on the poem. She encouraged all students to orally read the poems multiple times to foster comprehension, since multiple readings help promote oral fluency and bolster comprehension (Jenkins, Fuchs, Van den Broek, Espin, & Deno, 2003).

Ms. Rodriguez explained that all the students would not have similar elements, as poets do not use all poetic elements in each of their poems. Since students were practicing the same skill and since resources for poetry are plentiful, varying the content was relatively easy. Ultimately, the students in each group presented their findings in a similar fashion, so the differentiated tasks also looked quite similar.

In this case, Ms. Rodriguez was able to successfully differentiate the content without the students' knowledge. Therefore, they did not express discontent about their task or have notions that one group was "smarter" than the other. ♀

Recall that you can differentiate content by providing leveled readings of the literature used, but you can also differentiate criteria for completing the assignment. After the poetry unit, Ms. Rodriguez wanted students to create a script that retold an oral tradition as part of their oral tradition/storytelling unit. ♀ ♀

Ms. Rodriguez planned to assign students one of two lessons in which content was differentiated, depending on their readiness levels. She decided to determine these levels based on three different assessments . She used the final projects from the poetry unit and an additional preassessment writing sample to evaluate where students stood in their command of figurative language, story setting, wrap-up, and other skills that would be relevant to the script writing aspect of the new unit. Then she asked students to orally retell a portion of a story for two to three minutes. For this lesson, students worked in small groups, rating each other and receiving feedback from their peers and from Ms. Rodriguez. Ms. Rodriguez used this data as the third assessment to determine their level for the script writing project. ♀

Figure 3.2 shows guidelines for a project similar to the one Ms. Rodriguez used in her classroom.

Figure 3.2	Script writing project differentiated by content.

Lesson

Students will take an oral tradition from a variety of resources and create a script that they will use to orally retell a story that is about four minutes long.

Standard

NCTE: Standards 2, 3, 4, 6 (www.ncte.org/standards)

Less Challenging	More Challenging
Story selection	*Story selection*
The teacher chooses a story that is shorter and includes fewer events. The problem, resolution, and major events are more obvious and action packed. Character traits and emotions are more vivid and deliberately shown in actions.	The teacher chooses a story that contains more complex events. The problem, resolution, and major events are embedded within the story. There may be many events to help enrich the story, but these may not be relevant or needed during the oral retelling task. Character traits and emotions are more ambiguous.
Task	*Task*
1. Students will chart out the main elements of the story and create a script, using a graphic organizer to organize their thoughts.	1. Students will chart out the main elements of the story and create a script, using a graphic organizer to organize their thoughts.
2. When writing the script for the oral retelling, students will include:	2. When writing the script for the oral retelling, students will include:
___ Two instances of rich imagery ___ Three examples of sentence variety ___ Two examples of figurative language ___ One clear description of the main antagonist and protagonist ___ Three clear events ___ Two dialogue exchanges ___ Two instances of lingering and pausing ___ A clear resolution ___ A moral stated at the end	___ Four instances of rich imagery ___ Five to eight examples of sentence variety ___ Four examples of figurative language (at least one metaphor, simile, or personification) ___ Two clear descriptions of the main antagonist and protagonist (at the beginning and when the characters have evolved) ___ Three clear events ___ Three dialogue exchanges ___ Two instances of lingering and pausing ___ A clear resolution ___ A moral stated at the end

Differentiating Lessons by Processes

Lessons can also be differentiated according to the different processes students use to achieve the same curricular goals. *Process* refers to the methods students use to gain knowledge. It typically occurs after you have provided the lessons. The process stage is more student directed; it is when application of the information occurs.

There is a thin line between differentiating content and differentiating process, and many differentiated activities may fall into both categories. For example, students will use the varied content to learn the intended outcomes, and you may need to reteach information during the process stage depending on students' understanding and the outcome of their work.

Frameworks such as Howard Gardner's (1983/2003) multiple intelligences can be a helpful guide when differentiating by process. The application of such frameworks to guide teaching has been found to significantly lift student achievement (Bas, 2010). The following is a list of these eight intelligences:

1. Linguistic intelligence ("word smart")

2. Logical-mathematical intelligence ("number/reasoning smart")

3. Spatial intelligence ("picture smart")

4. Bodily-kinesthetic intelligence ("body smart")

5. Musical intelligence ("music smart")

6. Interpersonal intelligence ("people smart")

7. Intrapersonal intelligence ("self smart")

8. Naturalist intelligence ("nature smart")

Here's an example of how this can be put into practice. Let's say the class is studying a unit on novels that focuses on *Stormbreaker* by Anthony Horowitz. Lessons that explore story elements or character traits can be differentiated based on the eight intelligences (Horowitz, 2006). For instance, students can create a song (musical intelligence) or use motions (bodily intelligence) to exemplify traits of the hero, Alex Rider. Likewise, students could use word sorts (Joseph, 2002) to organize the words in appropriate groups (spatial intelligence) or memorize the specific spelling rules and use logical deduction (logical-mathematical or linguistic intelligence) to spell the words correctly.

Here's an example in which Ms. Rodriguez was able to use movement as an alternate route to help a student compensate for weak conceptual understandings.

One morning, Ms. Rodriguez noticed that one of her students had a difficult time using commas when writing sentences that began with prepositional or participial phrases. Initially, she tried a number of techniques to help him see that a comma was necessary after the phrase. She suggested that he could:

- *Highlight the phrase and punctuation with two different colors*
- *Leave a large space between the two parts of the sentence*
- *Refer to a comma prompt (an index card with the rule on it) at the beginning of class*

6 Data-Informed Instruction

However, none of these attempts proved fruitful. ♀ Knowing, from past performance, that the student was able to understand complex concepts once he used more hands-on approaches, she decided to see if movement could help him understand.

To begin, they read aloud together and decided where a natural pause made the most sense. They began to read the sentences with feeling, and they included a dramatic pause where the comma would be. Then they created an action for the comma, and they made sure to engage in it when they came to the pause where the comma should be included. With continued practice, the student was able to transfer the comma to his writing. Because of this differentiated activity, Ms. Rodriguez felt comfortable that this student demonstrated understanding of using commas to set off phrases (Common Core State Standards Initiative, n.d., L.6.2).

4 Continuous Assessment

2 Conveyed Standards

Another time, when Ms. Rodriguez was teaching basic paragraph writing skills to her students, she created a song for the elements of an example paragraph. ♀ The class included students whom she had identified through formative assessment data as ones who would struggle with this skill, but they were able to retain and recall the elements of the paragraph when she introduced it in song form. ♀ The song provided a scaffold similar to a mnemonic device and aided students who had difficulty memorizing the elements (the standards of the paragraph that they would be evaluated on). Mnemonics help facilitate memorization and can be very beneficial, especially for kids who have difficulty recalling information (Scruggs & Mastropieri, 2000; Wolgemuth, Cobb, & Alwell, 2008).

Ms. Rodriguez also used music as part of a novel unit on immigration. In this unit, seventh-grade students had a choice to share their family story in any medium (see Figure 3.3). One student, who had a learning disability, struggled with writing clear and organized stories, despite having strong ideas. ♀ ♀ However, because the student was musically inclined, this assignment allowed her to make the most of her abilities. She chose to share her family story through a song that she composed, and because she was able to choose the medium, her ideas flourished. While other students were drafting written versions of their story, she was composing music and lyrics that shared her family story. Her final product showed Ms. Rodriguez that she clearly had the ability to tell a story when given the opportunity to use a different type of intelligence in the process.

5 Student Self-Direction

Figure 3.3   Family story assignment.

"Every family has a story. Ours begins with _____." (Budhos, 2006, p. 19)

Chapter 3 of *Ask Me No Questions* by Marina Budhos (2006) starts off with a quote. The chapter continues to explain how Nadira and Aisha's family story begins with water. Please fill in the above-mentioned quote with the appropriate word or phrase that fits your family story. Your family story can go back as far into time as you would like. Or, it can be a story from your generation, especially if you are an immigrant. After, you will share a specific story that will help the reader to understand why your family story began with your chosen word. The story can be presented in any way you like (short story, poem, song, video, picture collage, comic strip . . .).

Differentiating Lessons by Products

It is also possible to differentiate by products. A *product* refers to a method that a student uses to show his understanding. Ideal products are closely aligned to the objectives and standards of the unit and lesson. Students can create long- and short-term products. Long-term products are more in depth and usually occur at the end of a unit in the form of a culminating activity that demonstrates student learning on all objectives of the unit. Short-term products focus on students' demonstration of understanding on a smaller scale, typically as a result of one or a few days of lessons. When generating ideas for products, you will not only consider the standards, curriculum, skills of the unit, and lessons; you will also create the methods of evaluation.

When you have clearly identified the objectives of the lesson beforehand, you can give students the opportunity to show their mastery through different products. ❢ Product is another area in which teachers can provide choices to students, which, as we have noted, increases effort and motivation (Brooks et al., 1998). When students have options, they also feel ownership in their learning and have an opportunity to pick the most relevant and applicable ways to show their understanding. ❢

Conveyed Standards 2

Student Self-Direction 5

Ideally, you should teach students to use results from formative assessments and interests to guide their decisions as they make choices about which product to select. For example, let us say that you want your class to present various types of gods and goddesses in Greek mythology and their relationship to each other. Some might choose to write a brief report using scaffolds and explicit paragraph instructional strategies as described in

Graham and Perin (2007). Others might create a poster to show the same information.

The big idea is that the product is not the end goal; it is a vehicle that indicates mastery of the standard. As you teach students to master a concept, you might allow them to choose from items in a standard menu to complete varied final products (see Figure 3.4). As with lessons, you should be flexible when creating products. Products that take student learning into account and are sensitive to the needs of learners have the potential to be powerful in the classroom (Tomlinson & Eidson, 2003).

Figure 3.4   Menu of product options.

Select one option from the menu below to represent your understanding of the current topic. The project will be scored on the accuracy, clarity, and completeness of the explanation of the English topic and skill, as well as the quality of the presentation of the material.

Poster	Song or Poem
Design a poster that conveys the main problem and resolution of the novel.	Write a song, rap song, or poem that explains the main problem and resolution of the novel.
3-D Image Design a 3-D image and a diorama-type box that represents the main problem and resolution of the novel.	Written Explanation Write a one-page explanation of the main problem and resolution of the novel.

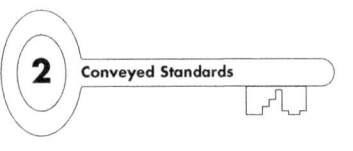

2 Conveyed Standards

Finally, it is critical that you take steps to define and convey ways to reach mastery to students for evaluative purposes for each assignment. ❓ You may find that objectives are easier to evaluate than criteria such as presentation and effort, which can be subjective. It is important for you to have specific criteria to avoid ambiguity and subjectivity in scoring. Specific criteria will also help you assess the different learners and differentiation that may have occurred in the class. A well-defined rubric that highlights skills, presentation, and effort will make it easier for you to evaluate a project that is a result of choice. We encourage you to create detailed rubrics for clarity. A well-crafted rubric makes explicit your expectations on assignments (Arter & McTighe, 2001; Jonsson & Svingby, 2007). It tells the student what is important when completing the assignment, and it tells you what to look for when assessing the product.

One way to account for differentiation is to create multiple rubrics that highlight the same skills but vary according to product. This way, the rubrics still provide explicit information about the ways the final product will be assessed without stifling the different creative aspects of each product (Jonsson & Svingby, 2007; Wiggins, 1998). Because the rubrics will be similar for the most part, especially if the objectives are the same, teachers may only have to make small adjustments to the presentation section of the rubrics.

As we have emphasized throughout this chapter, regardless of how instruction is differentiated, teachers are encouraged to accurately define the skills and level of mastery, and to use these definitions to consistently evaluate students through varied formative assessment. These steps will ensure that lessons hit the right targets, that the evaluation process not only is clear but also measures identified skills, and that students are working at their instructional level.

4 How Do I Differentiate Lessons?

The previous chapters have highlighted some of the benefits of differentiation. In this chapter we continue to examine the format for differentiated lessons. In the first section, we discuss:

- Identifying standards
- Using data from preassessments
- Teaching whole-class lessons
- Creating tiered lessons

We wrap up this section with an analysis of a differentiated lesson. Throughout the chapter, we ask:

- How can you continue to address the needs of students throughout each unit?
- How can you make the changes necessary to address the needs of each student in each activity?
- Keeping in mind that both student and instructional characteristics can differentiate lessons, how can you create specific activities to reach all students regularly?

To address these questions, we provide information on how you can make continuous changes to lessons based on student feedback.

♀ ♀ We include specific, in-depth examples of various ways to tier lessons. In the final section, we offer a framework on how you can tier lessons through six specific strategies:

1. Making small adjustments

2. Challenging all learners

3. Minimizing task differences

4. Crafting sophisticated questions

5. Increasing goals

6. Setting appropriate group work

Using any one of these six strategies, you will be able to tier activities with more ease and success for your students.

FORMAT FOR DIFFERENTIATED LESSONS

The extended vignette that follows illustrates how you can differentiate in real time and reveals the thinking behind instructional decision making processes. Although the idea of differentiating activities for each lesson may seem daunting, you will find that minor alterations may be the norm for differentiating in most instances.

Ms. Chan, who is the focus of the vignette, is a middle school English teacher who teaches mixed-ability students. Some have been diagnosed with language-based learning disabilities or perform significantly lower than their peers. Others understand instruction quickly and tend to get bored easily. This vignette shows how Ms. Chan used formative assessment to differentiate a unit on analytical writing. Specifically, it highlights the:

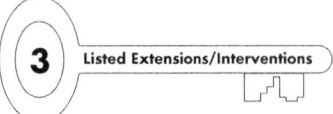

- Standards Ms. Chan wanted to address in her lessons ♀

- Possible interventions and challenges she could offer ♀

- Preassessment she used to identify students' readiness levels ♀

- Whole-class instruction she administered after the preassessment
- Tiered activities she administered after the preassessment ♀

For an overview of the portion of the unit that Ms. Chan used in her classroom, see the unit plan in Figure 4.1.

Figure 4.1   Differentiated lessons for analytical paragraph unit.

Unit Topic:

Analytical paragraph writing in which students will use the writing process to plan an organized paragraph that stays on topic, is developed with relevant facts and logical reasoning, includes smooth transitions between ideas, and uses appropriate language. Students will also practice comprehension skills to identify the relevant examples to support their points in writing.

Specific Standards:

  Core Standards: RL 6.1, RL 6.5, W 6.1, W 6.2, W 6.4 (www.corestandards.org)
  NCTE Standards: 1, 3, 5, 6 (www.ncte.org/standards)

Preassessment:

  1. Have students outline and write a paragraph based on characteristic traits of a character from a novel.

  2. Have students complete a comprehension test where they answer six short-answer questions on the novel. The questions employ different comprehension skills (summarizing, inferring, drawing conclusions, retelling, giving opinions with rationale) so that the teacher can further specify where the difficulties in comprehension lie.

Predictable Misconceptions:

  1. Students who are strong at reading comprehension will have no difficulties with organizing their paragraphing, whereas those who struggle with comprehending will also have difficulties with organizing their writing.

  2. Students who write strong creative stories will know how to organize and write analytical paragraphs better.

Motivation/Introduction:

  Either introduce or review the writing process: plan, organize, write, edit, revise. Students will watch "The Writing Process" video podcast on mspatel.podomatic .com. Discuss the benefits of engaging in the writing process: *"It may take longer to*

(Continued)

(Continued)

plan and organize in an outline than it would to simply write a paragraph. You will be able to write a more organized and logical writing piece with a greater number of detailed and relevant examples if you plan and organize beforehand, because you will have reflected already on, 'What should I include?' before you get to the actual writing. So, at that point, you can spend time thinking of adding some transitions, using more sophisticated vocabulary, and correctly following grammatical and mechanical rules."

Formative Assessment:

1. Teachers and students will evaluate various student-written analytical paragraphs (either the entire paragraph or rewritten sections) for organization, quality of examples, and analysis.
2. Students will set goals based on their results, and students and teachers will evaluate how well they have met them.
3. Students will answer comprehension questions.

Lessons

Day 1

1. Teacher will review the elements of an analytical paragraph.
2. Teacher will hand out an outline graphic organizer and discuss the components of the outline. Explicitly show how the outline includes all the essential elements of the paragraph.

Day 2

3. Teacher will complete a model outline of the example analytical paragraph with students.
4. Teacher and students will compare the outline they wrote for their preassessment with the model outline and will see that although the outline is completed in note form, it includes all relevant details.

Day 3

5. Students will rewrite a section of the model, using their own words.

Homework: Students will review comparing their outlines to the model outline created in class and will note goals for improvement.

Day 4

Objective: Students will write their own outline either based on a short story or one chapter of the novel they are reading. All students will be assigned the same character.

1. Students will break up in groups and complete a T-chart. On one side they will brainstorm a list of character traits for the assigned character; on the other side they will write out specific examples from the book that highlight the characteristic traits they have found.

Tiered support for lesson on Day 4:

- Students who can better express their ideas through images and drawing can draw rough diagrams of information in lieu of fully writing out specific examples.
- Some students who write slowly and have difficulty with legibility will be provided with a photocopy of the chapter so that they can highlight the examples in the chapter itself and write a few words or phrases in the margin. (Since the preassessment was timed, the teacher can compare the quantity written and analyze handwriting formations by each child to identify those students who have difficulty with the actual handwriting process.)

2. Once students have about five traits, they will receive an outline to complete. They will write their preset goal on a sticky note and keep it on their desk to remind them of their outlining goals. The model outline will be on the board for the students to review during the entire process.

Tiered Activities:

1. Extension/support: The teacher will assign specific traits to some students after consultation. Some traits will be easier, with clear, identifiable examples listed in the chapter, whereas some will be more sophisticated and need more inferential thinking to come up with examples. For example, in the novel *Homeless Bird* by Gloria Whelan (2001), the main character, Koly, can easily be concretely defined as hardworking, loyal, friendly, and brave. Some more sophisticated traits to define her would be misinformed, optimistic, naïve.

2. Comprehension support: For those students who have difficulty comprehending the chapter, the teacher will meet with a small group and plot a sequence of main events (provided by the teacher in random order) of that chapter in flowchart form in their notebook with illustrations and sentences. Then they will move on to completing a paragraph with only one characteristic trait subtopic (rather than two), where the students will have to choose one characteristic trait from a choice of two.

3. Characterization support: Students struggling with identifying traits will define traits of the main character through text-to-self activities. They will be asked to take on the persona of the main character and discuss how they would feel and act. Through these discussions, they will be able to identify relevant defining traits of the character.

4. Characterization extension: Students will brainstorm ideas for a chapter through a different perspective, highlighting different motives based on various traits, and create a comic strip.

Class Discussion:

Hold a whole-class discussion wrapping up the key points of each lesson, such as outlining, identifying key characteristic traits, locating relevant examples, or organizing the paragraph.

Assessment:

For the final assessment at the end of the whole unit, students will plan and write an analytical paragraph on a different piece of literature.

Identifying Standards

Ms. Chan wanted to plan a unit that would hit multiple standards and enable students to connect their novel study to writing skills. In prior units, students had engaged in the writing process with a research-validated strategy called "POWER" (Archer & Hughes, 2010); Ms. Chan knew that she wanted students to use this again. (See Figure 4.2.)

Figure 4.2 Using POWER to internalize the writing process.

Planning: The brainstorm stage—get all your ideas out on paper.

Organizing: Organize the ideas that you brainstormed in some type of outline.

Writing: Use the outline to help you write.

Editing: Go back and check for mechanical and grammatical errors.

Revising: Go back and check that all your content makes sense, and that all essential elements of the written product are included completely and clearly.

(See http://ctl.uoregon.edu/pd/cf10/presentation/1034 for more information on the writing process strategy of POWER.)

Based on the standards of the National Council of Teachers of English (NCTE, 2009), the Common Core State Standards (Common Core State Standards Initiative, n.d.), and individual school standards, Ms. Chan also determined that she wanted her sixth-grade students to write a clear, coherent, and organized analytical paragraph, as exemplified in Figure 4.3. She wanted this paragraph to contain relevant and specific details, definitions of key terms, as well as defined and relevant topic and conclusion sentences (NCTE Standards 5, 6; Common Core writing standards). ?

2 Conveyed Standards

Figure 4.3 Standards for elements of an analytical paragraph.

Topic sentence: A sentence that introduces the paragraph's topic and main points.

Transition words: Words or introductory phrases that connect points and ideas.

Subtopic: A transition sentence that reintroduces the main point that will be discussed immediately after the sentence. This sentence is only needed if multiple points are being addressed in a paragraph.

Examples: Specific story examples to support your point.

Analysis: A logical argument that clearly explains how the examples support the topic sentence. Analysis should include inferential information.

Conclusion sentence: A sentence that wraps up the paragraph.

Ms. Chan also wanted to focus on comprehension skills because she recognized that:

- *Reading and writing are reciprocally related*
- *Students use writing to help make meaning of what they have just read (Collins & Madigan, 2010).*
- *Writing strengthens reading comprehension (Graham & Hebert, 2010).*

She was also aware that weakness in writing and comprehension may be tied not only to either reading or writing but possibly to both. To strengthen students' comprehension skills throughout the novel study, she decided that as a way to help students understand the general story plot and character development, she would ask them to identify:

- *Various traits of a character throughout the novel*
- *The situations the character is in*
- *The character's motivating actions (NCTE Standard 3).*

Ms. Chan decided to ask students to write an analytical paragraph based on traits of a character in the novel Homeless Bird *by Gloria Whelan (2001; NCTE Standards 4, 6).* ♀ *Before she designed her preassessment, she predicted what it would reveal about her students' needs. Then,*  *based on those predictions, she planned for and listed potential differentiation tasks that would serve as interventions (Wilson & Bertenthal, 2005). At this point, the activities were rough ideas that became formalized once the preassessments were analyzed. Finally, she designed a preassessment (Wylie & Wiliam, 2006) on analytical writing that included both planning the piece of writing and writing the piece.* ♀ *This* 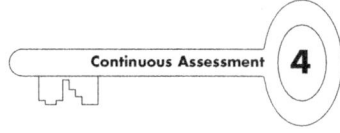 *preassessment asked students to outline and then to write about two characteristic traits of a specific protagonist from the last novel they had read.*

When you think about the tiered activities *before* you create the preassessments, you can create preassessments that specifically target the exact data you will need to inform which tiered activity each student needs to do. ♀♀ Of course, once you collect the preassessment 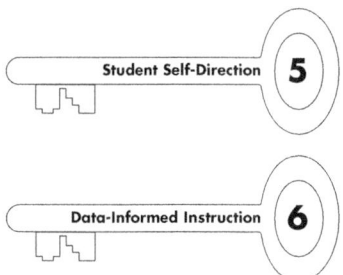 data, you and the students can reevaluate the activities needed in the lessons based on the student results.

Using Data from Preassessments

A week later, Ms. Chan began the unit by asking her students to complete the preassessment. Again, this assignment asked students to outline and then to write about two characteristic traits of a specific protagonist from the last novel they had

3 Listed Extensions/Interventions

5 Student Self-Direction

read. As she reviewed the preassessments, Ms. Chan was surprised by the variety of results. Some students could not write a well-supported, organized paragraph with relevant examples that stayed on topic. Few were able to write a somewhat organized paragraph with some solid examples and a few basic transitions. Most needed further assistance in developing their points by crafting a logical argument, using appropriate transitions between points, and accurately outlining their supporting points before writing. The preassessment also confirmed her concerns that a few students lacked basic comprehension skills.

Ms. Chan used the chart in Figure 4.4 to identify which skills each student was able to master independently. (Later in the unit, the students would use the same chart to evaluate themselves.) The results helped Ms. Chan craft unit lessons, and they helped students set appropriate goals for their writing, thus putting them in charge of some aspects of the decision making process for their learning.

Figure 4.4 Individual student chart.

Topic sentence with subtopics (2 points)	
Subtopic 1 (1 point)	
Example 1 (2 points)	
Definition of trait 1 (1 point)	
Analysis (2 points)	
Subtopic 2 (1 point)	
Example 2 (2 points)	
Definition of trait 2 (1 point)	
Analysis (2 points)	
Conclusion sentence (1 point)	
Transition words (1 point) Words used:	
CUPS (capitalization, usage, punctuation, spelling; 2 points) List mechanical errors:	
Stays on topic (Yes or No: 1 point if Yes)	
Total points:	

For those skills that receive only one point, students receive full credit if that sentence or sentences are provided in the paragraph. For those skills that receive two points, not only does that sentence need to be included, but it also needs to be developed with relevant information.

Teaching Whole-Class Lessons

During the introductory lesson, Ms. Chan reviewed the essential elements of an analytical paragraph. Then she provided students with a model paragraph, because she recognized that providing students with models helps them create mental models of the genre (Crinon & Legros, 2002), and it eases anxiety associated with a new task (Macbeth, 2010). She asked the students to identify all essential elements in the model and to complete the chart in Figure 4.4; this exercise helped them learn how to score a paragraph.

As Ms. Chan went over the model analytical paragraph that she had shown her students, she used a whole-class chart to make decisions about what to emphasize next (Figure 4.5 shows four entries). ♀ Reading the chart vertically, she noticed that most students had difficulty with topic sentences, examples, and analysis, so she chose a new example paragraph that modeled these well. (See Figure 4.6, which is based on Homeless Bird *by Gloria Whelan [2001].) She also noted from the chart, reading it horizontally, that Student 4 had mastered most basic elements and needed enrichment. She then noted those students (1 and 2) who would need extra support.*

Data-Informed Instruction **6**

Figure 4.5   Whole-class performance monitoring chart (for teacher).

Key: Topic sentence (TS); Subtopic 1 (S1); Example 1 (E1); definition (D1); Analysis 1 (A1); conclusion sentence (CS); transition words (TW); capitalization, usage, punctuation, spelling (CUPS); topic (T).

	TS	S1	E1	D1	A1	ST2	E2	D2	A2	CS	TW	CUPS	T	Total
Student 1	0	1	0	1	0	1	1	1	1	1	0	0	1	8
Student 2	0	1	1	1	0	1	1	1	0	1	0	0	1	8
Student 3	1	1	1	1	1	1	1	1	0	1	1	1	1	12
Student 4	2	1	2	1	2	1	2	1	2	1	1	0	1	17
Class totals	3/8	4/4	4/8	4/4	6/8	4/4	5/8	4/4	3/8	4/4	2/4	1/4	4/4	

5 Student Self-Direction

After students analyzed the new model, Ms. Chan handed back a copy of the preassessment task with a blank copy of the individual student chart (refer to Figure 4.4). ♀ For homework, she asked students to compare their paragraph to the new model provided in class. As part of this homework, students attempted to score their own paragraphs and set a specific goal based on the results and on the feedback Ms. Chan had provided with their preassessments, which also included specific comments about suggested goals they could address.

Figure 4.6 Model analytical paragraph.

In Chapter 1, Baap, the father of Koly, was compassionate and fearful. First, Baap was compassionate. During Koly and Hari's wedding reception, coconut cakes were served. Koly loved coconut cakes. Since Koly was a girl, she was supposed to eat after the men. Unfortunately, when it was her turn to eat, all the cakes had run out. Being a man and the father of the bride, Baap was one of the first to eat, and he made sure to save Koly a cake. When he said goodbye to Koly, he secretly gave her the treat. Someone who is compassionate thinks of others, is caring, and is willing to sacrifice for that loved one. This shows Baap was compassionate because he cared a lot for Koly and was willing to give up something for her. He thought about her interests and saved his delicious coconut cake for his daughter so that she would be able to enjoy the treat. Secondly, Baap was fearful. He loved his daughter dearly and was fearful that he may have made a mistake in promising her to Hari. He realized that something was amiss the day before the wedding, when he went to the Mehta's village and learned how ill Hari was. However, according to the culture he knew it was bad luck to cancel the wedding or change the date, so he went along with the plans reluctantly and full of anxiety. A fearful person is concerned about the facts presented and feels powerless to change them. This shows that Baap is fearful because, although he realizes that something is wrong, he feels he has no authority to change it. Therefore, he becomes concerned about his daughter's well-being and hopes that things will be okay for her. In conclusion, Baap is a compassionate man who is fearful for his daughter's well-being at this point in the novel.

The next day, Ms. Chan gave the students the individual chart she had filled out with specific comments and suggested goals. She also made sure to collect the students' homework charts and goals to ensure that they were in agreement on the scoring of the paragraph. Since reviewing this work would take time, Ms. Chan quickly asked the students to write the raw score from their homework on their individual student white boards. She looked at their boards to note any significant differences in scoring between her assessment and theirs, and she

1 Supportive Classroom Climate

made a point to confer with those students first. ♀ She also asked the students to indicate their understanding of the goals she had suggested with a thumbs up (approve/understand) or thumbs down (reject/question) procedure. Since students were used to these procedures and Ms. Chan had already created a supportive classroom environment, they felt comfortable honestly assessing and sharing their level of understanding openly. Later, in conferences with students, Ms. Chan addressed differences in scoring between her students' perceptions of their writing and her own.

Creating Tiered Lessons

Once Ms. Chan taught the students methods for incorporating the writing process (brainstorming and outlining) into their analytical writing, the students began to engage in tiered activities to reach mastery on elements they had struggled with during the preassessment, either in groups or independently at their specific level based on recommendations made by Ms. Chan and among themselves. 🔑*

Data-Informed Instruction **6**

Ms. Chan worked for 15 to 20 minutes with students who would benefit from specific comprehension instruction while the rest of the class worked on the foundational task of organizing their planning information. 🔑 *Since the students were well into the year, they were familiar with this classroom environment, so most did not question the reason why some kids worked with the teacher whereas others worked independently or in other smaller groups.* 🔑 *For those students who were able to complete the outline easily or had shown mastery of the comprehension skill in the preassessment, Ms. Chan suggested alternative extension comprehension activities that focused on other characters of the novel (see Figure 4.7).*

Supportive Classroom Climate **1**

Figure 4.7   Sample comprehension extension activities.

1. Create a T-chart for the character Maa, focusing on the values that she seems to prioritize. List five values, and give specific examples that show how she practices these values.

2. Pretend that Koly's brothers Gopal and Ram were at the wedding. What would their reactions be? Provide evidence from the text that supports why you think they might react as you predict.

3. Indian culture is evident throughout this book. Provide defining examples of this. You may make a picture (or a series of pictures), write a poem, create a vocabulary list with key words and definitions, or write a paragraph.

Ms. Chan observed students as they worked and, in response, adjusted the pace of the writing process. 🔑 *She also asked those students who had finished their outline to move on to the writing stage instead of completing an extension activity. Students began to write their drafts. During the revising and editing phases, Ms. Chan asked certain students to work on adding more sophisticated enhancements, such as intricate vocabulary, smoother transitions, and multiple examples. These students had created more demanding goals, and they were able to address those goals while their peers focused on foundational skills in comprehension or planning and outlining. As students worked, Ms. Chan continued to circulate around the room, answering questions and offering further support and feedback to all students.*

At the end of the class, Ms. Chan brought the class together to wrap up the activity. Together the class reviewed an element from the skill, and students openly reflected with their class on their experiences. (Ms. Chan always brings the class together at the end of each lesson to discuss or reflect at least one element of the lesson to continue to cultivate a feeling of community for a positive learning environment.) ♀

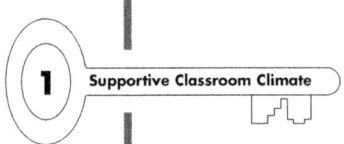

Analysis of a Differentiated Lesson

As we have emphasized, the first step to creating a differentiated lesson is to clarify the lesson standard that all students are expected to master. ♀ Ms. Chan did this by asking her students to identify the writing process and use it to write an analytical paragraph. Teachers also need to list and assess prerequisite skills. In Ms. Chan's lesson, prerequisite skills included identifying the different steps of the writing process and using the terminology learned in class for the five steps of the writing process (planning, organizing, writing, editing, revising). Since the students' final product would be an analytical paragraph, it was also important for Ms. Chan to assess the students' paragraph writing skills. ♀ Afterward, students reflected on their process to complete the assessment so that Ms. Chan could evaluate the students' understanding of the writing process.

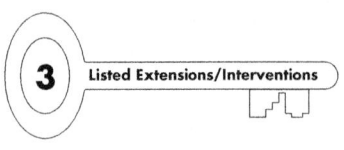

Preassessments remain invaluable in helping to plan for differentiating lessons at the start of the unit and again when the lesson begins. ♀ You should plan for common challenges in advance and prepare strategies to address them. Similarly, you can also prepare enrichments before a lesson. Ms. Chan used the preassessment data to alter some of the tiered activities she planned even before she administered the assessment.

As you introduce a lesson, plan to explicitly discuss the objectives of the unit as you motivate students. ♀ During Ms. Chan's introductory lesson, she asked students to recall the steps of the writing process and elements of an analytical paragraph. ♀ Next, plan whether you will tier differentiation by content, process, or product and by readiness, interest, or learning profile. ♀ In this case, Ms. Chan differentiated by readiness, and she gave a more abstract, advanced challenge to those who were ready.

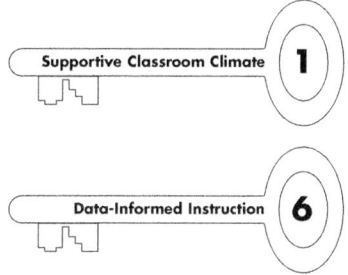

In fact, the lesson in the initial vignette did not include differentiation; Ms. Chan did not introduce differentiation until the second lesson. The first lesson was a whole-class instruction based on reviewing elements of a paragraph and further discussing the methods of using the writing process to complete a paragraph. In the second lesson, Ms. Chan asked the students to create their own outlines based on characteristic traits of a character in the novel they were reading. Naturally, this activity also assessed and utilized the students' comprehension abilities and their understanding of the plot and the interplay between the characters and the events. Therefore, after the initial planning activity, Ms. Chan planned mini lessons around comprehension strategies for students who struggled with the skill.

As the lesson given by Ms. Chan demonstrates, lessons should generally follow this path:

1. Open together

2. Branch off into different tiers

3. Reconvene at the end

As students demonstrate mastery or show a need for additional instruction, teachers need to have activities on hand and ready for use, as well as independent practice. These activities might include a page of extensions, a packet of related extensions, or an in-depth task.

The lesson should always conclude with some type of whole-class evaluation and reflection so student learning can be evaluated—ideally by students themselves, with an element of feedback and possible future steps included.♀

SIX STRATEGIES FOR TIERING ACTIVITIES

Tiered activities are at the heart of differentiation because they match instruction to a student's readiness level. As we have emphasized, differentiation raises student achievement when activities are tiered to meet the student's appropriate level of instruction (Pullen, Tuckwiller, Konold,

Maynard, & Coyne, 2010; Richards & Omdal, 2007; Vaughn et al., 2010). ♀ Formative assessment can help guide you as you make appropriate decisions when tiering activities. The following sections focus on six specific strategies for tiering activities:

1. Making small adjustments

2. Challenging all learners

3. Minimizing task differences

4. Crafting sophisticated questions

5. Increasing goals

6. Setting appropriate group work

We have chosen to focus on these strategies because they will help you tier activities with relative ease and foster your students' academic growth as you use formative assessment to guide your decisions.

Making Small Adjustments

When we have worked with English teachers to tier activities, we have often found that some of the most promising tiers involve small adjustments: just tweaking tasks to build in scaffolded supports or more complexity. In this section, we will look at how three seventh- and eighth-grade English teachers allowed for differentiation to occur in their short story unit.

All students needed to use the writing process to write a fictional story. The teachers used data from previous observations to design three graphic

organizers to help students organize their information (Figure 4.8a, 4.8b, and 4.8c), ♀ and then they used the data to help students choose the most beneficial graphic organizer for their needs. As Baxendell (2003) notes, graphic organizers that are clear-cut are most effective. Therefore, each of these organizers is straightforward. Moreover, they allow students to map the story, which has been found to raise student comprehension (Stetter & Hughes, 2010).

The graphic organizer in Figure 4.8a helped students to plan and organize their story using an arc that highlighted the peak of action in their stories. Although this graphic organizer is depicted in one specific arc, students knew that they would be able to draw their own arc depending on their story. The graphic organizer in Figure 4.8b helped students to sequentially order their story using the story elements as a scaffold.

Figure 4.8a Story arc planning sheet.

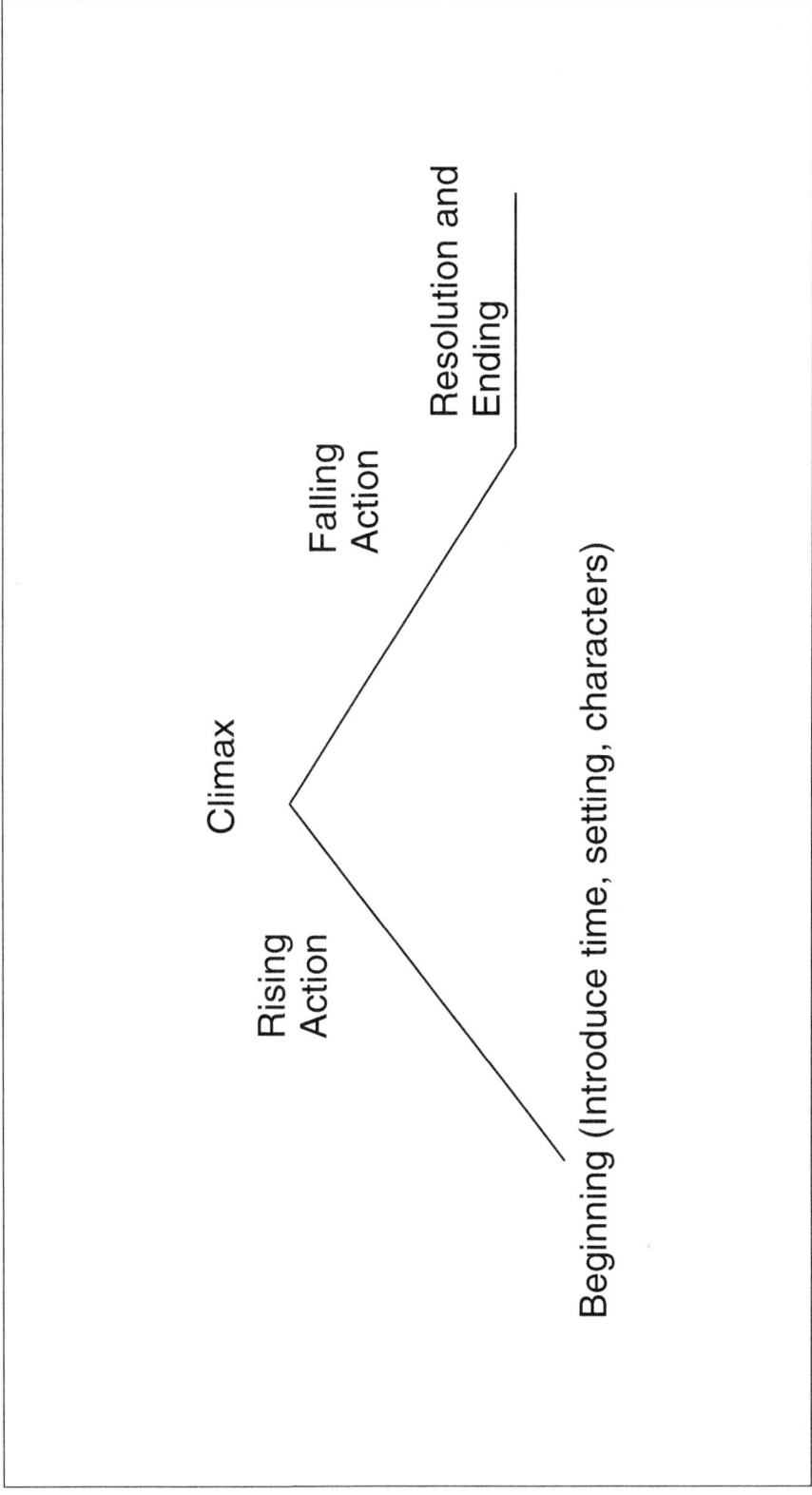

Rising
Action

Climax

Falling
Action

Resolution and
Ending

Beginning (Introduce time, setting, characters)

Figure 4.8b Story element planning sheet.

Setting (time and place):
Main characters (with description):
Main problem:
Events:
Resolution:
Ending:

Figure 4.8c Thinking map planning sheet.

Your thinking map should include the following information: setting, characters (protagonist and antagonist), exposition (starting event), major problem, events, resolution, and ending. You may use a combination of words, phrases, sentences and images to create your thinking map. Label each box with the correct story element first.

Label: _____

Label: _____

Label:_____

Label: _____

Label: _____

Label: _____

The graphic organizer in Figure 4.8c helped students who benefit from putting all their ideas on paper, either through images or words, and then organizing them into sequential steps. Each box can be labeled as the appropriate story element once it is on paper, and the boxes can be cut and ordered sequentially if needed.

Differentiating often involves making these kinds of tiered adjustments to the middle section of a lesson. When you tier activities, you will typically make these changes during the guided or independent practice portion of a lesson. In many school districts, English teachers are required to use instructional class time as independent work periods, where the students have an opportunity to pick an activity from a menu of choices. You can easily include tiered activities here.

Earlier in this chapter, we looked at lessons that evolved from Ms. Chan's decision to ask students to write an analytical paragraph based on traits of a character in the novel *Homeless Bird.* As these lessons showed, tiering activities can often mean giving one group extensions by

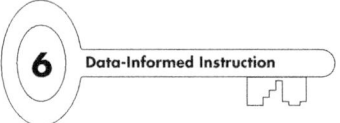

having them work on more sophisticated tasks or having them move to the next step of the lesson. ? While students who have reached mastery move on, other students who need scaffolded support can still be working on other remedial or standard level activities appropriate to their needs.

In fact, in Ms. Chan's class, as students found themselves in the editing and revising stages, Ms. Chan further differentiated lessons by their goals.

Ms. Chan asked students to set a goal related to writing style and/or grammar and mechanics. ? Based on the students' goals, she planned mini-tiered lessons on word choice, comma usage, complex sentences, sentence variety, and run-ons/fragments. She planned to teach these through embedded activities such as sentence-combining practice and through students' revision of their own writing—approaches that are more effective than isolated grammar drills at improving grammar (Graham & Perin, 2007). Let us take a brief look at how that worked.

To ensure that all students' goals were addressed through tiered activities, Ms. Chan allowed students to make choices from a chart with topics of editing and revising elements (Figure 4.9). ? This process:

1. Provided students with the opportunity to choose their goals by evaluating previous written samples

2. Narrowed down the options so that Ms. Chan did not have to plan an infinite number of lessons

Each choice on the chart addressed a weakness that Ms. Chan had observed in the classroom. She conferred with students who had initially picked an inappropriate goal, and she helped these students change the goal once both she and they had reached a consensus. Ms. Chan was careful to never dictate a change but used Socratic questioning, dialogue, and the preassessment to help each student recognize that changing the goal was important; in this way, the change was ultimately more of the student's decision.

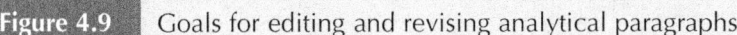

Figure 4.9   Goals for editing and revising analytical paragraphs.

Set one goal to help you edit and revise your paragraph. Refer back to the comments made on your paragraphs to make your goal. Your goal can address the following topics:

__ Adding more sophisticated vocabulary

__ Using commas correctly

__ Creating complex sentences with coordinating conjunctions

__ Avoiding run-ons and fragments

__ Using sentence variety to spice up your paragraphs

It is important to keep tiering lessons in perspective. If you spend time elaborately tiering lessons, you may not achieve much more in student learning than you would by making a simple, quick adjustment to allow students to work at their instructional level. Often, you are already doing this intuitively in your daily work with students. As a trained practitioner, this is what you are naturally skilled at doing!

At the same time, remember that differentiated instruction often works best when you preplan different ways to tier instruction. ❓ For example, let us say you suddenly recognize that you may have overestimated students' background knowledge. Perhaps you have started teaching a lesson with the assumption 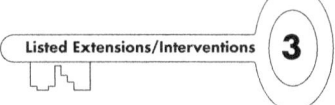 that the students know how to identify a particular element within a unit, but now you realize that some or the majority of the class is having difficulty. At that point, you may spontaneously begin to think of lessons to help the students gain the understanding they need, thus creating mini-tiered lessons in an impromptu fashion. This happens, as it is the nature of

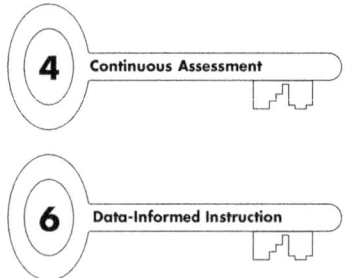

working with students. ❢ ❢ Yet, with preassessments such as anticipation guides (for instance, know–want to learn–learned charts), you assess the skills and understandings students have for a topic or certain elements *before* beginning that lesson. As Jacobs (2002) notes, when you accurately know what students bring to reading, you can effectively choose strategies to connect their prior understanding to their new understanding. This knowledge will help you make more refined tiered assessments, and it will reduce anxiety for both you and your students.

Challenging All Learners

As Ms. Chan's lessons demonstrate, in a mixed-ability class, all students can work on similar tasks and concepts, yet at different readiness levels, designed to meet the learning needs of each student. Ultimately, each child's broad goal in Ms. Chan's lessons was the same—to write an analytical paragraph based on characteristic traits of a character from the novel to the level set forth by standards. However, as you plan lessons, you must remember that the routes students will take to get to that final product may differ from one another. Furthermore, the level of expectation for the final product may also vary depending on the student's initial understanding. When you are able to alter the level of expectation among your students, you will be able to prepare lessons where each student is challenged at an appropriate level.

Ms. Chan asked all students to practice planning and outlining their paragraphs because the preassessment indicated that none of the students had fully mastered outlining skills. For example, the data showed that some students were writing either too much or too little. Others included irrelevant information, skipped parts, or did not complete the outline. During the planning process, she put students into groups according to ability, based on the outline students had completed during the preassessment, to discuss ideas. She provided questions for each group to help promote appropriate discussion. These questions helped challenge each group to add more sophisticated information to their planning. ❢ In this way, students were challenged appropriately while they worked on the same task, even though some students received additional scaffolds as needed to approach the task.

During the outline stage, Ms. Chan used two ways to further challenge students who finished before their peers:

1. Since reading comprehension was also a focus of this unit, she asked those who completed the outline to also complete

higher-order comprehension activities that asked them to make worldly connections based on the cultural themes seen in the story, make predictions, and draw inferences through the events and characters.

2. If comprehension was not an area that the student needed to work on, Ms. Chan encourage students to move on to the next stage of the writing process and required them to write with more sophisticated vocabulary, complex sentences, and further elaboration of some of the points. ♀ Ms. Chan continued to scrutinize their goals, she worked with them to ensure that those goals were addressed, and she encouraged them to set more sophisticated goals as needed.

Continuous Assessment **4**

Ms. Chan recognized that it was important for the class to know that while students can be at different stages of the writing process at the same time, they will still produce the same final product, though to differing degrees. ♀ At the end, she explained to the class that all students were expected to achieve proficiency with certain standards, and that she would then provide them with enrichment activities appropriate to their level. Each student would also have the opportunity to revise and edit his or her work. Students who finished beforehand would be provided an extension activity that was more project based. (See Figure 4.10, which is based on *Homeless Bird* by Gloria Whelan [2001].)

Conveyed Standards **2**

Figure 4.10 Project-based analytical paragraph extension.

Imagine Koly had been keeping a diary from the time she had heard that her parents had planned her wedding. Create at least four diary entries that would highlight her feelings when she heard the news of her wedding, during events leading to her wedding, the day before the wedding, and the day after her wedding. Each entry must clearly identify Koly's voice and moral dilemmas that she is facing. Remember that you have to put yourself in the shoes of Koly—a young Indian girl living in the villages of India in the early to mid-1900s. She would not have the same cultural background, luxuries, or thinking as you would, nor would she expect to live the life that you do. Be sure your entries are true to the character and the novel.

The entries can be a combination of written, pictorial, and audio responses. If you think of other creative ways to share your entries, please get my permission first. You may also work with a partner, with my permission.

As you work with your students, you may find that it will often take more than one lesson to get through the foundational material needed for some to be ready to tackle the challenges. If you have a prescribed curriculum, this can mean that you need to decide which tasks are less central and can be moved through more quickly to save time. When prioritizing tasks, consider the following:

- The school's curriculum
- Standards
- Results of the preintervention assessment
- The daily data you informally collect from your lessons with your students

For example, a prescribed curriculum may ask you to ensure that students can write a five-sentence expository paragraph with relevant examples. If this is the case, then focus on having students master writing the paragraph with all essential elements and relevant details. Do not emphasize other extension skills—like using sophisticated vocabulary and varied transition words—for all students; offer them only to those that have mastered the expository writing and need a further challenge.

Minimizing Task Differences

Tiered activities should not be viewed as rewards for competence. Consequently, they should not be more appealing than other tasks unless all students will be able to engage in those activities at some other time. ♀ All tiered activities should link a  common objective, skill, or theme if possible. Of course, it may be difficult to make a scaffolded activity less appealing or more appealing than another, and students will have different views of the activities' appeal based on their personal interests. For example, for some students, creating a monologue on paper for a character may be less appealing than acting one out. In any case, you will need to make the similarities of the assignments and workload apparent to the students. In this case, for those who are disappointed to miss the acting opportunity, you will want to provide an incentive or promise that a similar drama activity will be assigned to everyone in the near future.

When tasks are closely related, students can engage in shared discussions. For example, if all students are working on monologues, then students can discuss format and purpose collectively as a community. The shared discussion, especially about more sophisticated English skills, can be tiered with scaffolds and other background information so that all students can actively contribute.

In a differentiated class, students will be working on different activities either in isolation, in groups, or with the teacher during the same period. Students need the opportunity to work in this fashion so that they are practicing skills at their instructional level. However, it is important to regroup and reflect as an entire class at some point in each lesson to discuss the skills learned, their applications, and their relevance in the real world. This is done most successfully if the activities for all students are closely related. In Ms. Chan's class, for example, the students worked on some variation of the analytical paragraph or comprehension skills; this common goal allowed her to conduct a whole-class reflection or discussion at the end of the class. ♀ In your classroom, you can regularly remind students of the main product they are all working on. This will help them see that even though they may be working on different tasks, the end goal is similar for all.

Supportive Classroom Climate **1**

Crafting Sophisticated Questions

Sophisticated questions typically are more open ended. You can use them as an effective strategy to help students think critically (Black, Harrison, Lee, Marshall, & Wiliam, 2003). With some thought, you can craft sophisticated questions for all aspects of the English curriculum. In particular, you can create enrichment activities that ask students to apply, analyze, synthesize, and evaluate. You can also use Benjamin Bloom's (Bloom & Krathwohl, 1956) classic framework to craft sophisticated questions, and you can select words from charts such as the following, which are widely available on the Internet.

Designing Questions

Category	Example and Key Words
Knowledge: Recall data or information.	**Key Words:** *define, describe, identify, know, label, list, match, name, outline, recall, recognize, reproduce, select, state.*
Comprehension: Understand the meaning, translation, interpolation, and interpretation of instructions and problems. State a problem in one's own words.	**Key Words:** *comprehend, convert, defend, distinguish, estimate, explain, extend, generalize, give examples, infer, interpret, paraphrase, predict, rewrite, summarize, translate.*

(Continued)

(Continued)

Application: Use a concept in a new situation or make unprompted use of an abstraction. Apply what was learned in the classroom in novel situations.	**Key Words:** *apply, change, compute, construct, demonstrate, discover, manipulate, modify, operate, predict, prepare, produce, relate, show, solve, use.*
Analysis: Separate material or concepts into component parts so that the organizational structure may be understood. Distinguish between facts and inferences.	**Key Words:** *analyze, break down, compare, contrast, diagram, deconstruct, differentiate, discriminate, distinguish, identify, illustrate, infer, outline, relate, select, separate.*
Synthesis: Build a structure or pattern from diverse elements. Put parts together to form a whole, with emphasis on creating a new meaning or structure.	**Key Words:** *categorize, combine, compile, compose, create, devise, design, explain, generate, modify, organize, plan, rearrange, reconstruct, relate, reorganize, revise, rewrite, summarize, tell, write.*
Evaluation: Make judgments about the value of ideas or materials.	**Key Words:** *appraise, compare, conclude, contrast, criticize, critique, defend, describe, discriminate, evaluate, explain, interpret, justify, relate, summarize, support.*

Note. See http://www.nwlink.com/~donclark/hrd/bloom.html, where this chart and other useful resources are posted.

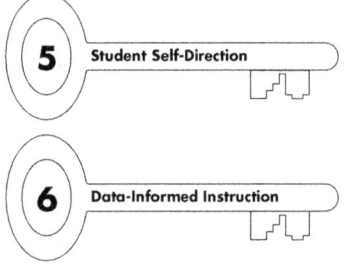

To help students think critically, you can provide the questions; however, depending on the skill and grade, you can also invite students to create their own questions, with varied levels of sophistication, based on a task and their interests. 🔑🔑 If comprehension pre-assessments reveal that some students have mastered all basic knowledge and comprehension skill questions, you can encourage them to begin crafting higher-order questions. For example, before the lesson, Ms. Chan had prepared an enrichment project-based activity for those students who showed mastery of basic comprehension skills and finished the analytical paragraph (Figure 4.11). This activity does not have one correct answer, and it asks the students to apply critical thinking as they analyze and evaluate the characters' actions. (See Chapter 5 for an in-depth discussion of higher-order thinking and crafting sophisticated questions.)

Creating sophisticated questions can serve as a valuable enrichment activity. For example, one seventh-grade class we worked with discussed themes in the novel *Ask Me No Questions* by Marina Budhos (2006). The teacher modeled appropriate ways to create a question that the students would ultimately answer in a five-paragraph essay. Students who were capable created more sophisticated thematic questions by using the model as a guide and adding their own flair, whereas other students followed the model as a direct roadmap and simply changed a few words (see Figure 4.11).

Figure 4.11   Examples of sophisticated questions for a mixed-ability class.

- **Teacher example:** How does the theme of secrecy emerge in the novel?
- **Student A (basic question):** How does the theme of perseverance emerge in the novel?
- **Student B (sophisticated question):** How does the theme of change around immigration affect the lives of the main characters of the novel?
- **Student C (even more sophisticated question):** How does the theme of change cause the main characters to question their morality?

In another example of enrichment, we also worked with a class of seventh graders who were writing paragraphs about the science fiction short stories they had read. The teacher organized them into two groups based on the results of the formative assessment. ♀ As the teacher provided scaffolding to the group that required more help with writing and comprehension throughout the main activity, the more advanced students worked on the enrichment activity to infer real-world connections from the content of the story (see Figure 4.12). In this way, all students were able to work on their own level yet still practice some logical reasoning.

Data-Informed Instruction   **6**

Figure 4.12   Examples of analytical paragraph activities for a mixed-ability class.

Main activity:

"Dr. Susan Calvin from the story Robot Dreams *was justified in shooting Elvex."* Your assignment is to defend or refute this statement by writing an analytical paragraph that includes three relevant reasons and examples from the story.

Enrichment activity:

"Dr. Susan Calvin from the story Robot Dreams *was justified in shooting Elvex."* Your assignment is to defend or refute this statement by writing an analytical paragraph that includes three relevant reasons from other texts, movies, historical or modern-day facts, real-life technological advances, or your own opinions.

Increasing Goals

When you foster an environment where goal setting is required and then have students set their own goals, you enable them to become more reflective and willing to edit and revise their work (Patel & Laud, 2009). Goals help students structure their efforts by prompting them to focus on the components that are important to the assignment. Goals also help them track their progress throughout, and they serve as a motivator (Schunk, 1990). The preassessment tasks not only drive instruction but also help students set specific goals to acquire the skills being taught.

Goals should be quantifiable, relevant to the task, and attainable within a short time. Depending on readiness, teachers can work with students to craft more or less sophisticated goals. For example, one student may have a goal of writing one concluding sentence as a wrap-up, whereas another may have a goal of writing a concluding paragraph. Both students aim to conclude their work at their respective instructional levels. ♀ ♀ Students in Ms. Chan's class used the paragraph models discussed in class and feedback from the teacher to create specific writing goals that they would address to improve their analytical writing.

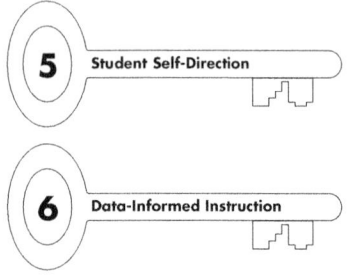

Teachers can also alter the number of goals a student has to meet, depending on formative assessment and student readiness. The goals can be based on content (relevancy of examples, analysis, answering a question with depth, adding sentence variety, including a descriptive setting) or mechanics (grammatical rules, spelling, paragraphing). Essentially, increasing the number of goals allows students to focus on more than one specific skill, thus making it a more sophisticated and enriching task.

Setting Appropriate Group Work

Although group work is at the center of student-centered learning, it can get a bad reputation. If not planned well, lessons can lose focus. Another danger is that they can be run by only one or two students from each group, which hurts the sense of community rather than fostering it. ♀ One successful form of group work embeds tiered activities. This means that the different members of each group can work on differing parts of the activity, enabling them to successfully complete their task, work cooperatively as a team to complete the final product, and learn at all levels.

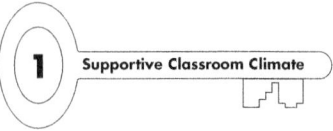

Here is an example in which we used formative assessments of comprehension skills to make appropriate groups for an activity that was tiered within. 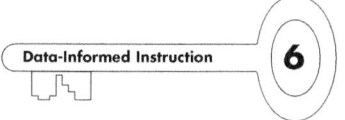 For one lesson, we asked our seventh-grade students to show their overall understanding of the first half of *The Watsons Go to Birmingham—1963* by Christopher Paul Curtis (1995). As we formed groups of three or four students, we did not group them in terms of ability; rather, we ensured that there were different tiered tasks within the one activity that each group had to complete. We did not create the groups randomly; rather, we made sure that we had identified a student in every group who would be able to complete one of the different tasks successfully.

We asked each group to map out a sequence of events to show their comprehension (Stetter & Hughes, 2010). Curtis's book is enriched with many events and rich details, and we wanted the students to identify the main point of each chapter, create one image that represented each chapter's main event, and write a three-sentence summary of the event. The flowchart in Figure 4.13 shows what the final product was supposed to look like.

Figure 4.13   Flowchart used to map sequence of events.

Chapter 1	Chapter 2	Chapter 3	Chapter 4	Chapter 5

Write a multi-sentence summary, no more than five sentences long, underneath each chapter image.

Chapter 6	Chapter 7	Chapter 8	Chapter 9	Chapter 10

Write a multi-sentence summary, no more than five sentences long, underneath each chapter image.

We required each member to engage in a task at all times. The students naturally started working on parts of the task they were more comfortable with. Some groups were slow to start and benefited from our support in identifying appropriate tasks for each group member to complete.

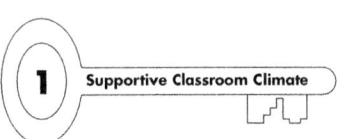

As we walked around, we saw and heard students: ♀

- Supporting group members who were having difficulty
- Encouraging the group to stay on task
- Negotiating the best answers
- Assigning different new tasks when a group member finished one
- Discussing the most appropriate answers

Throughout the activity, students who struggled with general comprehension of the book created the visual images with group consensus, whereas those who had shown mastery in this skill dissected the text for the essential pieces of information.

There are many ways to set appropriate group work. When setting group work, be sure to consider the instructional needs of all students and ensure that each has a task that meets her or his level. Ms. Chan broke students into groups to brainstorm for evidence of the identified traits of characters to use in their analytical paragraphs. ♀ She created ability groups based on academic performance to ensure that students were working at their level, and she provided appropriate supports through tiered activities if needed. We discuss other ways to organize groups in Chapters 6 and 7, specifically highlighting appropriate cluster grouping to address the needs of students who require support or those who exemplify giftedness or are high achieving.

5 Time Management Strategies

As you begin to contemplate using the differentiation model in your classroom, a whirlwind of questions may fill your mind:

- Where should I begin?
- Do I have enough time to plan the lessons?
- Will I be able to address all the standards and complete my curriculum?
- Do I have space to create centers?
- How will my colleagues and administration respond?
- How much do I really need to differentiate to yield favorable gains?
- Will I get help from someone to implement this model?
- How will I evaluate all the different tasks?
- How will I grade, effectively comment on, and create all the various formative assessments?
- How will I organize the students and keep track of what they are doing?

Teachers commonly experience such anxiety when making the kinds of changes required in using formative assessment to differentiate instruction (Reeves, 2009; Talbert, 2010). In fact, according to Nazzal (2011), many new teachers report the following barriers:

- Lack of time
- Collaboration problems
- A sense of powerlessness

- Difficulty with organizational skills
- Fears about curriculum coverage
- Behavior management issues

Managing time can be a core factor in this anxiety. Even experienced teachers can be prone to bouts of uncertainty as they begin to implement differentiation in the classroom.

As you get started with differentiation, it is important to begin with what makes the most sense and feels the most comfortable. Begin by making small changes, and when that feels comfortable, branch out over time. This is how we began. We did not try to change our entire classroom, nor did we try to do it all at once. However, when we started we began to see immediate gains in student achievement! Even the smallest changes in our instruction yielded positive results and motivated us to make more changes. Eventually, we learned how to shift our focus to specifying measureable standards, ♀ identifying extension and tiered activities and homework, ♀ and creating varied formative assessments ♀ to evaluate student progress regularly so that our workload did not significantly increase. The key is deciding where to begin.

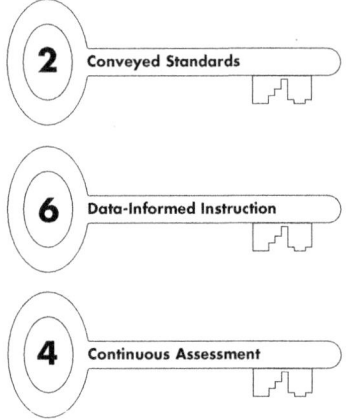

In this chapter, we will discuss some of the most prominent time management issues that arise as you differentiate English instruction. Specifically, we will provide suggestions on how to manage time effectively when you are:

- Planning lessons and units
- Managing students who are working on different tasks
- Assigning homework
- Grading

PLANNING LESSONS AND UNITS

Prioritize Your Time (Begin Small!)

English teachers often feel that they have limited time to complete all their desired tasks (Barmby, 2006; Wilson, 2002). Time is a finite resource, and teachers who have an ever expanding "to-do" list guard their time carefully. Therefore, you must constantly prioritize how to get the most value for how you spend your time. As you make planning decisions, you must regularly look at the big picture and ask if your efforts are most likely to result in increased student learning.

Research and our experience show that practices such as giving detailed feedback or planning tiered lessons that match students' instructional levels raise achievement, even when small changes in these directions are made (Hattie & Timperley, 2007). Of course, planning tiered lessons takes far less time and may make more sense than reviewing and giving detailed feedback to 100 or more students during lessons. Ideally, you should do both. However, when time does not allow for this, you can use shortcuts that are most likely to raise student achievement in the most time efficient ways.

For example, when you use formative assessments to provide feedback on various paragraph activities, you can create both a checklist of criteria to evaluate the students and a bank of common comments to provide students with feedback. This way you can simply check off the relevant comment rather than writing a separate comment on each paper. Of course, you will have to individualize some comments, but a bank of comments will help students identify the most common errors and receive individualized, specific feedback in far less time. Here are some possible comments that you can include in the bank of comments for feedback in expository writing:

- Your topic sentence does not clearly identify the subtopics you will be discussing.
- Your topic sentence does not clearly identify the topic/argument you will be discussing.
- Your _____ example is not relevant. It is off topic and does not help to support your point.
- Your _____ example would benefit from more specific detail on _____.
- You are missing the analysis in the _____ example.
- If you are having difficulty with analysis, start off with "This shows . . ." or "This example shows . . . ."
- Use a transition word to introduce the _____ example. It will help the paragraph's coherency.
- Your conclusion paragraph is just like your topic sentence. Try to add some flair. Perhaps you can _____.
- You have not indented the paragraph.
- Place a comma after the transition words.
- Can you combine both sentences in your _____ example?

As you begin a new unit, you can create a unit planning overview: a to-do list that includes all the relevant elements in planning that unit. Be sure to include:

- Time needed to plan and organize the changes
- Anticipated results based on each change

Afterward, using the standards as a guide, identify which changes will be implemented first, highlighting those that are most essential for students to master.

Let us look at an example of how one teacher planned a unit on mastering the use of coordinating conjunctions.

Ms. Avery is a general education teacher in a suburban setting with 24 students in her class. She wanted to see her students master using coordinating conjunctions in their writing through practicing sentence-combining skills, a research-validated way to enhance overall grammar (Graham & Perin, 2007). To achieve this, she inwardly debated whether she should tier the lessons with excerpts from the novels students were reading or have students choose from a menu of projects based on the novels. Although Ms. Avery knew that tiering assignments yields the most favorable results in achievement and may be the quickest to plan, since the resources are readily available, she wanted to engage her students by providing choice (Brooks & Brooks, 1999) and promoting creativity as they practiced the writing skill. She wanted students to engage in an authentic activity so they would buy into the grammar skill and transfer it to their own writing, thus improving their language skills in writing.

Ms. Avery decided to have students choose from a menu of choices and create one of the following to display to their grade level peers: a poster, PowerPoint presentation, poem, song/rap, lecture/lesson, 2-D or 3-D images, or a free-choice activity (pending her approval). ♀ She planned to identify students' understanding by having them complete a similar preassessment task that asked them to locate the coordinating conjunctions in a passage and then create complex sentences using coordinating conjunctions and sentence combining. After talking with her colleagues, who would be using a similar plan in their own classrooms, Ms. Avery expanded on the preassessment and decided to ask her students to engage in three different activities:

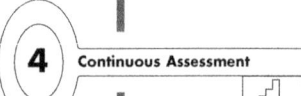

4 Continuous Assessment

Identification: Identifying coordinating conjunctions used in sentences from their novels.

Project development: Creating a presentation from the menu: a poster, PowerPoint presentation, poem, song/rap, lecture/lesson, 2-D or 3-D images, or a free-choice activity.

Assessment: Correctly combining five provided sentences using coordinating conjunctions.

7 Differentiation of Student Work

Ms. Avery's colleagues volunteered to create a part of the task, which reduced the time she spent on the task herself. ♀ Further, the teachers each created an advanced, medium, or basic assessment and shared the assessments with one another so they had a bank of resources to choose from. The teachers decided they would mark the third part of the activity, but they would ask the students to self-score the first two parts of the activity with a self-scoring rubric (Figure 5.1).

Using the rubric, the students would reflect on both their perceived level of difficulty in completing the task and their overall experience. This collaboration allowed Ms. Avery to create an activity that addressed tiered instruction and offered creative ways to increase student's engagement. The end result was a valid assessment measure that not only asked the students to reflect on their work but also provided teachers with an opportunity to use formative assessment to see each student's level of mastery.

Figure 5.1   Project self-scoring rubric.

Excerpt I chose was from _____
by _____.

The reason I chose this excerpt was _____.

Indicate the level of difficulty you experienced in finding the coordinating conjunctions that were used correctly:

(5 = difficult, 1 = easy)   5   4   3   2   1

difficult   easy

The creative project I chose to complete was (circle one):

Poster   PowerPoint presentation   2-D/3-D images   Song/rap

Poem   Lecture/lesson   Other:_____

Score for my project (circle your grade):
Excellent (E), Very Good (VG), Good (G), Satisfactory (S), Needs Improvement (NI)

Project presentation/effort:	**E**	**VG**	**G**	**S**	**NI**
Content (accuracy of information):	**E**	**VG**	**G**	**S**	**NI**
Language (clarity of explanation):	**E**	**VG**	**G**	**S**	**NI**

Strengths of the project:

Areas of improvement needed in the project:

The rules of coordinating conjunctions in sentence combining that I had not mastered were:

As a result of completing this project, I have mastered:

Further questions I have/final reflecting comments:

Teacher comments:

After a few days, Ms. Avery collected the completed projects, assessments, and self-scored reflections. Not only did she have various assessment measures (National Council of Teachers of English [NCTE], 2009, Standard 6) for this one task, but she also knew from students' comments that they were excited to share their projects with classmates: "I have been waiting to share my project for days." "Can we go see what the other classes have done?" "Oh, I love this. Next time, I will try to incorporate music in my project!" ♀ This assessment followed NCTE Standard 1, which asks teachers to consider students' interest as paramount in assessment. Ms. Avery had successfully ensured that students were able to complete an authentic and engaging task that, with her colleagues' help, involved minimal planning time.

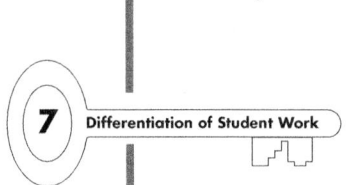

To further tier activities around sentence combining and coordinating conjunctions, Ms. Avery graded the assessments (the third part of the activity) and read the self-scored reflections to gauge the students' level of mastery. The formative assessments highlighted that, although students thought they had attained mastery, they did not know how to combine sentences using the coordinating conjunctions, or they were unable to recall the conjunctions themselves. Afterward, Ms. Avery placed each student in one of four homogeneous groups based on level of mastery: ♀

1. *Those who were not able to recall and identify all essential coordinating conjunctions in writing*

2. *Those who were not able to correctly use and punctuate using coordinating conjunctions to combine sentences*

3. *Those who had a combination of errors from Group 1 and Group 2*

4. *Those who had mastered both identification and usage of coordinating conjunctions in writing*

Group members in the first three groups reviewed their assessments by comparing their work with a model. Those in the mastery group completed an extension activity of responding to literature as they created their own complex sentences using coordinating conjunctions. At this point, Ms. Avery also differentiated their homework (see Figure 5.2). ♀

Ms. Avery was able to set and prioritize her goals when planning these lessons to start implementing differentiation into her lessons in small steps that were comfortable for her. The support she received from colleagues further helped her differentiate lessons, and she ultimately accomplished more than she had anticipated—even a formative assessment—without using extensive valuable planning time.

	Class Activities	**Homework**
Group 1	Corrected assessment with homogeneous group	Coordinating conjunction grammar activity
Group 2	Corrected assessment with homogeneous group	Coordinating conjunction grammar activity
Group 3	Corrected assessment with homogeneous group	Coordinating conjunction grammar activity
Group 4	Extension activity: Write a response to literature while using sentence combining and coordinating conjunctions.	Extension activity: Create an assessment using coordinating conjunctions

Figure 5.2 Differentiated class activities and homework.

When Ms. Avery began to try differentiating her lessons in manageable steps, she realized that even one change had a domino effect and that the changes were easier to make than expected. Her initial anxieties and uncertainties dissipated as she carried on with lesson planning and worked with her colleagues, realizing how the changes could happen with minimal effort.

Use a Unit and Lesson Planning Checklist

When planning units or lessons, you can use the planning checklist in Figure 5.3 or customize it to your needs. Do not plan to complete each option for every unit you create—that would become too daunting. Instead, as you create units and use this checklist, remember to prioritize based on:

- Students' needs
- Standards
- Curriculum
- Resources

It is important to note that whole-class or traditional lessons should still be included, since they will be necessary for some tasks.

Furthermore, to help with time management, you can complete the checklist with colleagues and then divide up tasks, as Ms. Avery did. We also find that working with our colleagues is essential to coming up with the most relevant, dynamic, successful, and least time-consuming ideas.

Figure 5.3   Options for planning and prioritizing time for unit differentiation.

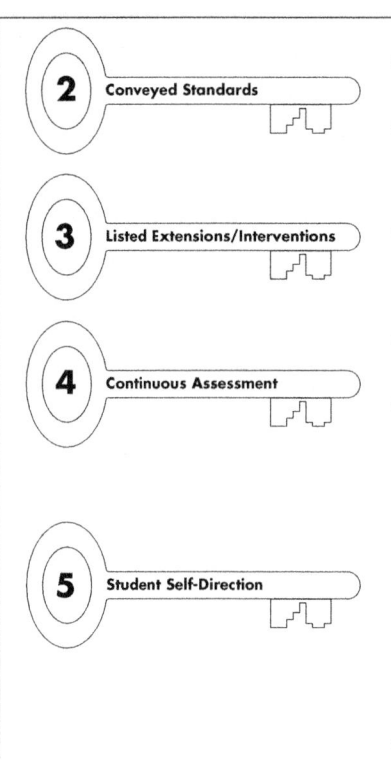

- Clarify unit *targets* and norms and how you will convey them (e.g., via list/rubric). ♀
- Decide which targets are more essential and prioritize. ♀

- List possible supports for students who struggle and determine which data results would suggest using which supports. ♀

- Design or find a *preassessment* for the unit (plan a structure for having students self-score it). ♀
- Plan for ongoing *formative assessment* to monitor learning and inform next steps: ♀
  - Make formative assessments that can be collected (e.g., homework, exit slips, reflection sheets).
  - Have students indicate where they are in their understanding and steps they will take to improve. ♀
  - Create a checklist of requirements for individual assignments.
  - Create a class checklist so that you can quickly keep track of student achievement.
- Use assessment data and co-plan next steps for how to *tier lessons* (challenges and supports). ♀
- Create options for *differentiating challenges and supports* in the unit with: ♀
  - Challenge activities (research using the Internet, classroom, and teaching resources for higher-ordered, inquiry-based, and research application activities; consultation with a learning specialist for challenging activities or opportunities for interdisciplinary, real-world application).
  - Support for lower-achieving students (research using the Internet, classroom, and teaching resources for scaffolded and simplified supports and other graphic organizers or plenary tools; consultation with a learning specialist or special educators for specific strategy-based instruction).

  - Choice activities as supplemental work. ♀
- ♀ Create *tiered homework, assignments, and assessments.*
- Also, use the **following tips for prioritizing** to get the most "bang for your buck":
- Do not reinvent the wheel: Do a quick 15-minute scan of teacher's editions and the Internet for ideas and tasks for tiers. Revisit the resources for more in-depth analysis once final decisions about activities have been made.

- Create a separate document of resources and the information you have found through your research so you can access them quickly.
- Begin with small, manageable tiers—just draft or find a challenge list to begin.
- Convey targets through preassessments—or just in a handout students can reference regularly.
- Strive to keep students on the same topic. However, if crunched for time, it is better to offer unrelated challenges than to have kids do too easy work that bores them.
- Create an individual student and classroom checklist to help keep you organized when collecting information on student performance.
- Do not change everything. There will still be a need for some whole-class lessons. Embed tiered activities and differentiated lessons within traditional lessons.
- Work with your colleagues. Together you can create strong, more applicable, more effective lessons and reduce the amount of individual work and planning.

Cut Scoring Time by Designing Feedback Systems

A typical English teacher can have more than 50 paragraphs, essays, or written responses to grade at any given time. Traditionally, teachers may feel it is important for the "expert" in the classroom to give feedback on all work in the classroom. However, it is important for you to come to three realizations:

1. You do not need to grade every assignment. In fact, students' writing achievement improves when all assignments are not graded because they do not feel the pressure of a grade and are willing to take more chances (Lindemann & Anderson, 2001).

2. You can assess assignments for specific elements or student-specific goals (Many, Taylor, Wang, Sachs, & Schreiber, 2007). 🔑

Student Self-Direction 5

3. You can help students use different modes of scoring to self-assess or peer-assess **(Diab, 2010; Yang, Ko, & Chung, 2005)**.

The following sections focus on the latter two elements.

Creating Answer Keys

You can reduce scoring time by having students self-, peer-, or group-blind-score written work using models, checklists, answer keys, and consultations. Although it may take you some initial preparation to create models, answer keys, and checklists and prepare blind student samples, it will not take you as much time as grading multiple class sets of written work. Plus, there is additional value for the students as they engage in this type of peer- or self-scoring **(Diab, 2010; Yang et al., 2005);** this makes the preparation time worthwhile. When students have the opportunity to review their peers' writing after guided practice, they learn to appreciate and effectively critique the work and, in turn, reflect on their own writing (Diab, 2010).

One method for creating answer keys is to make them as you create the assessment; this ensures that the key will be made. Initially, it is important to create answer keys for the students that are exact replicates of expected work; in this way, nothing is left to interpretation. These initial answer keys should have as much detail as possible and should explicitly show students the correct answer. For example, if students are to answer comprehension questions based on a novel, the answer key should take the form of complete sentences so students clearly know the expectations. As students become more skilled in self-scoring with a model or an answer key, you can provide less explicit keys.

Here is how Ms. Avery handled this process during the start of one school year. First, she designed an activity that asked students to answer seven short questions based on their reading from the night before. She wrote a detailed answer key and then gave students the assignment. When they passed it in, she graded the papers herself, providing feedback based on the key. Next, Ms. Avery returned the papers along with the detailed answer key. This way the students not only received detailed feedback on their work but also could see how to use a key to self-, peer- (individually), or group- (work together with a group of students to) score papers.

Although this process takes time, investing in it early in the year helps students to be more self-sufficient in evaluating written work later in the year. As you create keys, you might even be able to work with a group of teachers to divide up the work; each of you could write acceptable answers for a few of the questions.

These detailed answer keys should be considered models that:

- Provide students with an answer that is acceptable
- Offer students a tool to score work
- Serve as an aid for students to structure and organize their future work

Figure 5.4 provides a partial example of one type of appropriate model.

You can create other models for ambiguous assignments where there is more than one correct answer. For example, there are many acceptable responses for an assignment that asks students to make a personal connection to an event they have read about in a novel. In this situation,

| **Figure 5.4** | Model for coordinating conjunctions for sentence combining. |

Example 1: We like to visit the museum. We like to visit the zoo. (*and*)

Answer 1: We like to visit the museum and the zoo.

> Note: This sentence uses the coordinating conjunction *and*. There is no comma before the conjunction because two complete sentences were not combined. If you combine the sentences like this, you can include a comma:

Answer 2: We like to visit the museum, and we like to visit the zoo.

Example 2: The antagonist is a bad guy. I feel bad for him. (*but*)

Answer 1: The antagonist is a bad guy, but I feel bad for him.

> Note: In this example, the coordinating conjunction *but* is used. There is a comma before the conjunction because two complete sentences are combined.

you may provide a model of a correct answer for the students to refer to versus *the* correct answer. You should go over the model in a whole-class discussion to convey the essential required elements. You should also create a checklist of the required elements that the students can refer to at a glance. We will discuss this in more detail later in the chapter.

Attending to Specific Elements

When you evaluate students' work, you can help focus their learning by attending to specific elements of the assignment. The element that you decide to comment on should address one of the curriculum standards or individualized student goal(s). Detailed feedback that addresses one of these elements with future targets will be as beneficial as detailed comments on all elements of the assignment.

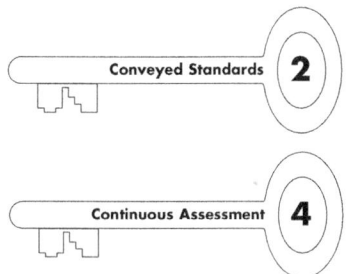

Feedback is a form of scaffolding for students, and commenting on just a few clear goals and objectives on a few topics is very effective (Many et al., 2007; Shepard, 2005). Providing feedback on every element or correcting every mistake is not advisable. Descriptive feedback that explains why work is incorrect is more helpful in raising student achievement than evaluative feedback that simply states that a response is right or wrong (Cho, Schunn, & Charney, 2006; Dinnen & Collopy, 2009). Figure 5.5 provides examples of both types of feedback for comparison.

It is also important to understand that the idea of "bleeding on paper," or using red ink to correct and address every error, may become too daunting for the student. Some students may shut down and refuse to respond to comments, viewing the feedback as unhelpful. Students report more improvement when teachers provide descriptive feedback (Cowie, 2005).

Figure 5.5	Examples of evaluative and descriptive feedback.

Evaluative feedback: Your paragraph is missing relevant details. Also, please check for spelling errors.

Descriptive feedback: Although your paragraph has a detailed topic sentence, you need to develop your examples. You have only one major example and no specific references to the book. Can you think about an example to show how the protagonist is evil? In your topic sentence you also state that the protagonist is clever but don't provide an explanation. Can you explain in your own words, then provide a specific example?

As you prioritize feedback, remember that students find comments based on content and ideas more helpful than those based on conventions (Matsumura, Patthey-Chavez, Valdés, & Garnier, 2002). In fact, students tend to improve errors in content and organization more quickly than errors in conventions. This does not mean that you should not comment on conventions, but those comments should be more structured, more focused, and attend to specific conventions at a given time. Perhaps you can focus on one or two conventional comments per assignment or over several assignments; this can help avoid overwhelming the student. According to research, some of the more helpful conventional comments address both sentence fluency and structure (Dinnen & Collopy, 2009). Let us take a look at how Ms. Avery successfully used feedback in her classroom.

Ms. Avery asked students to complete the formative activity of using coordinating conjunctions in combining sentences. This activity is structured and has specific correct responses. Therefore, she recognized that she could provide students with a specific answer key rather than a model so that they could initially score their own papers.

Afterward, she collected all papers and reviewed the errors. The next day, she introduced a few more sentences and discussed some of the common errors in mini lessons with students. She then asked the students to fill out the structured feedback form shown in Figure 5.6, based on their initial scoring and the mini lessons. ♀ Ms. Avery then went around the room to quickly identify the students who seemed to understand their errors and those who were able to make the correct changes.

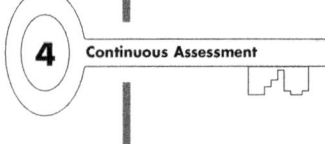

4 Continuous Assessment

Figure 5.6 Example of a structured feedback form for explicit assignments.

Essential elements of coordinating conjunctions:

1. Use one of the following coordinating conjunctions: *for, and, but, nor, or, yet, so.*

2. Use a comma before the coordinating conjunction when two sentences are combined.

3. Do not use a comma before the coordinating conjunction when there is only one sentence.

Models:

No coordinating conjunction: The weather forecaster has called for rain, which will be heavy at times.

Coordinating conjunction combining two sentences: The weather was bad, so we decided to stay at home and watch movies.

Coordinating conjunction with one sentence: My baby sister enjoys the spring but hates the thunderstorms.

I got _____ of the 10 correct.

> Choose one sentence that you got incorrect. Copy it here just as you wrote it:
>
>
> Fix the sentence using the models as a guide:
>
>

The type of error I made was:

___no coordinating conjunction

___incorrect punctuation

___other: _____

The form in Figure 5.6 is appropriate for a more explicit assignment that has one specific response. However, as we mentioned earlier, many English assignments do not elicit only one specific answer. Figure 5.7 provides a structured feedback form for those types of assignments. Here is how Ms. Avery used this form with students in the middle of a unit on expository paragraphs, after the majority of students had become familiar with the elements of the paragraph.

5 | Student Self-Direction

During independent work time, Ms. Avery consulted briefly with each student and set an individual goal of addressing one of these elements: writing complete and sophisticated topic and conclusion sentences, generating examples, analysis. ⚲ She then asked students to fill out the goal on the form and to consult the model in their binder. Later, she evaluated their work by checking the relevant issues on the form and adding comments as needed. She also helped students set a future target. Finally, students used the feedback to revise their work.

In this way, as Ms. Avery looked at the students' work, she only needed to comment on a specific goal; she did not need to provide feedback on every element. This format helped Ms. Avery manage her time more effectively and confer with many more students.

| **Figure 5.7** | Example of a structured feedback form for open-ended assignments. |

Goal on topic/conclusion sentences, examples, or analysis (set by teacher-student consultation):

Model: Consult the model *in your binder.*

Comments:

- missing element (introduction sentence, conclusion sentence, example, analysis, transition words)
- missing details
- lack of relevance (there are many details, but they do not address the topic or argument)
- does not follow paragraph form (topic sentence, three examples, analysis after each example, conclusion sentence, at least two transition words)
- more specific connections to novel needed
- opinion needed

Additional comments/future target:

Student revision: Based on the comments and the model, please revise by making the appropriate changes.

Using Rubrics as Self-Feedback or Peer Feedback Tools

As another time-saving tool, you can have students use ready-made rubrics to self-, peer-, or group-score work. ❢ Preparing the rubric ahead of time ensures that you have specified and expressed to your students the standards to be mastered. You can have students create their own rubric, have them use the same rubric that teachers will use to assess their work, or use rubrics available from various resources like the Internet (see Figure 5.8) or professional literature. Often, few if any changes are needed to make these ready-made rubrics relevant to your specific assignments.

Conveyed Standards 2

Figure 5.8   Online resources for rubrics.

www.readwritethink.org (Provides detailed English lessons and rubrics.)

rubistar.4teachers.org (Provides templates for making paper and online, interactive rubrics.)

www.rubrics4teachers.com/languagearts.php (Provides rubrics for language arts topics.)

www.rubrics4teachers.com/middleschool.php (Provides rubrics for middle school lessons.)

www.teach-nology.com/web_tools/rubrics (Provides a collection of rubrics and indicates where rubrics can be created.)

www.webenglishteacher.com/rubrics.html (Provides a variety of rubrics organized by language arts topics. Also allows for teachers to create rubrics online using various templates.)

If possible, it is always best to have students assess assignments using the same rubric that you will ultimately use to score that assignment or a similar assignment. This will help you with time management because you will be able to use one rubric for multiple purposes, and it will help students understand the grading criteria on the rubric and the level of complexity needed for each grade value. Essentially, this should help your students to:

- Evaluate their work with greater clarity
- Achieve at higher standards
- Better reflect on their work

For example, research has shown that during a writing unit, students produce better final drafts if they review a model, list criteria, and self-assess their first drafts with the same rubric that teachers will use to evaluate their final products (Andrade, Du, & Mycek, 2010). This also saves you time because you do not need to read and assess every draft. To standardize the evaluation process, you can read a sample story with students and then evaluate it together using the rubric.

Have Students Write Clear, Specific, and Focused Reflections

The reflection process is a valuable part of learning. We do not recommend that you evaluate students' reflections; the point of reflections is for students to be honest about the process, their learning, and personal strengths and weaknesses. However, you can review reflections from time to time to clarify the students' perspectives of their learning.

Encourage students to reflect on their work and progress regularly, but do not feel compelled to read every reflection. In fact, it may be beneficial to have students write longer reflections that can be private and "for their eyes" only. Then, at certain key times you can ask for clear, specific, and focused reflections. Here are some great times to choose:

- A midpoint of an assignment
- After a formative assessment
- After practice sessions for a key element of the unit or lesson
- At the end of the unit
- After the students have engaged in self-scoring or peer scoring

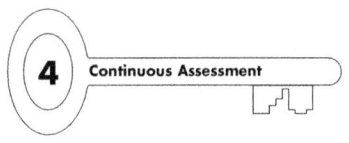

This way you can simply collect the reflections and, based on the comments, decide if you need to look at an individual's work in greater detail. ⚱ This will also help to reduce the amount of time you will need to spend looking at specific assignments.

To prompt a reflection, you might pose a few short-answer questions and ask the students to respond. To help keep the reflections condensed, you could provide a maximum amount of sentences (five sentences) or page limit (half a page). You should be sure to ask the students to reflect not only on the final product but also on the process and the changes and learning that have occurred.

Initially, you will need to spend more time teaching students how to effectively self-reflect. Without systematic and explicit instruction, there may be minimal positive gains. With this instruction, students will be able to reflect on independent work and assess peer work effectively (Rolheiser & Ross, 2001). Once you spend the extra time at the beginning of the year, continued opportunities of reflection will promote more positive experiences (Rolheiser & Ross, 2001). Therefore, you should encourage students to reflect regularly, but again, you should read only summaries of these reflections, possibly for major assignments or those that are pivotal for a unit.

In addition to allowing your students to reflect regularly and independently, you should require students to add a specific goal to these reflections. Therefore, each reflection students engage in should specify a future target. The goal tracking sheet in Figure 5.9 is a useful tool to help students capture their goals in writing. It also provides you

with a snapshot of each student's progress. If you feel that a student is on a basic goal for too long, you may have to intervene. This is also a quick way for you to get a sense of their reflections throughout the process. Since the goals on this sheet are self-directed, students will feel empowered and in control of their own learning—and they will gain a true sense of the purpose of the assignment.

Figure 5.9 Goal tracking sheet.

Skill or assignment:

Goals are set after each reflection. The goal can be the same if mastery has not been met. You are setting only one goal at a time. If you are still working to meet the same goal, simply write "Same as Goal _____."

Goal 1:	Date:
Goal 2:	Date:
Goal 3:	Date:
Goal 4:	Date:
Goal 5:	Date:

MANAGING STUDENTS WHO ARE WORKING ON DIFFERENT TASKS

As you review a difficult class assignment or homework focused on writing, you may often determine that some students need more review with the lesson, whereas others are ready to move on. An immediate response to differentiate tasks might be to ask some students to continue with the day's lesson or to work on the challenges posted in the room or in assignment packets. Any differentiation, even a small one, is better than none. The following sections offer examples of how you can effectively and efficiently manage students who are working on different tasks.

Manage Flexible Group Time

During a unit, students will be grouped according to their instructional level on a regular basis. However, it is essential to note that flexible groups should also be one of the central practices in any differentiated class. By *flexible*, we mean that group configurations should regularly change and are not static (Radencich & McKay, 1995). Flexible grouping acknowledges that all groupings—large groups, small groups, teams, partners, and individuals have value (Ford, 2005). Therefore, flexible groups are not always homogeneous or heterogeneous. ♀ You will use the data from the assessments and the lesson objectives to drive the decisions you make for groupings.

Only on rare occasions should groups be chosen at random. Ideal times are at the beginning of a unit (when skills are usually similar) or in activities in which different skill levels will be able to work successfully together, such as engaging in an anticipation guide. After introducing the lesson, you will have to decide how to organize groups. Your aim will be to use a variety of structures in grouping. Ford (2005) suggests that no grouping pattern is inherently bad; however, a teacher's overuse of one grouping pattern without informed decisions can lead to problems such as lack of engagement, frustration, boredom, and feelings of entitlement or stigma. So, to maintain a positive classroom environment, be sure to use a variety of groupings based on the objectives of the lessons. ♀

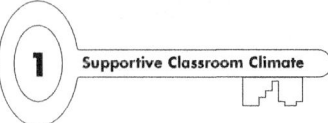

Flexible groups are broader than cooperative learning or tracked groups. Let us take a quick look at each type:

- *Tracked groups* are formed once at the start of the year and remain the same the entire year.
- *Flexible groups* change regularly based on independent learning, progress, and growth.
- *Cooperative learning groups* frequently use only heterogeneous groupings. Again, these kinds of groups are appropriate during exploratory, anticipatory, or initial lessons. Furthermore, this type of grouping is appropriate for activities that are differentiated within.

As students work in groups, meet with individual students or groups of students to provide scaffolded instruction, or circulate the room to collaborate with groups when necessary. ♀ Parking Lot (Figure 5.10) is a great method to help teachers manage time, attention to each group, and student questions. The "parking lot" is essentially a display that makes it easy for students to post questions (typically on a sticky note) and for you to see and address them.

Data-Informed Instruction **6**

Figure 5.10   Parking Lot form.

The question I have is:

I have tried to answer the question by:

So far I think:

Name(s):

Post Directions and Guidelines to Minimize Questions

As we have noted, it is essential for you to go over an activity with the whole class or an intended group. It is important to discuss the sequence of steps and expected outcomes and answer any questions that arise. However, although you will address many of the questions for clarification at this point, you can also expect that as students process or discuss the activity with their groups, more questions will arise that are central to the sequence or elements of the assignment. To avoid a second round of questions, you can post directions or guidelines in the classroom or provide a copy to each student or group. We have found that doing this for a simple activity avoids confusion and reduces students' dependence on the teacher. An example appears in Figure 5.11.

| Figure 5.11 | Example of directions for a simple activity. |

Activity:

Respond to an assigned question on the chapter you just read by writing a one-page response in your notebook. Once you are done, meet with your assigned partner to share your response and reflect.

Directions:

1. Review the chapter that you read last night.

2. Read the question that you have been assigned and jot down three points you will discuss in your response to that question.

3. Write a one-page response in your notebook. Once you are done, read it over (quickly) to make sure you can clearly identify the three points you wanted to discuss. Do not edit your written work for grammatical errors at this point, since I am concerned with content.

4. Once you are done, meet with your assigned partner, exchange notebooks, and read your partner's response.

5. Provide two comments on your partner's work: one positive and one constructive criticism. The comments should be only about the content. Do not comment on grammar.

6. Self-reflect on the process and your work in your notebook. Answer these questions: What did I do well? What have I learned from my partner's work? Compare your self-review with your peer's review of your work.

Provide for Additional Independent Work

To avoid idle time when some students finish their assigned work before their peers, you can either assign them activities or allow them to choose activities themselves. One teacher we know creates a folder of activities, organized by topic, so students can work on specific skills when they have finished their work. This teacher either allows the students to pick the task that they want to complete or assigns tasks based on specific academic strengths and weaknesses.

Another teacher we know creates two types of menus. First, each student gets a personalized menu with a list of three to five supplemental activities to choose from to address specific needs. Then, each student gets a copy of a whole-class menu that lists a variety of activities that students can choose from to enrich the unit or skill the class is working on. The teacher also posts this whole-class menu in a prominent spot in the classroom. 🔑 Each individual menu is derived from the student's performance on formative assessments, whereas the whole-class menu consists of enrichment activities.

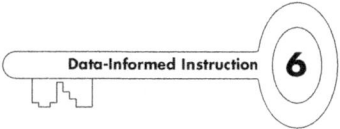

Here is another way you can provide independent work. Let us say your class is working on developing vocabulary skills in a novel study. In this case, you specifically want to develop students' consciousness, or "an awareness of and interest in words and their meanings" (Graves, 2006, p. 4). As an additional independent assignment, you decide to ask the students to document and define any unknown words in the first two chapters of the novel. Following this activity, they will create word webs that include the word, its definition, a synonym and antonym, a silly mnemonic or sentence to help them retrieve the definition, and a sentence using the word in context—all to make learning of the word concrete (Blachowicz & Fisher, 2011). The variety of tasks in the word web will elicit different responses and will naturally enable differentiation.

You can also create learning centers for students who finish their work early. (See Figure 5.12 for suggestions based on NCTE's standards for the English language arts.) You might locate a variety of engaging standards-based games, activities, and challenges at each center. If space is an issue, you can create mobile centers or boxes to house the materials, which students can then work on in an open area.

Figure 5.12 Suggestions for learning centers.

Reading and Comprehension

Independent reading: Students read a book of their choice that may be leveled, genre specific, or free choice (NCTE Standards 1, 2, 9).

Short comprehension activities: Students practice refining specific comprehension, interpretation, and evaluation skills on a variety of fictional and nonfictional and other literary passages with answer keys attached so they can self-check (NCTE Standards 1, 3, 6, 11).

Timed reading of short passages: Students work on fluency and comprehension skills by reading passages and working on intonation, rate, and understanding (NCTE Standard 3).

(Continued)

(Continued)

Literature circles/book clubs: Students read and discuss books in groups (NCTE Standards 1, 2, 3, 4, 9, 11, 12).

Drama activities/tableaux: Students use various drama techniques to reenact literature or create a story, event, or conflict (NCTE Standards 1, 2, 3, 4, 12).

Character profiles: Students analyze characters and create 2-D or 3-D profiles based on traits, motivations, and events experienced (NCTE Standards 1, 2, 3, 11, 12).

Making novel-specific bookmarks: Students synthesize the main events of the book and create bookmarks that can be viewed by other students in subsequent lessons and years as a book review (NCTE Standards 1, 2, 3, 11, 12).

Writing

Sentence combining: Students complete sentence-combining activities using content from literature or other textbooks (NCTE Standards 4, 6).

Rewriting a piece of writing: Students engage in the final steps of the writing process where they revise, edit, and rewrite their work for a better written product (NCTE Standards 5, 6).

Editing and revising practice sheets: Students make appropriate editing and revision changes on their own writing samples, highlighting and changing errors in mechanical, grammatical, and organizational errors (NCTE Standards 5, 6, 10).

Creating a script/writing a monologue/performing the monologue: Students engage in writing for drama activities (NCTE Standards 4, 5, 6).

Descriptive writing: Students practice descriptive writing using stylistic elements for a given scenario (NCTE Standards 5, 6, 12).

Genre-specific practice: Students engage in individualized genre-specific skill work in reading, writing, or comprehension.

Vocabulary and Spelling

Vocabulary activities: Students develop their vocabulary by engaging in various research-validated vocabulary activities: word mapping, cloze passages, word sorts, morphology of words, studying and researching etymology of words (NCTE Standards 6, 10).

Greek-Latin roots and prefixes: Students study words through exploration and inquiry of Greek and Latin prefixes (NCTE Standards 6, 7, 8).

Creating crossword puzzles: Students create crossword puzzles and challenges based on words read from literature or from a certain topic. Crosswords can be created based on inquiry-based projects as well (NCTE Standards 1, 2, 7).

Word sorts: Students sort words with similar spelling patterns and learn how to spell those words (NCTE Standard 4).

Taboo: Students practice word retrieval and develop vocabulary by playing Taboo (NCTE Standard 4).

Mad Libs: Students practice parts of speech while completing cloze passages in Mad Libs (NCTE Standards 4, 12).

Other

Grading assignments based on rubrics: Students self-assess, peer-assess, or practice assessing sample assignments using rubrics (NCTE Standard 11).

Using the Internet to practice skills if computers are present in the classroom: Students practice specific skills such as spelling using the computer (via programs like Lexia, SOS; NCTE Standard 8).

Centers offer an ideal opportunity for you to both provide additional independent work and differentiate instruction. Centers do not need excessive planning and can actually save time. It often takes students several days to complete center activities, which frees you up to complete other tasks, such as conferring with individual students or reading reflections. In addition, students enjoy the student-centered learning that takes place in centers.

To keep centers manageable, try to limit the number of centers open at the same time and the number of students per center. Centers should have no more than six students at once. Four is ideal, but with classroom sizes on the rise, it may be hard to limit some groups to only four students. You may want to vary the types of activities in centers to allow for some groups to be larger than others. In fact, you can stagger centers so that half the students are engaging in independent work while the other half are in centers; ask students to make a swap halfway through the class.

ASSIGNING HOMEWORK

Debate concerning the effectiveness of homework has questioned its necessity (Gill & Schlossman, 2000). However, research shows that the effectiveness of homework increases with each grade. An effective amount of homework for middle school students is about 60 to 80 minutes each day (Cooper, 1989, 2007).

Homework should be viewed as more than the completion of classwork that there was no time to do in school. As you consider homework assignments, keep in mind the following:

- Tasks assigned for homework should enhance learning.
- Tasks should be limited. No task should take an excessive amount of time to complete.
- Homework should be purposeful. It should either introduce new content or provide practice of a skill learned in class to promote further independence and mastery (Marzano & Pickering, 2007).
- Homework should not be considered busy work.
- The best homework assignments are differentiated based on amount of time spent, level of difficulty, medium of final work, and skill. ♀

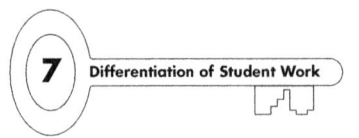

7 Differentiation of Student Work

You may wish to create a plan that charts out the sequence of homework early in the unit and then follow that plan in subsequent lessons.

To save time, limit the variety of homework you hand out. If there are four different groups, four different homework types will suffice with minor changes for some students. Also, try to keep homework skill based. Then the overall assignments among students in the class will remain consistent. For instance, if spelling is the skill being addressed, give all students some type of spelling work.

Of course, certain skill-based assignments may differ significantly depending on the student. One way to deal with this issue is to create two levels of homework assignments: common (in which all students work on similar tasks or the same exact task) and individual (skill based, focusing on the individual's needs). ♀

Vary the Amount of Time Spent

One way to differentiate homework is to provide different time frames of engagement for each student. ♀ For instance, if your students need to read the same novel but are at different reading levels, you can provide a maximum time limit for reading rather than a specific number of pages to read.

If you use this approach, it is important that you require students to keep a log noting the start time, end time, and total time of engagement and identify the number of pages read. (See Figure 5.13.) This log will keep the students accountable and organized because their reading will be tracked. You can then:

- Refer to the logs to check how much reading students have completed
- Evaluate the amount of reading they are able to complete
- Compare their figures to their peers'

If students are reading very few pages, you may decide to provide scaffolds. ♀ Therefore, you can also use the reading log as a formative assessment to guide instruction in either support or enrichment. Chapters 6 and 7 delve deeper into how formative assessment can be used to support or enrich learners.

It is also helpful to get parents involved and ask for their signature to ensure that the students adhered to their time frame. In our classrooms, we have found that this method limits students' frustration and negative views toward homework and reading. Conscientious students will want to complete the whole assignment, so as you assign pages and set maximum time limits, be sure to predict as accurately as possible the time it will take most students to read the assignment.

Continuous Assessment **4**

| Figure 5.13 | Reading log. |

Assigned Time	Start Time	End Time	Total Reading time	Start Page	End Page	Parent Signature

Keep in mind that if you use this model, your students will be at different parts of the novel. If you want to make sure that all the students stop at a major shift so that the entire class can engage in a worthwhile discussion, make sure you instruct them to do so. Also, be sure to tell your students the due date of reading to that specific point well in advance so that even those who will need extra time can reach that point with ease.

You may also want to ask the students to engage in an honor code in which they promise to discuss events of the story only with those who have read up to that portion of the book. ♥

Vary the Level of Difficulty

One of the most logical methods of differentiating homework assignments is to vary the difficulty of the work. ♥ As we have emphasized, it is important to keep the skill the same but vary the level of expectations among the students. For example, let us say that your seventh-grade students are working on descriptive writing in fictional writing. You require each student to use sentence variety, adjectives, and other descriptor words in their writing. In a homework assignment, you give some students more structure in creating their setting with certain words and scenarios; you give others free range. In this way, each student works on the same skill, but the specific assignment varies in degree of sophistication.

Plan Homework in Larger Chunks

Earlier in the chapter, we mentioned creating a homework planner to help organize assignments throughout the unit. You can plan homework assignments in one-week chunks (or longer chunks) to minimize additional workload and help facilitate students' organizational skills.

Collect certain parts of the homework for marking or simply check for key elements at the beginning of each lesson. Students can also engage in self- or peer-scoring their homework throughout the week; you might simply check their reflections.

Collect final products and then use the data from formative assessments

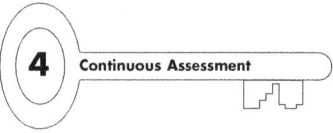

to decide to what degree you will assess them. Remember, some types of formative assessment should be collected throughout the unit. ♥ These assessments will give the best sense of a student's level of understanding and how homework has contributed to that.

Support Students Who Do Not Turn in Homework

If students do not turn in homework, you will want to determine why. Ask them to complete a time management form in which they detail how they spent their time (Figure 5.14). Students who did not understand the homework will fill out a checklist of efforts made so that you both can assess the problem and find an individualized solution. You might provide this list after every missed homework assignment or after a student misses a number of assignments.

Figure 5.14   "Why I didn't do my homework."

Explain what you did understand and exactly where you got stuck.

What efforts did you make to complete the homework?

- I called a friend from class.
- I conducted online research.
- I reread directions carefully, rewrote them in my own words, highlighted two to three important words in them, and looked back at prior models.
- I checked an alternative resource for another explanation.
- I asked an adult for help.
- I reviewed my notes from class.
- I brainstormed ideas but got stuck.

You will also want to work with students to create a time management strategy.

If students continue to have general difficulty despite these efforts, further differentiate support by asking a parent or guardian to send a weekly e-mail or note in the study or homework book stating whether homework has been completed. Of course, some parents face organizational challenges as well. In that case, perhaps a grandparent, other household member, or even another faculty member the student has connected with may be willing to step in.

If you have 100-plus students, you cannot easily stay on top of initiating e-mails regularly for missing homework. Asking parents to initiate a weekly check-in can help you with time management. Spending time finding out how best to get parents to check in (e.g., having a grandparent do it) will save you inordinate amounts of time down the road.

If you find that you are asking multiple students to check in with their parents, you might want to create a checklist for the parents that asks them to focus on key pieces of information. Alternately, you might post assignments with models on the Web. This will reduce the amount of time you spend noting missing information or other concerns for parents.

GRADING

Grading needs to convey where a student is in relation to mastering expected standards. However, grading can also serve as powerful feedback that should be understandable to students. For example, a B on a test tells little, but a checklist of mastered and unmastered concepts on the test is far more helpful, even (or perhaps especially) if the students fill it out.

As we have noted, students should not be graded on certain formative assessments, such as preassessments or homework that provides practice at achieving standards. A numerical score on these assessments has a negative effect on students, even if further comments are provided, because students focus only on the grade and miss out on the learning opportunity (Black, Harrison, Lee, Marshall, & Wiliam, 2004). With that in mind, homework effort should be shown in an effort grade that is separate from a grade for mastery and standards. Also, as we have emphasized, you need not grade everything students submit. Students can self-score preassessments, and you can give them the option of redoing a similar preassessment so that they can see their progress as they work on the activity again.

To make informed, evaluative decisions, teachers should make sure that all students are assessed on essential unit standards. Here are some suggestions for grading tests and assignments: ❢

- Count a rewrite as part of the class participation grade, or as a weighted homework grade.
- Based on how students did on the preassessments and formative assessment along the way during the unit, create a slightly more challenging task on a test that asks students to use higher-order skills. You can make these challenges optional or required.
- If students take a more challenging test and score a slightly lower grade than those who took an easier test, weight that grade differently when calculating the final scores.

- If the student has mastered all of the unit standards on the tests and only the more sophisticated questions are incorrect, then take that into consideration as you figure out the final grade for the course.
- Similarly, you can leniently grade students who attempt more challenging tasks if they have mastered the class standard and only struggled with elements of the task that were higher than the standard.

Teachers are at the heart of making the change to differentiated lessons. Although the idea of differentiation seems daunting, we encourage you to remember to make small changes and think about the lesson before teaching it. With your busy workload, it is critical to not only identify the standards that will be mastered in the unit but also to preplan as many extension and intervention activities as you can. Ultimately, you want to shift your focus to the most effective practices that will help each student improve academically without adding to your workload. As this chapter has shown, you can redistribute your effort by organizing your class, using assessment to drive and differentiate instruction, involving students in decision making, and differentiating not only classwork, but homework as well.

6 Supporting Students Who Are Low Achieving

Coauthored With Shira M. Cohen-Goldberg

Every student we have the honor to teach presents a fresh mystery. The opportunity to discover how each student can best be stretched or supported presents one of the most fulfilling and rewarding aspects of our work. Among students with learning challenges, the sources of underlying difficulties can be as varied as executive functioning (Altemeier, Abbott, & Berninger, 2008), dysgraphia (Nicolson & Fawcett, 2009), and even different subtypes of dyslexia (Katzir, 2009). Some of these students may share similar patterns, such as difficulty with decoding multisyllabic words or writing organized paragraphs. Yet no two students share the same profile of difficulties. Therefore, for each student, it is necessary to regularly gather formative assessment data for each foundational skill. This is especially important because preconceptions about students' difficulties may bias teachers. Each assessment allows students a new opportunity to surprise teachers—often in wonderful ways.

You can collect formative assessment data on the kinds of foundational skill challenges students with these difficulties face. By assessing, addressing, and ameliorating such challenges, you can allow these students access to the higher-order tasks described in other chapters. Therefore, the three major sections in this chapter provide an overview of how to use formative assessment to build proficiency in foundational areas. These sections do not provide an exhaustive overview of the foundational difficulties students may experience; instead, they model how to use formative assessments in general to guide provision of additional supports in these major areas. Each section is organized according to the three steps recommended in Practices 2, 3, and 4:

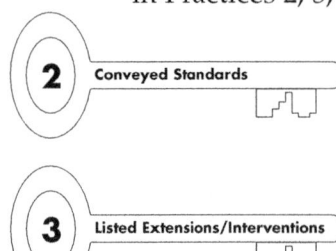

1. Specify measurable learning standards. ♀

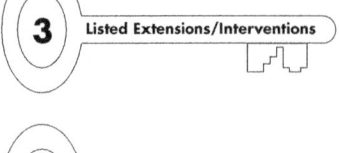

2. List possible accommodations and research-based interventions. ♀

3. Determine what data to collect from students so that you are able to select the best support options for enabling all students to master each standard. ♀

Teachers often begin by collecting abundant data and then do not know what to do with it all. These steps will help you avoid the common phenomenon of finding yourself swimming in data with no rudder to guide your direction. The sections that follow provide models for how to carry out these three steps in each of the following broad areas:

- Foundational reading skills (decoding and fluency)
- Reading comprehension skills (recall of basic facts, main idea, and vocabulary)
- Writing skills (organization and sentence variety)

FOUNDATIONAL READING SKILLS (DECODING AND FLUENCY)

> *Ms. Rodriguez noticed that two of the sixth-grade students in her third-period English class were struggling with completing both in-class and homework reading tasks. She wondered if they might be having difficulty sustaining their attention spans during the tasks. However, as she observed them reading aloud in class, she noticed that they both read in a halting, labored way. She decided to explore whether they might have reading difficulties before addressing any potential issues with attention spans.*

To begin, Ms. Rodriguez brainstormed strategies she could use to support the students. These strategies ranged from helping them practice specific decoding skills and providing opportunities for them to read more fluently to offering accommodations such as audio books and leveled readers. After making this list, she thought about what kinds of data might help her decide which supports would be best to offer. She considered efficient ways to assess the students' reading speed relative to peers. She also wondered if they had difficulty actually decoding words, and if so what patterns were difficult for them.

Ms. Rodriguez decided to do a three-minute whole-class decoding exercise to measure her students' reading speed. (This is explained in the following sections.) When this exercise confirmed that the two students were reading more slowly than their peers, Ms. Rodriguez asked them to remain after class to complete a three-minute decoding survey and a one-minute running record so she could see the specific nature of their difficulties. She found that the first student showed difficulty with decoding unfamiliar three-syllable words. The second student had solid decoding skills but read more slowly. Ms. Rodriguez shared feedback on the results with each student and then collaborated with them to design individualized plans to increase their reading rates.

Decoding and Fluency Standards

As we have mentioned, teachers should clarify measurable standards they expect students to meet. Both decoding and fluency standards are some of the more finite and easily definable skills to specify in measurable terms. ♀ Fluency standards can be found through sources such as Hasbrouck and Tindal's (2006) oral reading fluency assessment norms.

Conveyed Standards 2

For example, according to Hasbrouck and Tindal, students in the fall of sixth grade should read 127 words per minute. Teachers can collect local norms or use Hasbrouck and Tindal's. Moreover, since fluency involves more than just rate, standards have been set regarding how expressively students read and how well they use meaningful phrasing in ways that preserve the author's syntax. Figure 6.1 is an example of a rubric that can be used to measure this.

Decoding standards often recommend that, for material to be considered to be at a valid instructional level, students should be able to read at least 95% of it accurately with no decoding errors (Fuchs, Fuchs, & Deno, 1982), and that they should be able to read at least 98% of grade level material for them to be considered to be at an independent level (Caldwell & Leslie, 2010; Wixson & Lipson, 1991). Yet little empirical research on these standards exists, and some research has found that, with scaffolding, students will still benefit from what they read when these percentages are as low as 85% (Stahl & Heubach, 2005).

Figure 6.1		NAEP Oral Reading Fluency Scale, Grade 4: 2002.
Fluent	**Level 4**	Reads primarily in larger, meaningful phrase groups. Although some regressions, repetitions, and deviations from text may be present, these do not appear to detract from the overall structure of the story. Preservation of the author's syntax is consistent. Some or most of the story is read with expressive interpretation.
	Level 3	Reads primarily in three- or four-word phrase groups. Some small groupings may be present. However, the majority of phrasing seems appropriate and preserves the syntax of the author. Little or no expressive interpretation is present.
Nonfluent	**Level 2**	Reads primarily in two-word phrases with some three- or four-word groupings. Some word-by-word reading may be present. Word groupings may seem awkward and unrelated to the larger context of the sentence or passage.
	Level 1	Reads primarily word by word. Occasional two-word or three-word phrases may occur—but these are infrequent and/or do not preserve meaningful syntax.

Source: U.S. Department of Education, Institute of Education Sciences, National Center for Education Statistics, National Assessment of Educational Progress (NAEP), 2002 Oral Reading Study.

Decoding and Fluency Accommodations and Interventions

After you define standards, you can list realistic accommodations and interventions to offer students who do not meet these standards. ♀ Interventions actually address and ameliorate the underlying skills themselves. Accommodations, in contrast to interventions, are external scaffolds that help students access textual content.

Accommodations

Two potential accommodations include audio books and leveled reading materials. You can obtain audio books for free at many libraries via interlibrary loan. Additionally, organizations such as Learning Ally provide audio books at a minimal charge, as do online sites such as Audible .com. Teachers can encourage students to listen to audio books as they read, since listening to a fluent model helps build prosody and rate (Estevez & Whitten, 2011). Moreover, students with decoding difficulties often tire quickly when reading (Jainta & Kapoula, 2011; Wipprecht, 2007), and audio books may help them conserve energy so that they have the endurance necessary to comprehend more lengthy texts.

You can also provide leveled books for students who show that they cannot decode grade level material. This scaffolding can give them access to grade level content through simplified text. Figure 6.2 lists resources for obtaining leveled reading materials.

Figure 6.2   Online resources for leveled reading materials.

Abridged or Controlled-Text Novels

www.bearportpublishing.com

www.capstonepub.com/category/LIB_PUBLISHER_CAP

www.continentalpress.com/pages/subjects/reading_hilo_1.html

www.edconpublishing.com/index.php?route=product/category&path=41_14

www.glencoe.com/gln/jamestown/

www.heinemannclassroom.com/content/home_hilo

www.highnoonbooks.com/HNB/abouthnb.tpl

www.orcabook.com/client/client_pages/Orca_Soundings_Info.cfm

www.perma-bound.com/curriculum/differentiated-reading-materials/differentiated-reading-materials-s-to-v.faces

www.sdlback.com/shopResult.aspx

www.wieseeducational.com

Hi-Lo Compendiums or Passage Selections

www.donjohnston.com/catalog/stffrm.htm

edHelper.com

www.kurzweiledu.com/default.html

shop.scholastic.com/webapp/wcs/stores/servlet/ProductDisplay_60247_-1_10001_10002

Research-Based Interventions

Once you have listed accommodations, you can list interventions to offer students. As mentioned, in contrast to accommodations, interventions address and strengthen underlying skills. For example, interventions for decoding and fluency should work on building word level decoding skills or passage level fluent-reading skills.

Should teachers teach decoding skills? The National Council of Teachers of English (NCTE) Commission on Reading (2004) cautions against offering phonics instruction to *most* middle school students as part of the general education curriculum, citing the National Reading Panel's finding that phonics instruction with most older students does not lift reading comprehension skills. This may be because decoding skills are considered "constrained" in contrast to reading comprehension skills, which are considered "unconstrained." Decoding is finite, so by middle school most students are able to decode most words they encounter. However, a *small number* of students do continue to face "word study" (Ivey & Baker, 2004) or decoding challenges (Archer, Gleason, & Vachon, 2003) that would most certainly impede fluency. These challenges are usually insufficiently addressed in middle school curricula (Catone & Brady, 2005).

How can these skills be addressed? Research has found that middle school students who have severe decoding difficulties and receive *additional support programs* that focus on enhancing decoding skills can make significant progress (Ehri, Nunes, Stahl, & Willows, 2001; Lovett, Lacerenza, Borden, Frijters, & Steinbach, 2000; Lovett & Steinbach, 1997; Shippen, Houchins, Steventon, & Sartor, 2005). In some cases, this progress occurs in as little as four hours of total practice time (Bhattacharya & Ehri, 2006). Yet, additional support programs are needed. To close the gap, adolescents with severe decoding challenges require more support for learning to decode than teachers can provide (Kamil et al., 2008).

Fluency growth seems to require even more intensive support. Even 10 to 15 minutes of daily research-based practice in additional support programs is insufficient to increase reading rates (Wanzek, Vaughn, Roberts, & Fletcher, 2011). Among studies providing even more instructional time than this, slow gains in fluency have been found (Torgesen, 2005). Although these gains did not close the gap between students with decoding challenges and their peers, they did make an enormous difference to the students, who more than doubled their rate of fluency growth. Therefore, to augment both decoding and fluency gains, additional support from teachers may be key, especially since the less severe the difficulty, the more likely the teacher's efforts will help students close the gap. Approaches such as having students engage in repeated readings (Roundy & Roundy, 2009) have resulted in students making significant progress.

If remedial support is available, you can work to align extra supports you provide in class with the approach used by additional remedial teachers. If such support is not available or if students show difficulties with decoding but do not qualify for support programs, you will find that the strategies we describe here offer realistic and research-validated ways in which you can address these difficulties.

For students who have decoding difficulties, it is vital to find the right type of decoding exercises. Research by Canney and Schreiner (1976–1977) found that teaching decoding rules in isolation did not translate into reading gains. Plus, you usually will not have time or training to teach these rules. Yet studies have shown that adolescents make significant gains in decoding after they simply practice segmenting multisyllabic words according to flexible guidelines rather than according to a rigid set of rules. Moreover, they can make this progress in just four hours of instruction spread over five weeks (less than 10 minutes daily; Bhattacharya & Ehri, 2006). In Bhattacharya and Ehri's study, students practiced segmenting words into syllables, then blending them back together.

In our classrooms, we have used this technique as a tiered activity. We have had students practice in pairs and individually with content-related word lists, as in Figure 6.3. Some students use the words for vocabulary enrichment, whereas others use them for decoding practice or for working on more sophisticated Greek and Latin roots. You could also set up a reading/spelling/fluency slot in class where you tier those skill-based lessons. Here is how this might work:

1. Provide a quick whole-class introduction of how to decode and define the words.

2. Give certain students extra practice. Ask them to use lines to segment words and then to draw scoops below the words to show how they would blend the syllables back together into the word.

The goal is for all students to be able to read the word list to a peer or teacher in less than a minute.

During free reading time or while students work on individualized tasks at the end of class, you can encourage students with difficulties to spend a few minutes practicing these skills. Again, just 10 minutes a day may result in significant gains for below-average decoders (Bhattacharya & Ehri, 2006). In our classrooms, we ask students to practice the same sheet or set of words about three times. The key is to provide them with embedded and repeated practice in segmenting words. You should also encourage students to follow the steps whenever they encounter unknown words.

Additionally, you can ask students to practice these kinds of decoding skills online at websites such as Skillswise (www.bbc.co.uk/skillswise/topic/recognising-letters-and-words). Keep in mind that students who receive special education support may learn specific rules for segmenting words. Be sure to work in consultation with resource teachers to ensure that students apply consistent rules as they do these types of activities.

Figure 6.3 Segmenting multisyllabic words for a social studies unit.

Group A: Research when and why an *i* following a *c* or *r* is often pronounced "ee," or when and why it makes a "sh" sound after a *t.* Draw a line between syllables to break the words into parts. Then draw a scoop underneath each word to show how you blend the parts back together.

Group B: Define these vocabulary words and make concept maps that illustrate their meanings.

Group C: If you already know the definitions, create a concept map showing connections between at least two words. Example: *Significance—distinguished—imperial.* Someone who has great *significance* to society is *distinguished*. One who is *distinguished* to the highest degree may be considered *imperial.*

Acoustically	Agrarian	Appreciation
Approximation	Censorship	Chivalrous
Distinguishable	Enlightenment	Exponential
Imperial	Inadequate	Indignant
Linguistic	Maturity	Significance
Transcription	Truculent	Variance

5 Student Self-Direction

Furthermore, to involve students in using assessment data to direct their own learning, give them goal planning sheets like those in Figure 6.4. ❓ After you return an assessment, which we will discuss in the section "Decoding Automaticity Assessments," help your students interpret the results and use those results to set goals. Then use weekly progress monitoring, such as one-minute reading probes written at students' grade level, to ensure that students are making progress with both rate and decoding accuracy. You can give these assessments right after class or during a free reading period so as not to take time from class.

You can also give students a practice log (Figure 6.5) to use in conjunction with the goal planning sheet. Practice logs give them ownership of and accountability for their own learning. You might give extra credit to students who complete this log, but a better incentive is to have them recognize how practicing these skills moves them toward overall improvement in reading.

Figure 6.4   Plan to improve decoding and fluency skills.

Based on my preassessment, I'd like to improve: speed, accuracy (circle one).
My current reading speed in one minute with a grade level passage is: _____

I would like to increase this to _____ by _____ (date).

The kinds of errors I made were:

_____

_____

_____

To improve my general reading rate, I will:

_____

_____

_____

Resources to improve my reading rate/accuracy are:

Times I will practice include:

Figure 6.5   Practice log.

Date	What I did	Adult Signature

My Graph (Words Read Accurately per Minute)

200											
180											
160											
140											
120											
100											
80											
60											
(Min)											
Dates:											

If your assessments reveal that students read slowly but accurately, you might intervene by asking students to practice fluency building through songs (Patel & Laud, 2007b) or repeated readings with materials such as Quick Reads (Vadasy & Sanders, 2008). Also, keep in mind that students may be accurate but not automatic at the word level. Research has found that when you ensure that students are not just accurate but also automatic at the word level, you can increase reading fluency (Hudson, Lane, Arriaza-Allen, Isakson, & Richman, 2011). Automaticity differs from fluency in that it is commonly associated with word level and word chunk level reading, whereas fluency is associated with reading at the passage level.

Students can also practice fluency at the passage level with online technology such as Read Naturally. You can ask students to work on Read Naturally outside of class time. You can also have students practice fluency at the passage level with Quick Reads, which are done in small groups or pairs at the end of class. Quick Reads are research validated (Vadasy & Sanders, 2008) and include five passages that use a common vocabulary bank. They are also valuable for building knowledge within content areas, since the passages focus on science and social studies topics. Addressing reading speed is important because it:

- Affects comprehension (Samuels & Farstrup, 2007)
- Can lengthen the time it takes to complete homework
- Has the potential to exhaust, demoralize, and create negative attitudes toward reading in students

On the other hand, if students struggle with decoding accurately, you can ask them to do brief decoding exercises a few minutes daily, again, just before or after class or school. If this is not possible, then you should ask parents, caregivers, or other adults to help students. Because the methods for addressing fluency are fairly straightforward in comparison to methods that address other reading skills, those who are not professional educators can still support students (Shaywitz, 2003). Share resources from leaders in the field of fluency, such as "Creating Fluent Readers" (Rasinksi, 2004), or summaries of this material (see Figure 6.6) with these adults and use them as guidelines prior to the adults' participation.

Decoding Automaticity Assessments

After you have listed possible accommodations and interventions, such as those just described, reflect on what kinds of data might help you decide which of these accommodations and interventions to offer. As an

Figure 6.6   Guidelines for parents for developing reading fluency.

Developing Reading Fluency

Research-based strategies that have been shown to increase fluency are repeated readings and assisted or modeled readings.

Select a 160- to 200-word paragraph. First, read the paragraph aloud to the child and be sure to model expression and phrasing (grouping words within sentences into meaningful phrases). Then, read the paragraph aloud together and be sure to read at a slightly faster pace than the child while modeling expression and phrasing. Time each reading. Reread it three to four times, since research shows that three to four readings fosters optimal growth in fluency.

Keep in mind that fluency is not just about speed. Faster is not always better. As you engage in this process, remember to:

- Read aloud with expression and phrasing. Stress important words and read words in meaningful groups or phrases rather than word by word.
- When doing repeated readings, read the paragraph at a slightly faster pace and model expression and phrasing.
- Encourage accuracy *and* speed.
- Additionally, have your child listen to audio books while reading along in the book. Be sure to use unabridged recordings.

initial screener, you can have students complete a whole-class decoding assessment in which they read a passage in which the spaces between words have been removed (see Figure 6.7 for an example). 🔑 This assessment, which is based on the Test of Silent Word Reading Fluency (Mather, Hammil, Allen, & Roberts, 2004), will identify which students read slowly. You can create passages aligned with the current curricular topic and increase the difficulty of the words throughout the paragraph, but especially toward the end.

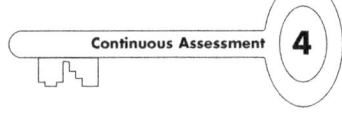

Continuous Assessment **4**

Distribute this assessment facedown and ask students to write their name on the back of the paper. Then provide directions, making it clear that students are not to turn over their papers until you have said so. You may want to provide a quick demonstration beforehand and, if needed, have students practice with three words. During the assessment, circulate throughout the room to ensure students are working correctly. Speak to any students who do not seem to be doing the assessment correctly. It is important to stop all students at three minutes exactly.

We have found that this assessment accurately identifies students with decoding difficulties in almost every case. Each time we use it, we see that students who are receiving remedial reading support come out at the very

| Figure 6.7 | Sample of a three-minute decoding assessment. |

Use a slash to separate the words in the following paragraph. You have three minutes to complete your work. I will ask you to stop when the three minutes are up.

Thelongestriverpassesninecountriesalongthewaybeforeitdrainsintothesealikemany greatriversthisriverismadeupofseveralsmallerriversithasthreemainstreamsitgathersits headwatersnearthehighlandseveryyearbetweensummerandfallmeltingsnow andheavyrainfallinginthehighregionwouldswelltheriverandcreatefloodsthisonce ayearoverflowhadbeengoingonforthousandsofyearsitwaseventuallyputtoastop afteradamwasopenedforuseintheyearnineteenhundredandseventytheancient peoplehadnoideaabouttherealcauseofthefloodstheythoughtitwasanactofagod becausetheydidnothavethekindofscientificundertandingsofnaturethatwenowhave developedinsteadtheyneededtoresorttosupernaturalbeliefsbecausetheycould notunderstandnaturalphenomenalikewedoinmoderntimes.

bottom of the list. Students who score just above those receiving remedial support can still benefit from decoding and fluency support, even if they have not been identified as needing remedial support.

Students in Grade 5 can separate about 45 of these words in three minutes. Students in Grade 6 can separate about 50 words in three minutes. (These norms may differ across schools, so collecting whole-class samples is valuable for finding local norms. We then set goals of having students reach the class average.)

After using this screener, consult with reading specialists or special educators to complete one- to three-minute individualized decoding and fluency assessments with the small group of identified students. Free grade level passages are available at Easycbm.com, dibels.uoregon.edu, and https://dibels.org/next/index.php. As students read these passages, you will be able to identify exactly where they fall in relation to grade level fluency rates. Moreover, as you listen to students read, you will be able to hear the specific decoding errors students make. Then you can use this data—combined with classroom observations you make as you watch students read and as you read individually with them—to choose appropriate accommodations and interventions.

If, for example, students show certain patterns while decoding unfamiliar three-syllable words, then you can target this skill with additional segmenting practice as modeled in Figure 6.3. Really Great Reading (www .reallygreatreading.com/resources/tools/diagnostic-decoding-surveys) offers free decoding surveys that are great for more specific analyses of decoding issues.

READING COMPREHENSION SKILLS (RECALL OF BASIC FACTS, MAIN IDEA, AND VOCABULARY)

Ms. Rodriguez noticed that Hamid's comments often seemed off base during discussions of material he had read. She knew from previous class assessments that his reading speed and decoding skills met standards, so she decided to collect formative assessment data on his comprehension skills.

Before beginning a unit on the novel Number the Stars *by Lois Lowry (1989), Ms. Rodriguez reviewed the reading comprehension standards that she expected of her students (Common Core State Standards Initiative, n.d.):*

- *Describe the plot*
- *Determine the main idea*
- *Recall and summarize facts*
- *Cite textual evidence to support what the text states explicitly and to support inferences drawn from it*

Ms. Rodriguez then listed out and researched possible supports that she could offer Hamid during the unit, such as paraphrasing, inference training, and reciprocal reading strategies. Next, she planned for ways that she could assess his reading comprehension before the unit so she could best target the supports she could offer. She decided on an assessment that she and her colleagues had created— comprehension questions (short answer and open response) to go with a brief story and expository passage. They had given these for several years and had collected local norms. Most students scored at least 75% of the total points possible. Students who scored more than 10 points below this showed difficulty in class. With the help of math teachers in their school, Ms. Rodriguez and her colleagues had compared scores on this assessment to state test scores the students had received. Since they respected the quality of their state tests and felt that they accurately measured the Common Core State Standards, they believed that demonstrating proficiency on these tests was a standard all students should achieve.

Hamid scored 58% on the preassessment, suggesting that he would score far below proficient on the state assessment. Ms. Rodriguez then used the assessment formatively to look for patterns that might suggest which areas of reading comprehension he most needed support with. When Hamid showed difficulty with most of the assessment tasks, she decided to start from square one—that is, helping him to develop reading comprehension skills at the most explicit and basic level: paraphrasing strategies. Although Ms. Rodriguez had already planned to teach paraphrasing to the entire class, she now was able to identify the additional support Hamid would require in mastering comprehension skills.

Conveyed Standards **2**

Reading Comprehension Standards 🔑

Setting measurable standards for reading comprehension is not as clear as setting standards for fluency or decoding. This may be because there are so many complex components that come into play when students work to understand what they read. According to the Common Core State Standards (Common Core State Standards Initiative, n.d.), reading comprehension standards include:

- Determining explicitly what a text says
- Making inferences about texts
- Citing evidence from texts orally or in writing to support conclusions drawn from texts.

For narrative genres, students should be able to determine central themes and summarize key supporting details. To engage with texts at the level delineated in the Common Core State Standards, students must first be able to show this basic comprehension.

Standards can also include scoring proficient or above a given stanine on a standardized test, such as the GRADE (Group Reading Assessment Diagnostic Evaluation). For instance, you can create reading assessment tasks, such as short answer or open response questions, and then score the class and use class norms to set standards. You can also correlate scores that students receive on your assessments to scores they receive on state assessments. In Ms. Rodriguez's case, the correlation was more than 0.8, or very strong. Since the class assessment is a strong indicator of what students will score on state assessments, Ms. Rodriguez concluded that these students were probably also proficient on the Common Core State Standards.

Alternatively, you can use standardized assessments such as Maze to set standards for reading comprehension at a basic level. For example, in the fall of sixth grade, students should be able to circle at least 22 correct responses to perform at the 50th percentile.

Reading Comprehension Interventions ♀[3]

3 Listed Extensions/Interventions

A recent meta-analysis on comprehension interventions for middle school students found several techniques effective in raising reading comprehension (Solis et al., 2011). These included:

- Strategy instruction
- Graphic organizers
- Checklists
- Prompt cards
- Review

In this section we will focus on the first technique: strategy instruction. Strategy instruction is an umbrella intervention that includes subelements such as mnemonics, questioning, and self-monitoring procedures. Essentially, strategy instruction involves explicitly teaching research-based strategies. As a specific example for how to use strategy instruction, let us look at how instructors in one study taught students specific steps to identifying main ideas to help them develop summarization skills (Gajria & Salvia, 1992).

First, the teachers explicitly modeled summarization skills for students. Next, they asked students to engage in guided and independent practice, and they offered feedback that emphasized mastery learning. During guided practice, instructors shifted responsibility for learning to the students. Throughout this process, they coached students in using Brown and Day's (1983) five summarization rules:

1. Superordination

2. Deletion of redundant information

3. Selection

4. Invention

5. Deletion of unimportant information

We have also used this strategy with our students. To make it more accessible and student friendly, we modify the language as we model and explain these rules to students. Figure 6.8 shows an explanation of the rules we model, followed by the questions we ask students to use to guide them in writing summaries. To support students with narrative passage summaries, we have designed a similar structure, again aimed at explicitly teaching reading comprehension strategies (see Figure 6.9).

Figure 6.8 Expository passage summary.

Replace lists or actions with superordinate terms. For example:

There were shirts, pants, and sweaters. → There was clothing.
They walked, rode bikes, and went on a bus. → They traveled.

_____

_____

_____

(Continued)

(Continued)

1. Select a topic sentence, if you can find one. (Main idea is what it is about. Topic sentence narrows this by defining what the author is saying about the main idea.)

_____

_____

_____

2. Create a topic sentence.

_____

_____

_____

3. Delete redundant information. (List here.)

_____

_____

_____

4. Delete unnecessary information. (List here.)

_____

_____

_____

Did I substitute category names for lists or events?
Did I delete repetitive information?
Did I find a topic sentence?
Did I create a topic sentence?
Did I delete unimportant information?

Craft your full summary here.

_____

_____

_____

_____

_____

_____

_____

_____

_____

Figure 6.9   Narrative passage summary.

What is your purpose for reading this?

_____

_____

_____

List what you already know about this topic.

_____

_____

_____

What do you predict this passage will cover?

_____

_____

_____

Identify text structure:

  Who are the main characters?
  When does the story take place?
  Where does the story take place?
  What does the main character want to do?
  What happens when he or she tries to do it that leads to a central conflict?
  How does the story end? (What event is the turning point or climax?)
  How does the main character feel?

Summarize content:

  What are the major topics of each paragraph and the bigger category these fit under?

  • Main idea _____

  • Supporting detail _____

  • Supporting detail _____

  • Supporting detail _____

  Is there a topic sentence in the passage (or the title)? Underline it and check off each detail that the topic sentence indicates will be discussed in the paragraph.
  If there is no topic sentence, write one here.

_____

_____

_____

(Continued)

(Continued)

What information can I delete because it is not essential to the bigger topic? Is any information repetitive? List both instances here.

_____

_____

_____

Craft your full summary here.

_____

_____

_____

_____

_____

_____

_____

_____

Keys to Literacy is a literacy organization that offers another set of comprehension strategies that have been validated by increases in state assessment scores in schools that use them, as described on their website (Keys to Literacy, 2012a, 2012b). The Key Comprehension Routine is a set of strategy activities that include foundational comprehension skills, such as:

- Using and generating top-down topic webs
- Taking notes
- Generating questions
- Summarizing

To increase the effectiveness of the strategy instruction, help students learn to use these routines in tandem (Duke, 2004; Gaskins, 1998; Pressley, 2000). These routines work particularly well within a secondary school setting because you can help students apply them to any instructional content area. This enables teachers of all content areas to provide extra literacy scaffolding.

When you provide comprehension strategy instruction within the context of learning other subject matter, such as history and science, you foster comprehension development (Biancarosa & Snow, 2004; Snow, 2002). One powerful aspect of the Key Comprehension Routine is that it may be used in all classrooms across a school. Thus, students in a given grade level can learn routines that are consistent from one classroom to the next.

Another simple strategy for strengthening reading comprehension is to have students self-monitor their reading comprehension (Joseph & Eveleigh, 2011; Solis et al., 2011). For example, you can ask students to keep small graphs in their notebooks to show how many reading comprehension questions they get correct (Figure 6.10). In our experience, students have found this motivating and teachers have valued the feedback. We often choose passages taken from abridged classics, such as those by the Edcon Publishing Group (as mentioned in Figure 6.2). Each story has 10 leveled passages. Students can use any reading comprehension passages that are leveled, such as the expository passages presented in the

Figure 6.10 Chart for monitoring comprehension strategies practice.

Date	What I did	Adult Signature

My Graph (Number of Questions Correct)

20												
15												
10												
5												
(Min)												
Dates:												

Reading for Content series by Carol Einstein (see eps.schoolspecialty.com/products/details.cfm?series=1651M). Students can often complete such passages in 10 to 15 minutes or less. This means they can read them before the lesson begins, during "DEAR" (Drop everything and read) time, before or after school, as homework, as work with tutors, or during other unstructured times of the day.

On the graph, we ask students to chart the number of correct answers they receive for each passage. They become motivated when they see that they are growing in achievement as they apply the strategies we are teaching in class. One caveat: This does not constitute strategy instruction, since students are practicing comprehension strategies and monitoring their growth in using them. Instead, the strategy instruction takes place when you introduce, model, and scaffold students in applying specific strategies, and provide feedback along the way.

You can also ask students who struggle with reading comprehension to fill out a second sheet—similar to the decoding and fluency planning sheets—that details steps they will take to shore up their reading comprehension skills (Figure 6.11). ♀ You can also use this form with students to debrief them on the results of a formative assessment.

Reading Comprehension Assessments ♀

Far more is known about the assessment of reading fluency and decoding skills than is known about how to effectively assess reading comprehension (Snowling, Cain, Nation, & Oakhill, 2009). Perhaps reading

Figure 6.11 Plan to improve reading comprehension skills.

Based on my preassessment, I'd like to improve:
The kinds of errors I made were:

_____

_____

_____

My plan to improve is:
Specific reading strategies I will practice applying include:
When doing personal reading, I will:
When reading for school, I will:
Resources to improve my comprehension are:

comprehension is more difficult to define or operationalize, given all the diverse components needed for understanding what is read. Also, it may be more difficult to determine what assessments of reading comprehension actually measure. For example, it is often surmised that oral language is a strong predictor, or correlate, of reading comprehension skills. However, different reading assessments measure different skills. For some assessments, oral language is a strong correlate of reading comprehension skills, yet for others, decoding skills are the strongest correlate (Keenan, Betjemann, & Olson, 2008). Therefore, different assessments may assess vastly different dimensions of comprehension. A first step in assessing reading comprehension may then be to define comprehension, which is challenging. The Common Core State Standards provide descriptions of what reading comprehension skills include, and it is thus essential to find optimal ways to assess these skills.

Standardized assessments and teacher-created assessments are two ways you can assess your students' comprehension skills. For instance, you might craft questions based on a chapter of a novel or other literature selection (e.g., poem, newspaper article). Your assessments can include short answer or open response formats. As we have emphasized throughout the book, before you design or select assessments, be sure to first clarify the standards that you expect students to meet and plan out potential supports that you can offer. This way, you can be sure that the assessment data are most likely to give you the information you will need to decide which additional supports to offer.

Also be sure to monitor students' progress so you can frequently assess whether the additional supports are helping. Standardized measures of reading comprehension for the whole class include options such as the GRADE. Alternatively, you can analyze scores from the prior year's state assessment. Research has shown that these are the best predictors of who will score proficient on the next state assessment, so you can use them to identify students who may require additional support (Denton et al., 2011).

Moreover, you can assess reading comprehension strategies through metacognitive surveys that assess which strategies students already use. One survey you might try is the Metacognitive Awareness of Reading Strategies Inventory (Mokhtari & Reichard, 2002), which is available at www.dayofreading.org/DOR10HO/MARSI_2002.pdf.

Vocabulary Standards ?

Conveyed Standards 2

An essential subcomponent of reading comprehension is vocabulary knowledge. Therefore, it is important to identify vocabulary standards and address these as well. You can expect students to know a bank of vocabulary words that are grade level appropriate. More important, you should ensure that they can use effective strategies to determine or clarify the meanings of unknown words or words with multiple meanings. According to the Common Core State Standards (Common Core State Standards Initiative, n.d., L.6.4, L.7.4, L.8.4), these can include using context, roots, or reference materials.

Vocabulary Supports ?

There are several research-validated ways you can support students' vocabulary learning. Teach students in ways that best facilitate depth of processing. This includes asking students to:

- Pair associations with synonyms
- Find antonyms
- Classify words in common groupings
- Generate a new definition
- Use the word in a sentence

Be sure to expose students to these words at least three times. Specifically, you will want to engage students in the following approaches (Elleman, Lindo, Morphy, & Compton, 2009):

1. Deciphering word meanings from context

2. Using word roots to figure out word meanings

3. Using word webs, in which associated meanings are attached to new words, to learn meanings of a specific bank of words (e.g., words from a novel students are about to read)

4. Creating images and using other strategies to memorize word meanings

Vocabulary Assessments ?

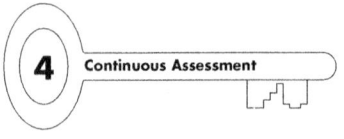

If preassessments show that students know the majority of words in an upcoming novel, then minimal vocabulary instruction may be needed for those words. In such a case, you might focus on more global approaches, such as using word roots and context to decipher meanings of new words. Alternatively, if students do poorly on preassessments involving a bank of words from a novel, then you can implement specific strategies for teaching those words, such as word webs or images. Again, the key is to:

1. Clarify standards

2. List potential supports

3. Determine what data you will need to select which supports to use

You might preassess students' vocabulary with a list of selected words before the class reads a novel. You can also assess vocabulary by analyzing words used in student writing. This reveals not only whether students can identify word meanings, but also whether they actually use varied vocabulary when they write. One structured way to do this, which we adapted from the Test of Written Language 4 (Hammill & Larsen, 2009), is to count words with three or more syllables or seven or more letters. We ask students to "also count unique, well-suited, and rarely used words that strike the reader as exemplary vocabulary choices." Teach students to evaluate their own work in this way a few times a year as a check-in. Set a standard and show models. We have found that, on average, students in sixth grade use five of these kinds of words per 100 words written. You should need to monitor the progress of only a small number of students for this.

For a more standardized option, build an assessment from a grade level word bank, such as one available from Wordly Wise 3000 Test Generator (eps.schoolspecialty.com/products/details.cfm?series=2818M). This test generator allows you to select from a bank of grade level vocabulary words, and it provides a global measure of each student's vocabulary knowledge. We have used these banks to create global vocabulary assessments and found that students score an average of 16 out of 20 words correct on grade level assessments. This assessment has accurately identified students who struggle with vocabulary. In fact, we have noticed that the students who struggle on reading comprehension assessments are the ones who score the lowest in their grade on this assessment, which underscores the important role of vocabulary in reading comprehension.

The vocabulary test generator gives you the option of creating assessments that measure a student's ability either to decipher the meanings of words in context or to define words that stand on their own. We use a mixture of assessments because we want to measure students' general vocabulary knowledge as well as their ability to figure out unknown words in context. The Wordly Wise 3000 Test Generator also provides excellent options for progress monitoring. EasyCBM is currently creating vocabulary assessment options, and these should be released soon.

WRITING SKILLS (ORGANIZATION AND SENTENCE VARIETY)

When Ms. Rodriguez collected a paragraph writing preassessment from her class on the topic of rivers, she immediately noticed that some students had not used topic sentences, transition words, or conclusions. As always, her class showed a wide range of ability in paragraph writing, so she knew she needed to offer both supports and challenges. One child who clearly needed extra support was Sophia. In her paragraph, Sophia had listed everything she knew about the topic with no organization at all. Ms. Rodriguez identified this as classic "knowledge telling," in which students list what they know without giving any attention to structure (McCutchen, 2006).

She decided to begin by listing out possible supports she could offer Sophia. Her school used a writer's workshop to teach writing. While this method seems to enhance motivation for writing, Ms. Rodriguez also knew that the minimal research that exists on writer's workshops has shown that students can actually lose ground with this method (Harris, Graham, & Mason, 2006). Therefore, she decided to supplement this approach with self-regulated strategy development (SRSD). SRSD has been found to be the most effective way to significantly raise writing achievement (Graham & Perin, 2007), and it has been used effectively by classroom teachers in their work with small groups and individual students (Helsel & Greenberg, 2007).

In this approach, teachers support students in coordinating the multiple demands of writing through a gradual release of responsibility that involves directly modeling a series of steps. Students learn to self-direct by using self-talk and self-encouragement as they write.

As students practice using the strategies they have seen modeled, they also score model writing samples, peer writing samples, and their own work according to specified criteria. After reviewing the Common Core State Standards, Ms. Rodriguez designed a rubric to help Sophia evaluate each writing sample. She created a scale that could be used to score the samples, setting a numerical overall standard that she expected all students to reach.

Writing Standards ♀

According to the Common Core State Standards, students should write clearly and coherently to address development, organization, and style as appropriate to task, purpose, and audience. You can delineate the exact standards you expect students to meet by designing rubrics that measure these skills.

Measuring writing skills, like measuring reading comprehension skills, is not a well-developed field. Collect writing samples from an entire grade and correlate the scores to standardized assessments of writing, such as National Assessment of Educational Progress (NAEP) or state assessments. Then establish specific standards by setting local norms. You can set cut scores that correlate highly to scoring proficient on standardized tests. You should expect all students to master this standard, represented by the numerical value received on the rubric.

Writing Interventions ♀

Listed Extensions/Interventions 3

Using Self-Regulated Strategy Development (SRSD)

This model has been used effectively in classrooms with regularly achieving students (Harris et al., 2006), as well as in pullout programs (Patel & Laud, 2007a). Given the extent of its research base in comparison to other writing programs as well as its built-in progress monitoring structure, it is a suitable strategy for a Tier II writing intervention within a Response to Intervention framework, and it has been successfully used in this way (Helsel & Greenberg, 2007; Sandmel et al., 2009). Further factors that fundamentally distinguish SRSD from other writing programs include:

- Mnemonics that bring together the steps needed for successful writing
- Systematic attention to providing scaffolds and emphasizing self-directedness
- Transfer to other settings and regular progress monitoring

Through progress monitoring, you will be able to ensure that students master each stage of the strategy before moving on to the next stage. To help them master each stage, you will introduce scaffolds and then gradually remove them as students become proficient at each stage. This process allows you to coach students to ultimately use the strategy independently in all the different settings in which they are asked to write. Specifically, the SRSD model has students cycle through six stages (Figure 6.12) as you support them in learning to use specific writing strategies.

As an example, an instructor in a recent study taught a paragraph writing strategy to fifth-grade students in a resource program (Patel & Laud, 2007a). As a preassessment before strategy instruction, she asked students to write a paragraph. Then she assessed requisite preskills—defining a topic sentence and adding supporting details, transitions, and a conclusion. Since students' preassessment paragraphs revealed that they did not apply any of these, she created a mnemonic, "UNITE," to help students develop these skills (see Figure 6.13).

Initially, she modeled these steps for students. She encouraged students to identify how using the strategy would be helpful to them, as well as when and where they might use it outside the resource room. The teacher also used a think-aloud, with student input, to demonstrate how

Figure 6.12 Six stages of SRSD.

Stage 1: Activate background knowledge
- Find out what students already know (preassess)
- Collect several baseline samples
- Build genre-specific knowledge and any preskills

Stage 2: Develop goals and rationale
- Present a mnemonic for the strategy
- Develop effort to learn it
- Have students determine when they will use it

Stage 3: Model each step of the strategy
- Have students evaluate modeled use of the strategy
- Evaluate preassessment performance and set goals
- Model self-talk for using the strategy and encouraging oneself
- Develop a self-talk bank
- Articulate value/principles of each step of the strategy

Stage 4: Help students memorize the strategy
- Use props such as ball tosses, sticky notes, exit quizzes
- Encourage overpractice

Stage 5: Engage in collaborative practice
- Use the strategy together
- Scaffold use of the strategy with graphic organizers, peer evaluations, and self-evaluations
- Have students practice the strategy alone at scaffolded levels of increasing independence
- Provide progress monitoring feedback until criteria are met for each step
- Help students design self-talk to direct themselves through the steps
- Connect strategy-derived successes to strategy use

Stage 6: Ask students to engage in independent practice
- Make self-talk and any strategy applications covert
- Practice and encourage transfer to other settings
- Fade all scaffolds

Figure 6.13 Mnemonic for paragraph writing steps.

Unload all you know in note form.

Note categories and arrange facts into each.

Identify categories in your topic sentence.

Tie detailed sentences together with transitions.

End with an exciting conclusion.

she wrote each sentence in a model paragraph. She then asked students to evaluate the modeled use of the strategy with a specific set of questions:

- Did the writer remember to "unload all I know" and make notes in the margin that listed major ideas?
- Did the writer identify specific categories in the topic sentence?
- What transitions did the writer use?

Next, the teacher asked students to review their initial preassessment paragraph and score it according to a chart similar to the one in Figure 6.14. Out of a total 12 possible points, they each scored fewer than five points.

After students scored their work, they set point goals and specific writing goals, such as, "I will use more effective transition words." They also reflected on the kind of self-talk they used when they were writing, including the talk they used to guide their writing decisions and encourage themselves. The teacher modeled effective self-talk examples, and students used this model to explicitly improve the quality of their own self-talk. They also continuously reflected on how the strategy could help them.

Students memorized the strategy, primarily through using it and reflecting on its daily use but also through activities such as saying a step of the strategy before catching a ball, or writing the steps on sticky notes as they entered class or on exit passes as they left class. Students continued to practice

Figure 6.14 Chart for monitoring paragraph writing.

Assignment:								
Topic sentence (3 points):								
Supporting details (1–3 points):								
Transitions (1–3 points):								
Conclusion (3 points):								
Total (12 points possible):								

12
10
8
6
4

Sample: #1   #2   #3   #4   #5   #6   #7   #8

the strategy as a group, then individually with structured peer feedback and self-feedback on their use of it. At regular intervals, they practiced writing new paragraphs and scoring themselves or having peers score them. This provided progress monitoring data that enabled them to see which elements of a paragraph they were mastering and which they still needed to develop. As a scaffold, the teacher gave lists of transition words to students who struggled with transitions, and she taught strategies for tying sentences together. Eventually, the students used all of the targeted elements independently. The teacher faded all of the scaffolds so that students ultimately used only covert self-talk and subtle notes they wrote to themselves in the margins to support their use of the strategy in other settings. Over several weeks, they mastered all elements and scored the highest possible number of points consistently.

Many of the six steps are typical activities that teachers choose to use in their classroom. The SRSD strategy differs in that it:

- Uses additional unique scaffolds (self-talk coaching and mnemonics)
- Systematically combines elements
- Introduces and then gradually removes scaffolds
- Explicitly fosters self-directedness

Through the six steps, you can focus on building essential writing skills:

- Brainstorming
- Organization
- Elaboration of ideas
- Revising
- Editing

The SRSD strategy organizes the skills in a coherent and comprehensive fashion. This coherency will facilitate classroom planning and help you organize lessons in a time-efficient manner.

The UNITE mnemonic also brings together the steps needed so that students can recall what they need to do. Mnemonics can also provide students with a convenient way to recall all the necessary elements in a story. For younger students, "BME" (beginning, middle, end) may be enough. For narrative writing, "WWWWhat2How2" (Graham & Harris, 1989) helps students recall narrative text elements (who, where, when, what is the goal, what happened, how did it end, how did the character react) and include them in their stories.

Designing Additional Strategies

It can be beneficial to design specific strategies to teach a sequence of steps that students should follow when writing (similar to UNITE). Keep in mind, however, that you should teach only two or three of these sets of strategy steps each year. In addition, the strategy should include a sequence of steps that lead to the problem's solution. Here are our recommendations:

1. The steps should be generalizable, meaning that they should work with all examples.

2. The steps should prompt students to perform an overt action (e.g., write the answer) or use a cognitive or metacognitive technique (e.g., find examples that demonstrate what someone is thinking).

3. The steps should be worded clearly.

4. The steps should be accompanied by a mnemonic device to help students recall them.

5. There should be no more than seven steps.

Essentially, according to Lenz, Ellis, and Scanlon (1996), the steps should use research-validated principles of learning, such as setting goals, activating background knowledge, and self-monitoring work. Steps should be essential and should encompass the entire process; they should not be a loose, non-cohesive collection of suggestions for separate tasks. The checklist that appears in Figure 6.15 is based on the work of Lenz and colleagues (1996). It can be used to evaluate the potential effectiveness of any strategy.

Figure 6.15 Features of an effective strategy.

Content
- Leads to a specific, successful outcome
- Is sequenced so as to facilitate an efficient approach to the task
- Cues students to use specific cognitive and metacognitive strategies
- Cues students to select and use appropriate procedures, skills, or rules
- Cues students to take overt action
- Can be performed in a limited amount of time
- Includes only essential steps or explanations

Design
- Uses a remembering system (i.e., mnemonic)
- Uses brief, simple wording
- Begins with action words
- Accomplishes the sequence in seven or fewer steps
- Uses words that are uncomplicated and familiar to students

Usefulness
- Addresses a common but important problem that students are encountering
- Addresses demands that students are encountering frequently over an extended time
- Can be applied across a variety of settings, situations, and contexts

Interventions for writing can include elements of the SRSD approach if the entire approach does not seem needed. Students can use the goal planning sheet that appears in Figure 6.16 to supplement their writing preassessments. ♀

| Figure 6.16 | Plan to improve writing skills. |

Based on my preassessment, I would like to improve:
The kinds of errors I made were:

_____

_____

_____

My plan to improve is:
Resources:
Websites:
Times I will practice:

My Graph (Number of Elements Correctly Used in My Writing)

20													
15													
10													
5													
(Min)													
Dates:													

Goals and plans can address basic mechanics (organization), basic content, and style. These might include any of the following skills: sentence variety, genre elements, word choice, rules of dialogue, complex sentences, capitalization, punctuation, coordinating conjunctions, paragraphing, spelling, smooth transitions between events, figurative language (metaphors, similes, personification), and vivid adjectives and adverbs. Let's look at an example.

In one classroom, we worked with several students whose assessments showed that they had mastered the basics of writing a simple paragraph. Consequently, we decided to encourage them to move on to writing more complex sentences. To begin, we adapted a rubric to measure usage of complex sentences (see Figure 6.17). We gave more weight to complex sentences than to compound ones, and we gave additional credit for introductory phrases (IP); in-betweens (IB), or parenthetical phrases; and tack-ons (TO) that add punch at the end of a sentence (e.g., "He ran quickly, *thinking he might never make it"*). Then we designed lessons to specifically teach and address these additional pieces.

Figure 6.17   Scoring unit summaries for sentence complexity and variety.

Topic Sentence (_____ /4 points):

1. List the main idea phrase from your topic sentence (TS) here. (1 point)

_____

_____

_____

2. List the three categories from the TS. (TS can be two sentences: main idea and categories.) (1 point)

_____

_____

_____

3. Describe how the categories are listed in a parallel structure (parallel structure means that the topic sentence tells specifically what is coming, and *in the same order* in which each topic is introduced). (1 point)

_____

_____

_____

4. Is my topic sentence smooth, with few grammatical errors, and those only in the kernel (first meaningful chunk of the sentence)? (1 point)

_____

_____

_____

(Continued)

(Continued)

Supporting Details (_____ /18 points):

	Transition word? (1 point)	Relates ideas? (1 point)	Compound? (1 point)	Complex? (2 points)	Introductory phrases, in-betweens, tack-ons? (1 point)
Supporting Detail 1					
Supporting Detail 2					
Supporting Detail 3					

Conclusion (_____ /3 points):

1. Describe how the conclusion restates and wraps up the main idea. (1 point)

_____

_____

_____

2. List the transition words used to introduce the conclusion (and these must be varied from summary to summary, so cannot always be "in conclusion"). (1 point)

_____

_____

_____

3. Describe how your conclusion is spunky and raises an interesting point. (1 point)

_____

_____

_____

To help students improve their sentence variety, we asked them to work on sentence combining (Saddler, 2005). We modeled complex sentences, noted them when we found them in texts we were reading, and then had students craft them. After students wrote their complex sentences, they reviewed them with peers for feedback. They then practiced writing paragraphs with more complex sentences and learned

Figure 6.18 Sentence-combining practice.

Combine each set of short sentences and fragments into one sentence.

1. Bader always orders cheese fries. Bader is not very adventurous. The reason why is because they're his favorite.

2. The tree fell on Kim's house. This was a sycamore. Because of the high winds. Her grandmother wasn't hurt. Casy showed signs of cowardice. Kim did not.

3. Tim's dog's name is George. He is a Golden Retriever. He loves to play Frisbee. He is clumsy. (contrast conjunction needed)

4. Alex's parents have given him a car. That is why he is now carefree. He can stay out later. He does not need to take a subway that runs only at certain times to get home anymore.

Combine each set of sentences into one sentence using the coordinating conjunctions listed below. Use each conjunction only once.

for	and	nor	but	or	yet	so

5. Some students remain on the sidewalks. Zach and Ted cut across the grass.

6. Ted and Kim have to park far from their classrooms. They are often late for class.

7. The administration promised to improve dining hall service. The quality of the food was actually worse this year. Alex was helpful and inventive. He introduced Mel to a new website of recipes.

Combine the same sentences into one sentence using the subordinating conjunctions listed below. Again, use each conjunction only once.

unless	because	even though	while	although	though

8. Some students remain on the sidewalks. Zach and Ted cut across the grass.

9. Ted and Kim have to park far from their classrooms. They are often late for class.

10. The administration promised to improve dining hall service. The quality of the food was actually worse this year. Alex was helpful and inventive. He introduced Mel to a new website of recipes.

how to self-score them. Figure 6.18 shows an example of an activity we assigned to students to provide them with extra practice with sentence combining.

Writing Assessments ♀

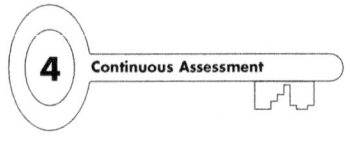

You can assess writing skills in varied genres through collecting writing samples in each genre. You can also ask students to jot down what they know. The key is to design a useful rubric that can guide you and your students in discovering what next steps they will need to take to improve their writing.

You can also use Quick Writes (Mason, Kubina, & Taft, 2009) to assess each student's writing abilities or as a weekly way to monitor the progress of students who show greater difficulties with writing. Ask students to spend 10 minutes drafting an outline and a writing sample. Then ask them to self-score the piece, and also score the piece yourself. Ask students to graph the results and set goals for improvement, independently or with your help.

Supporting students who struggle with mastering various areas of literacy can be one of the more challenging aspects of your work. Using formative assessments like those described in this chapter can enable you to better tailor your instruction to meet their needs. It will also enable you to see whether your teaching is working—and change course if it is not. Remember that students who struggle often have low motivation. Rather than just highlighting deficits, formative assessment can enable these students to see progress that they make. It supports all students in discovering how to learn more effectively.

7 Challenging Students Who Are Gifted or High Achieving

Who shows signs of giftedness or high achievement in class? How can you use formative assessment to tailor lessons that are engaging and appropriately challenging for them? Students who show giftedness and are high achieving will benefit from advanced curricula in English (Van Tassel-Baska & Brown, 2007). When teachers plan challenging lessons, these students will learn.

This chapter discusses how to identify students who show signs of giftedness or high achievement, and it offers research-based practices for differentiating instruction for them. When you teach students at their correct ability level, you will find that they generally gain independence more quickly and exhibit positive classroom behaviors (Rogers, 2007).

Students crave constant intellectual stimulation. Students who show signs of giftedness or high achievement thrive when lessons match their ability, connect to their lives, and cultivate higher-order thinking (Van Tassel-Baska, 2005). Although finding the resources to design and implement these lessons may be challenging initially, you can make small, manageable changes in lessons to help appropriately stimulate these students. This chapter provides detailed examples of enriching, sophisticated, and creative lessons that can challenge and keep students engaged in class. Specifically, it:

- Briefly explains typical classroom behaviors of students who show signs of giftedness or high achievement
- Provides a more in-depth and extensive focus on best instructional practices for using formative assessment to differentiate lessons for higher-achieving students
- Discusses the importance of challenging higher-achieving students
- Highlights strategies to avoid

The chapter wraps up with the teacher assessment quiz that first appeared in Chapter 1.

TYPICAL CLASSROOM BEHAVIORS OF GIFTED OR HIGH-ACHIEVING STUDENTS

Maxi is a seventh-grade student who has been identified as high achieving based on his academic performance and classroom behaviors. Maxi's teacher, Ms. Nakamura, has been an English teacher for the last 17 years in the same school. Maxi's class comprises 22 students with varying academic abilities: Some have a diagnosed learning disability, some are high achieving, and others are advanced English language learners. The following vignette shows what a gifted or high-achieving student might look like and illustrates typical classroom behaviors of these students.

When Ms. Nakamura reviewed Maxi's files at the start of the year, she learned that he usually sat in class, unenthusiastic and unmotivated. If he was not cracking jokes, talking to his peers, or asking inappropriate questions, he was acting as if the lessons bored him or did not matter. However, whenever a teacher called on him, Maxi responded with the correct answer. Past teachers reported that when an activity provided him with exciting choices or sparked his interest, he was full of zest and strived to complete the assignment perfectly. Most of his teachers noted that they enjoyed having him in the class because he asked thought-provoking and enlightening questions when he was focused. Also, he reached mastery fairly quickly on skills learned in class—usually after one or two attempts. However, they also reported that his disruptive or passive behavior was often a challenge to manage.

Using formative assessments, Ms. Nakamura learned that Maxi was a high-achieving student. Based on his academic performance and his classroom behaviors, she concluded that Maxi was a high-achieving learner. As a result, she provided appropriate high-level tiered activities throughout the year that kept him motivated, positive, focused, and learning. ♀

6 | Data-Informed Instruction

Gifted and high-achieving students often outperform their peers academically. However, high academic performance does not indicate giftedness. The gifted student:

- Poses unforeseen questions
- Is curious
- Generates complex, abstract ideas
- Can exhibit opinions from multiple perspectives
- Infers and connects topics well
- Prefers student-directed learning
- Is usually unmotivated by grades (Nova Scotia Department of Education, 2010)

The high-achieving student:

- Remembers the answers
- Is attentive
- Works hard to achieve
- Responds with interest
- Enjoys school
- Comprehends at a high level
- Memorizes well
- Gets *As* (Kingore, 2004)

Although it is important to understand that not all high-achieving students are considered gifted, for our purposes, it is okay not to differentiate between the two, since any student who has reached mastery on a certain objective will benefit from enrichment activities. The important piece is to identify students who will need limited or no practice on a skill and to be able to provide them with instructional activities that challenge them. ❢ Those who exhibit 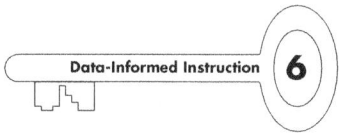 these behaviors will benefit in the differentiated classroom (McGrail, 1998).

In Maxi's case, his preassessment results and classroom behaviors helped Ms. Nakamura better understand him. Based on his ability to grasp information quickly, strong results on formative assessments, and classroom behaviors, Ms. Nakamura thought Maxi could possibly be identified as a high-achieving or gifted child (Figure 7.1).

Based on Figure 7.1, would you consider Maxi high achieving or gifted? His strong academic performance shows his high readiness and ability levels. His thought-provoking questions and desire to explore unknown concepts in depth expose his inquisitive nature and his ability to engage in depth when he decides to do so. Maxi's need to finish assignments perfectly and outshine his peers highlights his motivation and demanding and perfectionistic behaviors. However, when he is not

| Figure 7.1 | | The high-achieving or gifted child. |

Expected Traits	Unexpected Traits	Observations on Preassessment Tasks and Activities
High ability Delightful Inquisitive Creative Engaged Motivated	Demanding Impatient Perfectionistic Sarcastic Disruptive Introverted Bored	High level of mastery on preassessments or Able to reach mastery after limited practice (if preassessments do not indicate mastery)

stimulated or is asked to work on redundant assignments that he has already mastered, his outcries, lack of enthusiasm, jokes, and reluctance to work exemplify the unexpected traits of a gifted child, such as boredom and sarcasm. He does seem to fall into the category of high achieving or gifted.

On a positive note, Maxi's creativity shines through his ability to create sophisticated projects that show mastery of objectives for lessons that are taught in a new way. For example, during an immigration unit, most students wrote a paragraph, created a comic strip, or used a picture as a springboard for a narrative response. However, because Ms. Nakamura recognized that project-based activity fosters creative thinking (Swicord, 2011), she gave students additional options that allowed Maxi to share his family story in a way that he felt was more realistic and relevant (Thomas, 2000). He created a video documentary highlighting his family's story. Because he was offered the chance to cater to his interests in completing the assignment, Maxi was able to elevate the assignment and make his family story come to life. Ms. Nakamura saw many of these creative traits in Maxi regularly and believed that Maxi was not only high achieving but quite possibly gifted.

BEST INSTRUCTIONAL PRACTICES FOR USING FORMATIVE ASSESSMENT TO DIFFERENTIATE LESSONS FOR GIFTED OR HIGHER-ACHIEVING STUDENTS

When planning differentiated lessons for gifted or high-achieving students, you will need to decide on how to enhance your curriculum and the type of instructional practice you want to use (Koga & Hall, n.d.). In general, you can differentiate lessons for the gifted or high-achieving student using the three options highlighted in Figure 7.2. Once you reach a decision, you can create coherent and well-planned lessons using the best instructional practices in gifted education (Robinson, Shore, & Enerson, 2007; see Figure 7.3).

Figure 7.2 Modification options for gifted or high-achieving students.

Lesson Modification	Using tiered activities that are open ended and engage students in higher-order thinking.
Assignment Modification	Providing flexibility in lessons. Allowing students to be exempt from lessons, moving through lessons at a rapid rate, or allowing students to engage in independent projects that extend the curriculum.
Scheduling Modification	Creating groups with a specific purpose. Allowing flexibility of groups so that changes can be made; avoiding random, heterogeneous groups unless the tasks are appropriate.

Source: Roets, L. (1993). *Modifying standard curriculum for high ability students.* New Sharon, IA: Leadership.

Figure 7.3 Best instructional practices in gifted education.

1. Exemptions and curriculum compacting
2. Higher-order thinking activities: questioning and logical reasoning techniques, problem solving, enrichment, and choice activities
3. Independent study
4. Cluster grouping

Source: Robinson, A., Shore, B., & Enerson, D. (2007). *Best practices in gifted education: An evidence-based guide* (p. 166). Waco, TX: Prufrock Press.

As you consider best instructional practices, use formative assessment to guide instruction. ♀ These assessments will help you identify students who would benefit from exemptions or from curriculum compacting. When you make exemptions, be sure to replace already mastered material with higher-order thinking tasks. Allow students opportunities to engage in activities that are appropriate for their instructional level; this will encourage them to exert critical thinking and effort when completing tasks.

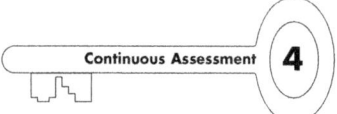

Continuous Assessment **4**

Exemptions

In a differentiated lesson, not all students have to engage in the same activity. For example, in a spelling instruction class, students who have mastered spelling words with a soft *c* should move on to a different spelling objective. You might ask these students to move on to mastering spelling words with the soft *g*, or they could practice correctly spelling words with unfamiliar endings such as *-gion, -gian, -gious, -tion, -sion, -cion, -tian,* or *-cian.* Furthermore, students who do not need any spelling practice could build their vocabulary by using words from certain spelling patterns in context. The following vignette shows how Ms. Nakamura proceeded to exempt Maxi from a spelling lesson when she recognized that he did not need the same direct instruction as his peers.

> *Since Ms. Nakamura recognized that Maxi did not need help spelling words using the pattern that his peers were studying, she asked him to use the words in context in his writing and in oral presentations. Later, she allowed him to develop his own bank of words that used the same patterns she was using with his classmates. When he reached mastery fairly quickly, Ms. Nakamura had an individual conference with him, and they agreed that Maxi would no longer need to practice spelling with his peers for this spelling pattern. Instead, she instructed him to use the class time to find sentences from* Holes *(Sachar, 1998) that grabbed his attention and could be used as examples to improve his own writing. As his peers worked on the spelling pattern, Maxi hunted for complex sentences, interrupters within sentences, sophisticated descriptions, and varied vocabulary. Ms. Nakamura knew this was the first step in helping Maxi to use more sophisticated language structure, language conventions, and figurative language in his own writing (National Council of Teachers of English [NCTE], 2009, Standard 6), and he enjoyed the extra challenge.*

As the vignette shows, your students will thrive when you engage them in activities that are based on the results of formative assessments to promote their individual growth.  When students master objectives, exempt them from completing the regular work assigned to the entire class. Instead, engage them in activities that allow them to reflect on the curriculum and to engage in critical inquiry within it (NCTE, 2009, Standard 4). According to Edwards (2005), critical inquiry that allows students to create something new, novel, or useful is extremely beneficial for students who show giftedness or are high achieving. Of course, critical inquiry is important for all students, but it is particularly essential to promote enthusiasm and motivation for students who show giftedness or are high achieving (Edwards, 2005; Van Tassel-Baska, 2005). Making exemptions and offering new choices and challenges will allow you to differentiate the lessons and reach students who have mastered the objectives.

Students who show giftedness or are high achieving may require fewer repetitions of practice to achieve understanding (Kingore, 2006). Therefore, they should be allowed to use their time to develop other skills or learn something in greater depth. When you identify by formative assessment that students have reached mastery even before instruction has started, exempt them from lessons altogether. In the vignette, the exemptions allowed Maxi to engage in a task that was similar to that of his peers but individualized to his needs.

Students who show giftedness often thrive when you give them the opportunity to learn something in greater depth through research and exploration rather than rote memorization (Van Tassel-Baska, 2005). Frequent formative assessment check-ins will enable you to gauge which students master objectives quickly and can benefit from enrichment tasks. ♀ Remember, you are the most important agent in assessment (NCTE, 2009, Standard 1), and frequent check-ins will help you track students' progress and move them to the next steps.

To appropriately differentiate instruction for this type of student, you will need to be flexible. For instance, you may have to provide extension activities midlesson when it becomes apparent that the student has met mastery. Ideally, you will have predicted this beforehand and will have prepared additional extension activities in advance. ♀ However, at times it will happen unexpectedly. We suggest that you create an extension activity folder for each unit or skill taught and then continue to develop activities specific to students

or to the unit in incremental steps. Or, you can use various resources such as the Internet and teacher guides to help you come up with a bank of ideas for enrichment activities. In due time, you will accumulate ample extension activities that you can use with minor modifications when enrichment activities are needed, depending on the objectives of the lesson and student ability. When you have nothing on hand, it may be beneficial to come up with activities on the spot based on students' affect, comments, and readiness. Alternately, ask the students to come up with an activity that will challenge them.

Standards specify that students should apply their knowledge of language structure and conventions when they discuss texts (NCTE, 2009). Consequently, as Ms. Nakamura regularly created enrichment activities for her class, she frequently concentrated on specific skill-based lessons in grammar, spelling, or writing that would help students communicate effectively with a wide variety of audiences for various purposes (NCTE, 2009). Although activities around some of these skills may be viewed as concrete, simple, or basic, Ms. Nakamura knew that with minor modifications she could develop activities around some of these skills that would enrich even the students who showed giftedness or were high achieving. Here are some of the steps she decided to take:

• She prepared writing prompts connected to real-world events for students to practice vocabulary words in context.

• She designed activities in which students practiced using more sophisticated words with the same complex spelling patterns so that students got both vocabulary and spelling practice from the same activity. For students to use the words in context successfully, they needed to learn their meanings and how they are used in sentences.

• She allowed students to create personalized spelling lists (see Figure 7.4). When the spelling and vocabulary skills were significantly varied among her class, she had the students create individualized spelling lists from context using spelling pattern guidelines.

• She kept a bank of quotes from celebrities, politicians, world leaders, journalists, bloggers, known adults from the school, and past students that her students could evaluate and analyze for grammar instruction. She developed this activity after reading a study that showed that analyzing grammar rants is a fun and productive activity to help students learn the rules of standard English and the direct link between language and communication of meaning (Linblom & Dunn, 2006).

Figure 7.4   Sample enrichment/extension activities for spelling.

Activity 1:

Word Bank

addition magician confusion connection caution section adaptation migration compassion condition introduction graduation discussion direction suggestion precaution mansion fusion reaction

Circle the unknown words and define the identified words using context or a reference book. Create a short story using at least four of the words you have circled, plus at least four other words from the word bank. The words should be spelled correctly and used correctly in context.

Activity 2:

Look for words that end with the suffix *-tion*, *-tian*, *-cian*, or *-sion*. Create a personal list consisting of three words in each category. Afterward, define each word and correctly use it in a sentence, phrase, or multi-sentence response to help define the word. After you have finished the entire activity, be a detective and try to discover the meaning of each of the suffixes.

Activity 3:

Decide which suffix to add to the following base words. Use resources to find out how to correctly spell the word with the added suffix. You will either have to drop letter(s) or add letter(s) to the base word to add the suffix. Identify the change you will have to make and then find another base word that would require a similar change.

Base word	Change to be made to base word	*-tion* or *-sion*	Rule	Other words
Alter				
Expand				
Participate				
Include				
Demonstrate				

Activity 4:

At the end of the novel *Holes* (Sachar, 1998), the warden is forced to sell Camp Green Lake to the state government, which turns the camp into a Girl Scout camp. Discuss the irony in this situation by doing one of the following activities:

1. Writing a blog post about the turn of events for a popular online newspaper.

2. Creating a newsletter by the Girl Scout organization on the acquisition of their new camp.

3. Writing a series of letters between Clyde Livingston and the Yelnats and Zeroni families.

Your response should include at least five words that fall into the spelling pattern you have been given and should be used correctly in context: _____.*

*The spelling pattern can be teacher directed, student directed, or teacher and student directed, as long as it works on a spelling skill the student needs.

Curriculum Compacting

One method for exempting students from regular practice is through curriculum compacting (Winebrenner, 2009). In this method, you literally compact assignments for units. When a formative assessment reveals that a student has reached mastery of certain objectives, you remove or shorten

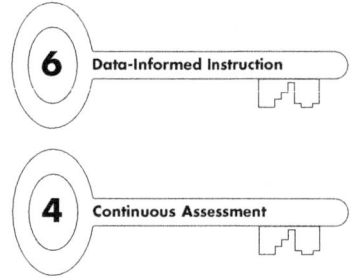

activities that practice those objectives. ♀ This grants the student more time to work on other, more stimulating content.

To compact lessons, you can follow three steps:

1. *Accurately identify the students who will benefit from compacting lessons.* Some students can appear to understand the concept yet may not master it until they practice it sufficiently. ♀ ♀

2. *Create a plan that discusses the activity and time frame for the exemptions and the alternative work that the student will do.* The plan should clearly list the activities so that the student can distinguish the regular activities from the extensions on the plan.

3. *Work with students to plan less structured and more open-ended independent activities that may relate to the real world and help answer a question.* This option will require you to form a partnership with your student as you create the plan (McGrail, 1998). ♀

For example, Ms. Nakamura planned a writing unit that emphasized sentence variety because she knew that students would improve specific writing skills if she gave them the opportunity to manipulate sentences while practicing those skills (Daiker, Kerek, & Morenberg, 1990). ♀ Before the lesson, she planned out the objective she wanted the students to master: the ability to identify, create, and comfortably use sophisticated sentences that began with adjectives, adverbs, and verbs. She designed a fair preassessment (NCTE, 2009, Standard 6) to identify her students' current knowledge of parts of speech and their ability to create these sentences without instruction (see Figure 7.5). ♀

To compare the preassessment data with her objectives, Ms. Nakamura looked at her existing plan for the class to review prepositions and prepositional phrases using the novel they were reading. She wanted the students to learn to introduce sentence starters for sentence variety (see Figure 7.6).

The preassessment data indicated that two students would benefit from curriculum compacting. Erin demonstrated mastery in correctly identifying nouns, adjectives, and adverbs in context. Samir not only mastered identifying the parts of speech, but he also used prepositions and prepositional phrases successfully. Further, he had mastered the other

Figure 7.5 Preassessment for sentence variety.

1. Identify the part of speech above each italicized word.
   a. The *tall* and lean *lifeguards cautioned* the kids to play around the *pool carefully.*
   b. She *was* acting *mysteriously* when her *calm* mother patiently asked her about the *crack.*
   c. *Running* to the door, the *excited* boys *screamed* with joy because they were at *Grandma's* house.
2. Circle the varied sentence in Activity 1. Explain your reasoning.
3. Change the simple sentences into complex sentences that use sentence variety.
   a. The girl anxiously took her test.
   b. The children were filled with excitement to open their gifts on Christmas morning.
   c. The old and decrepit house was abandoned.
   d. Alicia walked around the room in her bright blue, elegant dress with confidence.

Figure 7.6 Sentence starters for sentence variety.

1. Sentences starting with verbs (*-ing* and *-ed*):
   Running to the gate, Marigold was anxious not to miss her flight.
   Angered by the conflict, Hassem kept his mouth shut.
2. Sentences starting with adverbs:
   Joyously, Angel told her parents about her perfect attendance award.
3. Sentences starting with two or more adjectives:
   Stern and rigid, Ms. Moore was the math teacher feared by all.
4. Sentences starting with prepositional phrases:
   Before dinner, Mr. Shah put the pictures of his beloved grandmother back in his safe place.

three types of sentence variety in his own writing. Therefore, Ms. Nakamura decided to compact the curriculum for both students using similar unit plans (see Figure 7.7). ♀

Data-Informed Instruction **6**

Figure 7.7 Unit plans resulting from curriculum compacting.

Erin	Samir
1. Skip review of adjectives, adverbs, and nouns. Introduce prepositions and prepositional phrases: Create a word bank of prepositions, learn how to use them in sentences, identify sentences with prepositional phrases (especially those at the beginning of the sentence), create sentences with prepositional phrases.	1. Continue to practice the three other types of sentence variety.
2. Introduce and practice the four types of sentences: Identify sentences both in context (novels) and out of context (teacher-provided sheet of sentences), create sentences out of context, peer-edit created sentences to make sure they are correctly punctuated and logical.	2. Application of the four types of sentence variety (Part 1): Use the four types of sentences in short pieces of creative writing.
3. Application of four types of sentences (Part 1): Use the four types of sentences in short pieces of creative writing.	3. Application of four types of sentences (Part 2): Use the four types of sentences in an already written piece for both English and another class, such as history or science (for one piece only).
4. Application of four types of sentences (Part 2): Use the four types of sentences in an already written piece for both English and another class, such as history or science.	4. Other complex sentences: Sentences with dependent clauses used with correct punctuation, sentences with semicolons.
5. Other complex sentences: Learn other complex or compound sentence structures (choose the most applicable for the student): compound sentences with coordinating conjunctions (*for, and, nor, but, or, yet, so*), complex sentences that are balanced, sentences with dependent clauses used with correct punctuation, sentences with semicolons.	5. History/English research project: Pick a topic based on something Samir is learning in history. After researching the topic in full, write a historical fiction piece using sentence variety and other complex sentences.

*For both Erin and Samir, Ms. Nakamura eliminated the review of parts of speech.

Ms. Nakamura checked on Erin and Samir regularly to make sure that they were engaged. Then she moved them to the next step whenever they met mastery. Since Samir was more advanced than Erin, his plan included a real-world research project that asked him to use the writing skills to create a historical fiction piece. This research project also met Common Core State Standards on research and writing (Common Core State Standards Initiative, n.d.), which help students to build and present knowledge for all grades in middle school.

As you compact the curriculum, you will find that students will be at all different stages. Therefore, you should keep detailed and organized charts like the one in Figure 7.8 to correctly identify the activities students are completing. You will find that the initial time investment needed to create such a chart is well worth the payoff when you can easily focus on the listed criteria and allocate work more effectively. To make the charts efficient to use, limit entries to a few necessary criteria or criteria that are easy and quick to fill in with a few words.

Figure 7.8 Chart for tracking curriculum compacting.

Student Name	Activity	Date of Completion	Activity	Date of Completion	Activity	Date of Completion
Maxi	Spelling using irregular words, Sets 2 and 3	10/15	Independent spelling list of words with four syllables			
Lilac	Spelling using irregular words, Set 2	10/14	Spelling using irregular words, Set 3			

You may also find that you need more impromptu, simplified strategies to help facilitate activities at the differing stages of the students. Keep a folder for each of your classes in a central location, with a personalized page for each student. Walk around the classroom with a pen and sticky notes and jot down each student's progression. Note what activity each student is on and what progress has been made. Then ask the student to place the sticky note on the personalized page in the folder. This ensures that all sticky notes end up in one central location.

Higher-Order Thinking Activities

Use results from formative assessments and instructional practice to help you decide which students will benefit from—and should have time for—higher-order thinking tasks, including critical inquiry in the curriculum (NCTE, 2009, Standard 4). ⚲ When you compact

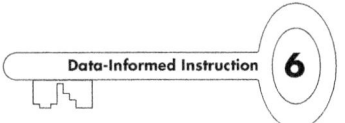

Data-Informed Instruction 6

the curriculum, you naturally build more time in class for students to work on tasks that are more challenging. Since higher-order thinking tasks usually have more than one correct answer, they:

- Engage students in critical and inquisitive thinking
- Ask students to apply, evaluate, and analyze information
- Challenge students who show giftedness or are high achieving because they foster problem solving, questioning, and challenging one's own ideas

Many students who are high achieving think they must know all the answers (Delisle & Galbraith, 2002). This common misconception escalates when we reward students for the correct answer and not for the process of thinking that comes with deriving the right answer. This false belief can create a feeling of personal failure, self-doubt, and distress, especially when these students do encounter failure or difficulty (Cross, 2002). Often, these same students are bored because they have not been challenged appropriately in their classrooms; many are even labeled as "slackers." It is important for you to address these perceptions. These students must learn that the process of tackling a challenging task is more important than identifying the actual correct answer. Students who show giftedness for creating quality work and performing at a high level must be able to learn, practice, and refine raw abilities (Gagné, 2003) such as thinking and questioning. Of course, all students will think, wonder, and question when coming up with an answer to an assignment; however, when the assignment is at the appropriate level for the student to exert effort in thinking, questioning, and wondering, then the student's engagement can grow. The latter practices are the best for all students to engage in.

As you work to create higher-order thinking activities in the English classroom, you will find that Bloom's Taxonomy (Bloom & Krathwohl, 1956) provides a useful framework, since the skills are organized from the least to the most cognitively demanding. The chart in Figure 7.9 shows both the old and new versions; the new version (Anderson & Krathwohl, 2001) may be more student friendly, since it uses verbs, or actions, to describe the skills. As you create activities for students who show giftedness or are high achieving, emphasize the last four skills on this chart. These skills align with the higher-order thinking tasks that these students should engage in. ♀

For example, let us say you are working with a group of students who have read the novel *Keeping Corner* by Kashmira Sheth (2007). You can ask students to complete any one of the activities detailed in Figure 7.10, at their

| Figure 7.9 | Aligning Bloom's Taxonomy with higher-order thinking tasks. |

Old Version	New Version
Knowledge	Remembering
Comprehension	Understanding
Application	Applying
Analysis	Analyzing
Synthesis	Evaluating
Evaluation	Creating

appropriate instructional level. In the figure, an activity for knowledge/remembering and comprehension/understanding is provided for comparative purposes.

| Figure 7.10 | Activities for *Keeping Corner* using Bloom's Taxonomy. |

Knowledge or Remembering	Define what it means when Leela is required to "keep corner."
Comprehension or Understanding	Summarize the conflict between Kanubhai and Bapuji (Leela's father).
Application or Applying	Classify typical expressions that Kanubhai, Kaki, Masi, Jaya, and Ba would have with Leela.
Analysis or Analyzing	Analyze how Leela's education helped to change Ba's (her mother's) traditional views.
Synthesis or Evaluating	Compose a poem that Leela would write to widows about her new life in Ahemdabad.
Evaluation or Creating	Judge what Masi's greatest flaw was and explain why it was appropriate for Masi to act the way she did.

You will likely find that some students need more than these types of enrichments. Gifted or high-achieving students learn in qualitatively different ways than their peers and need more than just harder and more advanced work. You must also be cautious about providing "harder" work that may not be matched to the specific differences in how these students think, and you should take steps to ensure that students do not perceive the work as "additional work" or "extra credit." Do not burden them with extra work simply because they finish the classwork early. Rather, as we have emphasized, give students opportunities to engage in higher-order thinking in activities that facilitate questioning, logical reasoning, and problem solving as well as other enrichment activities.

For example, in one classroom we worked with students who had read *Hatchet* by Gary Paulsen (2006). As a culminating activity, we decided to ask them to create a survival book based on the novel. We recognized that this assignment would allow them to synthesize and organize information, draw conclusions, and closely reexamine the book for survival tips. It would also enable them to practice writing skills.

At the same time, we wanted to provide ways to support the students who showed giftedness or were high achieving. We decided to ask those students to take the information from *Hatchet* to create a real-life survival book about a scenario that they might encounter in their own life. In response, some of the students, who were living in an earthquake zone, chose to read fiction and nonfiction work about the topic and then create a survival book.

This enhanced assignment allowed students to practice the same skills of comprehension and write at a more sophisticated level. In this context, the students solved relevant problems they chose themselves and showed their learning through a project. They also communicated information in a different genre, thus practicing adjusting their written language to serve a specific informative or explanatory purpose (NCTE, 2009, Standard 4; Common Core State Standards Initiative, n.d., W.5/6/7/8.2). The students who benefited from more than higher-order thinking tasks performed better because we allowed them to use a project-based approach (Grant & Branch, 2005).

Questioning

One form of higher-order thinking activities is questioning. There are two ways students can engage in questioning:

1. Answering questions through a discussion or written activity

2. Deriving questions from a discussion or written activity

Questioning increases students' literacy level and develops their higher-order thinking skills (Dantonio & Paradise, 1988; Taylor, Pearson, Clark, & Walpole, 2000). Further, authentic questioning used in the context of academically challenging tasks helps students improve their reading comprehension and literature achievement (Nystrand, Wu, Gamoran, Zeiser, & Long, 2003). Any activities that allow for questioning throughout the process can help students engage more actively in the assignment. When you ask students the right questions, you support critical thinking, which encourages students to become problem solvers and sparks their enthusiasm and interest (Hannel & Hannel, 2005). Through questioning, you can help students connect to the activity, critically analyze the content, and activate their creativity. Let us take a look at how this worked in Ms. Nakamura's classroom.

> *Tia, one of Ms. Nakamura's students, showed giftedness and demonstrated mastery on comprehension assessments. When the class worked on follow-up activities as part of a novel study on* A Wrinkle in Time *by Madeleine L'Engle (1973), Ms. Nakamura recognized that Tia's skills went beyond the typical comprehension activities of posing questions, making predictions, inferring, and making connections (National Institute of Child Health and Human Development, 2000; Nokes & Dole, 2004). To ensure in-depth analysis, Ms. Nakamura asked Tia to focus closely on the details of one character, IT. Using sticky notes, Tia posed questions that the character IT would ask throughout the series of events in the novel. Her task was to creatively answer the question, "Was the antagonist wrong in his actions?" Further, Ms. Nakamura asked Tia to compare the book to the movie. This tied in with the Common Core State Standard R.L. 7.7 (Common Core State Standards Initiative, n.d.), which asks students to analyze the similarities and differences between a written story and its filmed version.*

When you ask students who show giftedness or are high achieving to work on questions around moral dilemmas, you:

- Help them connect to the books
- Bolster their motivation and interest
- Add richer context, which may help them to see real-world implications more readily
- Help them determine the theme or central idea of the text
- Allow them to critically examine particular elements of a story (Common Core State Standards Initiative, n.d., R.L. 6/7/8.2, R.L. 6/7/8.3)

To answer questions around moral dilemmas, students must analyze, synthesize, and evaluate the information presented and come up with an abstract conclusion—one that cannot be readily defined as correct or incorrect.

Research shows that when students express their perspectives through discussion, they not only shape discourse but also build in-depth comprehension (Nystrand, 2006). Let us say that your gifted and high-achieving students are reading the story *Taking Sides* by Gary Soto (2003) and working on moral dilemmas. You can ask them to justify whether Lincoln Mendoza's actions were ethical at the final basketball game between his new school in the affluent town of Sycamore and his old school in the barrio of San Francisco. To facilitate your students' decision making, ask them to complete a T-chart like the one that appears in Figure 7.11. This challenging activity promotes the thinking process and elicits creativity, analysis, and logical deduction—all of which are integral and sophisticated areas of practice.

Figure 7.11   T-chart on Lincoln Mendoza's actions.

Using your book, find examples of Lincoln Mendoza's actions or thoughts about both his new town and life and his old town and life. Write the events and facts in note form, and be sure to include the page number. Afterward, take a stance on his actions and use complete sentences to justify whether you think his actions or thoughts were right. Keep in mind that you will have to defend your response to your group.

Lincoln Mendoza's Actions or Thoughts	Personal Justification

As you create questioning tasks, provide students with the opportunity to answer higher-order questions and create their own. They can create questions:

- In response to literature
- Before literature is read as an anticipatory guide
- In response to or for discussion
- To help promote project-based, inquiry-based, or problem-based assignments

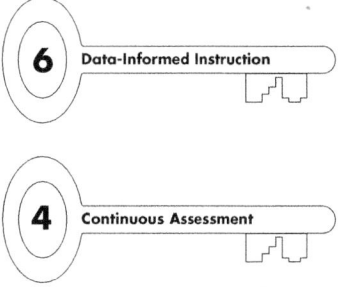

Use formative assessment as a tool to help you regularly promote inquiry through questioning for all students. Lessons that pose questions are the most effective, so you should ensure that all students, regardless of giftedness or high achievement attributes, engage in some type of higher-order thinking questions that promote deep learning and provide opportunities for multiple correct responses (Taylor, Pearson, Peterson, & Rodriguez, 2003).

Logical Reasoning

Logical reasoning is a skill that students engage in when answering questions and completing other higher-order thinking tasks. Logical reasoning requires students not only to comprehend information but also to apply, analyze, synthesize, and evaluate the information through various lenses. It encourages students to understand, interpret, and justify information using deduction.

Activities that employ logical reasoning can be written or oral. Many students who show giftedness or are high achieving are verbally advanced as well (Kingore, 2006; Van Tassel-Baska, 2003). One way to cultivate this skill in depth is to pose activities where students use logic, reason, and proof to defend or refute their answers. Their responses may include an additional oral component that asks them to present their logical reasoning in a different way. According to standards, students should practice speaking and listening skills because this helps them to present claims; organize their information using logical, accurate, and relevant descriptions; and use appropriate eye contact, tone, and pacing (Common Core State Standards Initiative, n.d., S.L. 5/6/7/8.4).

You can create the following types of activities to help students strengthen their verbal skills:

- Storytellings
- Factual presentations
- Monologues
- Debates
- Poetry
- Lyrics
- Advertisements
- Video blogs
- Journalistic reporting

For example, when we worked with seventh-grade students who showed giftedness or were high achieving, we asked them to write a scientific report after reading the novel *Never Cry Wolf* by Farley Mowat (2001). Specifically, we asked them to highlight Mowat's differing opinions about the "savage and wild" wolves using facts, evidence, and logic to support his claim that wolves are not dangerous creatures and have many humanlike qualities (see Figure 7.12).

To further facilitate students' advanced verbal skills, we had them create a presentation that Mowat might give to a group of scientists at a conference or a speech he might give at a press conference, using his data to support his points. This type of activity helps students make a more authentic connection between logical reasoning and the task. In the future, we might even collaborate with the science teacher to create a more authentic lesson. For example, students could conduct a modified experiment in science class based on a scientific question they had from the novel and then use the appropriate science lab format to complete the activity.

Figure 7.12	Scientific report format.

Title:

Date:

Purpose:

Materials:

Hypothesis:

Procedure:

Data (including tables and charts):

Results:

Conclusions:

References:

Problem Solving

When you allow students to engage in problem solving tasks that call for induction, intuition, and encountering new situations, you help them tap into higher-order thinking skills (Archambault et al., 1993; National Council for Curriculum and Assessment, 2006). For example, you can ask students who show giftedness to rewrite a descriptive portion of their story or of a published story without using adjectives and adverbs from a "Do not use" list. The list can restrict students from using the most readily used words and other frequently used sophisticated words. Or, you can individualize the lists and ask students not to use words that each of them uses regularly (see Figure 7.13). The students can then go on "word hunts" around the school, interviewing people for words or using the dictionary, thesaurus, and Internet to build a new word bank before they write (see Figure 7.14).

Figure 7.13 Personalized restricted word lists.

Look at the last five written assignments in your portfolio. Circle any adjectives or adverbs that you have used at least three times in any of the last five pieces of work. Write those words on this "Do not use" list. When completing your next descriptive writing piece, do not use any of these words.

Figure 7.14 Personalized word bank.

Use a dictionary, computer, or thesaurus, or walk around the school interviewing people and surveying signs, for rich and vivid words that you have not used in your writing but would like to use. Make a list below. After you are done, circle at least five words that you commit to using in your next descriptive writing assignment.

Problem solving activities allow students to produce inventive and revolutionary ideas. Furthermore, they ask students to tolerate a high degree of ambiguity. These factors drive gifted students (Johnsen, 2004). When you teach word study lessons, ask gifted and high-achieving students to complete a variety of analogies in various topics (see Figure 7.15). This process will tap into and strengthen their problem solving and logical reasoning skills.

We recommend the activity in Figure 7.16 for gifted students since it explores word definitions and various relationships (Van Tassel-Baska, 2003). It allows students to infer, deduce, and use reason as they develop a more sophisticated vocabulary. When you create vocabulary activities that incorporate analogies, you can select vocabulary words from novels being studied, words students are interested in, and words from real-life situations.

Figure 7.15 Types of analogies.

Synonyms—smart : intelligent :: sly : sneaky

Antonyms—dishonest : honest :: always : never

Part : whole—pencil : lead :: coconut : milk

Numerical—½ : 1 :: 5 : 10

Cause : effect—earthquake : tsunami :: heavy rains : flood

Person : situation—paleontologist : museum :: doctor : clinic

Geography—Manhattan : United States :: Mykonos : Greece

Measurement—pound : kilogram :: quart : liter

Time—winter : January :: spring : March

Although we provide some specific activities here, plan to take steps to explore additional inquiry-based learning lessons with students who show giftedness and are high achieving (Van Tassel-Baska & Brown, 2007). For instance, students can pose questions about problems or conflicts related to objectives in their lessons and seek to find the answers through research and exploration. Once they have found an acceptable response, they can create a project that illustrates and explains their response and rationale. This is a more holistic lesson that will involve students' planning and require a significant amount of time. Consequently, this type of lesson is recommended for students who have mastered the objectives early on and have the opportunity to invest an appropriate amount of time in completing the project.

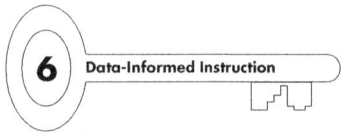
6 Data-Informed Instruction

Enrichment Activities and Resources

Any supplemental or developed activity for the student who shows giftedness and is high achieving can fall under the enrichment activity section. However, it is important to note that these activities are a necessity—not an enrichment—for these students. These activities enrich and extend the set classroom objectives, so they provide gifted and high-achieving students an opportunity to be challenged and learn something new. Enrichment activities can thus be thought of as extension activities in terms of the learning that will occur. The one difference between enrichment and extension activities is that students may need more time to complete an enrichment activity because it may involve multiple steps, projects, group discussion, and inquiry. Many of these activities help address

Figure 7.16 Create your own analogies.

Create five analogies using any of the words from the word bank. Be sure to clearly label the type of analogy you have created.

Word Bank:

vital (13) impression (14) veranda (12) frock (8) gaudy (14) heaps (14) satchel (13) chattels (14) placard (3) ardent (5) helter-skelter (14) blithely (5) Zionist (9) speculation (5) loathe (18) ardent (5)

Analogy	Type
Example: collar : frock :: buckle : belt	Part : whole

the NCTE and Common Core State standards that ask students to conduct research on issues and interests by generating ideas and questions and by posting problems.

Ultimately, when you design and evaluate enrichment activities and resources, keep the following traits in mind: ⚲

Data-Informed Instruction 6

- Does it *open out* the task and/or allow for *multiple solutions*?
- Does it tap into *abstract thinking* capabilities?
- Does it allow for *choice*?
- Does it allow for *divergent thinking*?
- Does it enable students the ability to *invent or design* something novel?
- Does it allow *flexibility in reasoning*?
- Does it allow students to *research* or think in greater depth about a topic or about the process?
- Does it allow students to *contribute to designing the task*?
- Does it help the student see *real-world applications*?
- Is it *inquiry based, project based,* or *problem based* (see Figure 7.17)?

Figure 7.17 Learning approaches.

Inquiry-Based Learning	A student-centered, active learning approach that focuses on questioning, critical thinking, and problem solving.
Project-Based Learning	An approach where students explore real-world challenges and problems and work in small groups to develop cross-curricular skills.
Problem-Based Learning	An approach where students develop skills and learn through the process of solving a problem. This approach can be thought of as inquiry-based learning when students have the opportunity to decide on the problem they will work on or solve.

Although there are many activities you can consider for each trait, the list in Figure 7.18 provides some examples. Each trait is grounded in research, has overlapping elements of higher-order thinking skills (questioning, logical reasoning, problem solving), and has been discussed in this chapter. ♀ You can regularly use formative assessment to accurately identify the types of enrichment students would best benefit from. Good lessons will use a combination of traits. Throughout the year, you can tap into these traits in different activities.

6 Data-Informed Instruction

As mentioned, you can keep folders with activities on hand for unexpected times when students are ready to move on. However, these should not be random, extraneous activities. Relevant and beneficial activities will have an overall parallel with the scope and sequence of the year and of the skills needed by students who show giftedness or are high achieving. You can also provide instant enrichment activities by asking students who have completed their work to answer questions that make them think differently about the assignment they are completing. You will find it beneficial to create a bank of these activities, organized by specific skills. ♀ Some skills to consider are reading, comprehension, writing, rewriting, spelling, and speaking, as all of these would address the NCTE and Common Core State Standards.

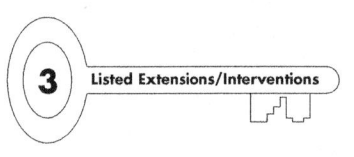
3 Listed Extensions/Interventions

We have also mentioned that students who show giftedness and are high achieving benefit from the opportunity of choice when completing enrichment activities (Smutny, 2000; Westberg, 1995). For instance, to provide students with choices for practicing comprehension, reading, and writing strategies, you could post on the board a menu of activities that take a variety of times to complete (see Figure 7.19). ♀

Figure 7.18 Examples of enrichment activity traits.

Enrichment Activity Traits	Examples
Multiple Solutions	**Nonfiction/Informational Unit:** Create an information brochure, documentary, podcast, flyer, or article about a societal issue that is important to you. Your work should inform the reader about the key facts, issues, and ways to help.
Abstract Thinking	**Poetry:** Create a poem emulating the style of *r-p-o-p-h-e-s-s-a-g-r* by E.E. Cummings.
Choice	**Shakespeare:** Choose from one of the following activities. 1. Create a soundtrack for *Romeo and Juliet* (Shakespeare, 1597/1992). Explain your rationale for each song selection. 2. Create a cast list for a new movie of the play. 3. Write a plot for the modern-day play.
Divergent Thinking	**Vocabulary Study:** Create a list of unfamiliar words from the novel you are reading. Commit to using at least three of them in your next short writing assignment.
Invent or Design	**Autobiography:** Create an autobiography.
Research	**Historical Fiction:** Research a time that interests you. Take some events and create a historical short story. Be sure the story includes vivid setting details to show the time frame.
Contribute to Designing the Task	**Writing:** Based on close inspection of writing samples, preassessments, and a conference with the teacher, create a list of skills you would like to work on in your writing.
Real-World Application	**Presentation Skills/Novel Study/Group Work:** Give an overview of the novel you read in literature circles, highlighting the main characters, conflict, and resolution. Discuss two major themes and give an appropriate review of the book. Your main goal is to keep the audience interested, highlight the book, and work in groups appropriately.
Inquiry-Based Learning	**Essay Writing/Theme study:** Create an essay question based on a theme you are interested in writing about from the novel you are reading. Write a five-paragraph essay to engage in the writing process.
Project-Based Learning	**Greek Mythology**: Using information from the book *Heroes, Gods and Monsters of the Greek Myths* (Evslin, 1984), work with your group to create a board game that introduces young children to the different gods and goddesses, their mythical powers, and their connections with other gods and goddesses.
Problem-Based Learning	**Anthology:** Take a stance on a problem that is present today in your community. Research the various viewpoints, decide on your position, and create an anthology that will explain your viewpoint. Your anthology should contain self-created literary work. You can create poems, newsletters, documentaries, articles, flyers, maps, charts, etc. Consider using multimedia tools as well.

| Figure 7.19 | Sample of general and specific comprehension, reading, and writing activities. |

Comprehension

- Read or reread the passage and engage in predicting, inferring, synthesizing, or connecting by answering an open-ended question. (See chart posted on wall.)
- Use art to interpret the major themes in this chapter. Art can be in the form of words, images, drawings, photographs, poetry, etc. Be sure to explain the links and provide evidence from the novel to connect with the art.
- Take an excerpt from a play and decide what background music would be appropriate for it. Create a movie with the words from the play and the music.
- Research periods in which a novel or play took place by reading nonfiction resources. Create a live diorama modeling a scene from the story or play that takes the historical information into account.

Reading

- Find a professional journal article on the topic or theme from the novel or nonfiction book and read the article. Note words that you don't understand and use the context and any other resources to understand at least two-thirds of the article. Jot down strategies that you used to read the difficult text.
- Change a dramatic reading into a comedy.

Writing

- Write the same setting from the story or event from someone else's perspective.
- Write out two themes you have observed in the book with specific examples. (See example posted on wall.)
- Practice voice by writing a personal narrative, and then collect an oral history and write a narrative of the oral history in the voice of the person who gave it.

At the same time, post lists and examples like the ones shown in Figures 7.20 and 7.21.

You can also use these types of immediate extensions—and other activities like completing sentence combining (Graham & Perin, 2007; Saddler, Behforooz, & Asaro, 2008) and analogy activities (Castillo, 1998; Van Tassel-Baska, 2003)—as supplemental tasks that students can work on when they announce, "I'm done." Guide the students to consult the menu of extension activities whenever they complete their work.

Figure 7.20 Open-ended questions for comprehension strategies.

Predicting: Based on the initial interaction between Moon Shadow and Ms. Whitlaw in the novel *Dragonwings* by Laurence Yep (1977), predict the relationship they will have. Create a scene and script that highlights that relationship.

Inferring: Pick a character from Chapter 4 of *Animal Farm* (Orwell, 1945/1996). Based on his actions and comments, infer his mood, personality, and thoughts. Support your rationale with evidence from the novel.

Synthesizing: Pick out the most important parts of Scene 2 of *Romeo and Juliet* (Shakespeare, 1597/1992) that affect the ending of the play.

Connecting: How would Holden from *Catcher in the Rye* (Salinger, 2001) react to the recent stock market crash? Write an inner monologue in his voice. Afterward, think about how you reacted to the market. Write your inner monologue. How do the monologues compare?

Figure 7.21 Writing activity demonstrating themes.

There are many themes observed in *Flowers for Algernon* by Daniel Keyes (1987). Choose two themes and write two examples, one to demonstrate each theme (see example in the following chart).

Theme	Example from *Flowers for Algernon* (Keyes, 1987)
Prejudice	Charlie, a man with developmental disabilities, has an IQ of 68. His coworkers at Donner's Bakery consistently taunt and tease him for his actions and behaviors. Unfortunately, due to his low IQ, Charlie is unable to understand their behaviors and thinks that the coworkers are his friends, which promotes further cruel treatment.
Identity	After Charlie's operation, he becomes more intelligent. One day when he is at the bakery, he realizes that one of the employees is stealing. He is conflicted and does not know what to do. Alice, his teacher at the community college, tells him to trust his heart. When prompted to do so, he realizes that he can, and is overjoyed that he is able to solve these types of ethical and moral dilemmas. He believes he is far different from the man he used to be before he got his surgery, and he is overjoyed by this fact. His desire to be smart has come true, and he is really enjoying who he is at this time. As a result, Charlie confronts the employee and forces him to stop stealing. Shortly thereafter, he is fired from the bakery because the coworkers can't handle the drastic change. This forces him to have flashbacks of himself presurgery and causes him to panic about his old self. He is conflicted overall about who he is now and who he was then.

Independent Study

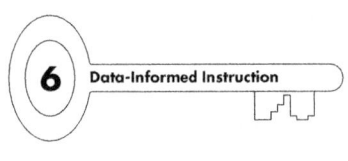

When a student's preassessment indicates substantial mastery of an objective, 🔑 you may have to create an altogether new unit for that student. Independent studies can help students build their skills as they find interest and challenge in the content. You can connect the projects in the unit to objectives the class is learning in one of two ways:

- By genre or skill (e.g., if the rest of the class is writing, the gifted student should be writing as well)
- Through content or subskill (e.g., descriptive writing, analytical writing, or first-perspective writing).

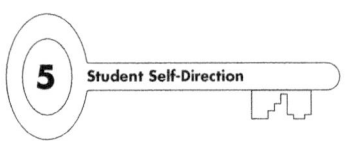

Once you and the student have agreed on a project, meet to discuss the details while other students complete independent work or practice skill building activities. 🔑 Work with the student to establish times when he or she will consult with you to track progress (via e-mail, Google Docs, or spontaneous check-ins during class). You will also want to use a learning contract to capture the guidelines and due dates of the independent study (see Figure 7.22). Students who show giftedness and are high achieving usually prefer to structure their own tasks and set their own deadlines, and they tend to learn more when they are allowed to set their own pace (Dunn, Dunn, & Price, 1984; Whitener, 1989).

There are many types of learning contracts. Be sure to use one that lists the following:

- Activity
- Anticipated objectives (Stanley, 2012)
- Action plan
- Deadline dates
- Criteria for evaluation

Although the learning contracts should be clear, limit the details. Too much information may prohibit flexibility, especially when the student is applying the learned information to the process and product. Rigidity may hamper the creative approach, flow of learning and level of engagement (Csikszentmihalyi, 1990), logical reasoning, and questioning, which may affect learning outcomes. The best learning contracts are those that you and your student either create together or mutually accept (Stanley, 2012).

Figure 7.22 Sample learning contract.

Topic _____

I have decided to create _____

Options: anthology, report, podcast, 3-D model, short story, poem, dramatic presentation, presentation with technology

I have chosen this way to create my project because _____

_____

My action plan with due dates:	
Procedure	**Due Date**

Final due date of project: _____

The rubric or grading criteria used to assess this project will be _____

(Attach the rubric to the plan, and write a brief summary in the box.)

Student Signature _____Date_____

Teacher Signature _____Date_____

Cluster Grouping

Cluster grouping occurs when you group students based on abilities around specific assignments. These groups are purposefully planned based on academic performance and formative assessment but remain flexible. Cluster grouping provides students with the opportunity to engage in intellectually stimulating conversations, challenges, and tasks at an appropriately advanced level with equally capable learners, thus possibly increasing academic outcome (Brulles, Cohn, & Saunders, 2010; Gentry & Kielty, 2001). Based on this evidence, cluster grouping can be beneficial for all ability groups. When you use cluster grouping in your classroom, students' achievement levels consistently grow and you develop a realistic level of achievement for your students (Gentry, 1999).

In fact, Gentry found that in regular education classrooms where cluster grouping occurred, more students were identified as high-achieving students after three years. Furthermore, Gentry's research showed that cluster grouping benefits not only the teachers and students in the classroom but the entire school ethos in the following ways:

- Creates opportunities for staff development, emphasizing a variety of instructional strategies
- Raises teacher expectations
- Creates a sense of ownership
- Reduces the range of achievement levels in classrooms
- Creates opportunities for collaboration with colleagues and administration

When you use cluster grouping, you will find differentiating instruction within the whole class even easier (Van Tassel-Baska, 2005). ♀ Specifically, when you group students with equally capable peers, you can easily:

6 Data-Informed Instruction

- Differentiate reading materials
- Modify depth of inquiry or types of assignments
- Teach mini lessons

For example, you can use cluster grouping to create groups when students are discussing novels in literature circles. Students who need support can work with others who receive support, and those who benefit from a challenge will have those opportunities as well. One of the most positive aspects of literature circles is that all students in the class are engaging in the same task and no one is pulled out for an extension or support activity.

As you set up these literature circles, you can either assign the books or give students a differentiated choice. Ask students who are gifted and high achieving to select from titles that are more challenging in terms of readability or content ♀. You can also ask them to read more challenging nonfiction books (Topping, Samuels, & Paul, 2008). Their discussions about nonfiction books may have significant real-life applications, which will further motivate them.

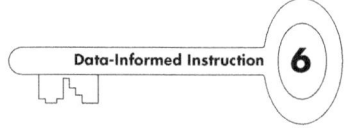

Another form of differentiation will take place among the groups and their types of discussions. As the facilitator, you guide the groups that are high achieving to engage in high-level discussions that go beyond discussing the plot, describing the characters, and making connections to oneself. Although personally connecting to literature promotes motivation (Rosenblatt, 2005), students who show giftedness and are high achieving can have discussions around characters' intent, moral ambiguity, connections to the real world, symbolism, and metaphors.

In a new model of literature circles, Daniels (2006) suggests abandoning traditional roles and having students code the literature for all the different roles. Students can use sticky notes, write in response notebooks, or note information in the margins of their own books if they have purchased them. This may foster a more authentic experience in engaging in comprehension strategies (Daniels, 2006). We suggest you start with the traditional literature circle form and move to this one for the groups that can handle engaging in multiple roles at the same time.

THE IMPORTANCE OF CHALLENGE

Some researchers believe that students who are high achieving will excel whether or not teachers put much effort into challenging them (Delisle & Galbraith, 2002). This may be true in some cases, yet other research shows the difference that good teaching and curriculum can make with these students (Tomlinson et al., 2005). If you do not teach students at their instructional level, their achievement can actually decrease because of the boredom and disengagement that results. Furthermore, we believe that because the content comes so easily to gifted or high-achieving students, they will not necessarily develop skill in perseverance unless we challenge them.

Here is an example. In one eighth-grade English class, we worked with a student named Garret who tended to zip through assignments carelessly. Fortunately, this did not dissuade his teacher, who believed that he was high achieving. She realized early on that he was not enthusiastic about the

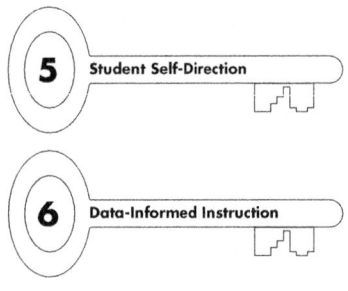

work because it was too easy. ♀ ♀ Through preassessments and learning contracts, she created challenging units and lessons, many of which took Garret significant effort to meet with success. He quickly learned that English lessons could be challenging, and that the only way to complete assignments successfully was to engage in the process with care and effort and through trial and error. As Garret's example illustrates, gifted and high-achieving students need frequent opportunities to sink their teeth into challenges so that when they reach higher levels, they will have the inner resources to persevere (Porter, 1999).

Fundamentally, you need to create a climate in which students are regularly challenged. ♀ This happens over time as you provide initial coaching and support and give students appropriate challenges. When students show talent in English and are accustomed to coasting in English class, you cannot assume that they will immediately and easily take to being challenged. But when you help them build their skills and learn how to approach challenges independently with perseverance, you give them a gift that will have enormous long-term value.

STRATEGIES TO AVOID

Two strategies that are frequently used—yet have little research support—involve advocating ad hoc peer tutoring and requiring that students master basic skills before tackling higher-order thinking challenges. However, while you may find some value in using carefully planned and well-supported peer tutoring models, particularly for a limited time and in specific circumstances, research shows that regularly asking students to explain topics to peers when they finish early does not offer them the kind of intellectual challenge they need (Nelson, Gallagher, & Coleman, 1993). Students whose teachers ask them to "help" other classmates regularly become resentful and angry. Many report feeling used—as if they are being asked to do the teacher's job (Reardon, 2009; Robinson, 2003). As a result, their motivation to complete their work dips and they underperform.

Also, some students who show extraordinary talent with higher-order thinking sometimes have difficulty mastering certain skills such as grammar, spelling, and paragraph organization (Baum, Cooper, & Neu, 2001; Fetzer, 2000). Many may also have a learning disability that makes mastering certain skills difficult (McEachern & Bornot, 2001). Although these students may be skilled at abstract, higher-order thinking, they may find activities that require rote memorization challenging (Fetzer, 2000). As a result, some teachers mistakenly preclude them from engaging with higher-order activities, fearing that students may never master basic skills if they do not take such action. Instead, provide students who fall under this category with specific and explicit learning strategies to strengthen the skills that need support, along with extension activities that facilitate higher-order thinking (Bisland, 2005). Give them multiple opportunities to master these standards, but not at the cost of missing out on more challenging work.

You must not fall into the rut of looking at the results of formative assessment without considering the whole child. As you look at the whole child, you can make wise decisions about when complete mastery of a skill, especially one that involves rote memorization, is necessary. Ultimately, you will find that students who show giftedness and are high achieving will have the chance to reach their true potential when you provide them with consistent, engaging opportunities to challenge themselves, exert effort, and—ultimately—learn (Bisland, 2005).

TO WRAP UP

At the start of this book, we asked you to take a differentiation quiz. Now that you have finished the book and become invested in some of these practices, you can retake it. Best of all, you can celebrate your growth in using *formative assessment to differentiate literacy instruction.*

Figure 7.23	Differentiating practices rubric.

Differentiating Practices Rubric

We all begin in different places and pursue different goals as we grow as teachers. This self-assessment provides an overview of practices that can enhance how you use formative assessment.

On a scale of 1–4, rate how frequently you do each practice:

1—I do this often, 2—I do this occasionally, 3—I've tried this, 4—I haven't tried this yet

Practice 1: Establish a Supportive Climate				
I foster self-directed, independent approaches to learning.	1	2	3	4
Students recognize that doing different work helps each student get what she or he needs.	1	2	3	4

(Continued)

(Continued)

Practice 2: Specify and Convey Standards				
I clearly convey objectives (targets) before beginning each unit.	1	2	3	4

Practice 3: List Extensions and Interventions				
I list potential extensions and supports before designing and then collecting formative assessments.	1	2	3	4

Practice 4: Preassess and Continually Assess				
I use diagnostic preassessment tasks before beginning each unit.	1	2	3	4
I systematically collect formal and informal assessment data all along.	1	2	3	4

Practice 5: Involve Students in Next Steps				
I use assessment data to tier homework, class activities, and assessments.	1	2	3	4
I have students self-score assessments and use the results to decide next steps to take.	1	2	3	4
I stress the importance of self-initiated learning that is based on teacher feedback and self-scored assessments.	1	2	3	4

Practice 6: Use Data to Challenge and/or Support				
I regularly use flexible groupings for differentiated tasks.	1	2	3	4
When reviewing homework or class participation during teaching, I enable students who "get it" to move on as I assist others.	1	2	3	4
I use an extensive bank of supplemental resources.	1	2	3	4
I have a bank of strategies for challenging students (e.g., open-ended tasks, higher-order questions, abstract projects, compacting contracts, and extension resources).	1	2	3	4

Practice 7: Differentiate Homework and Assessments				
I differentiate homework and hold students accountable for the different work they do.	1	2	3	4
I differentiate class assessments.	1	2	3	4

For a downloadable version of the "Differentiating Practices Rubric," *go to* http://www.corwin.com/books/Book237623.

References

Altemeier, L., Abbott, R., & Berninger, V. (2008). Executive functions for reading and writing in typical literacy development and dyslexia. *Journal of Clinical and Experimental Neuropsychology, 30,* 588–606. doi: 10.1080/13803390701562818

Anderson, L. W., & Krathwohl, D. R. (Eds.). (2001). *A taxonomy for learning, teaching and assessing: A revision of Bloom's Taxonomy of educational objectives* (Complete ed.). New York, NY: Longman.

Andrade, H. (2010). Students as the definitive source of formative assessment: Academic self-assessment and the self-regulation of learning. In H. Andrade & G. Cizek (Eds.), *Handbook of formative assessment.* 90–105. New York, NY: Routledge.

Andrade, H., Du, Y., & Mycek, K. (2010). Rubric-referenced self-assessment and middle school students' writing. *Assessment in Education, 17*(2), 199–214.

Archambault, F. X., Westberg, K. L., Brown, S. W., Hallmark, B. W., Zhang, W., & Emmons, C. L. (1993). Classroom practices used with gifted third and fourth grade students. *Journal for the Education of the Gifted, 16*(2), 103–119.

Archer, A., Gleason, M., & Vachon, V. (2003). Decoding and fluency: Foundation skills for struggling older readers. *Learning Disability Quarterly, 26,* 89–102.

Archer, A., & Hughes, C. (2010). *Explicit instruction: Effective and efficient teaching.* New York, NY: Guilford Press.

Ardoin, S. P., McCall, M., & Klubnik, C. (2007). Promoting generalization of oral reading fluency: Providing drill versus practice opportunities. *Journal of Behavioral Education, 16,* 55–70.

Arter, J., & McTighe, J. (2001). *Scoring rubrics in the classroom.* Thousand Oaks, CA: Corwin.

Asimov, I. (1986). *Robot dreams.* New York, NY: Berkley.

Bangert-Drowns, R. L., Kulik, C.-C., Kulik, J. A., & Morgan, M. (1991). The instructional effect of feedback in test-like events. *Review of Educational Research, 61*(2), 213–238.

Barmby, P. W. (2006). Improving teacher recruitment and retention: The importance of workload and pupil behavior. *Educational Research, 48*(3), 247–265.

Bas, G. (2010). Effects of multiple intelligences instruction strategy on students' achievement levels and attitudes towards English lesson. *Cypriot Journal of Educational Sciences, 5*(3). Retrieved from http://www.world-education-center.org/index.php/cjes/article/viewArticle/158

Baum, S., Cooper, C., & Neu, T. (2001). Dual differentiation: An approach for meeting the curricular needs of gifted students with learning disabilities. *Psychology in the Schools, 38*(5), 477–490.

Baxendell, B. W. (2003). Consistent, coherent, creative: The 3 C's of graphic organizers. *Council for Exceptional Children, 35*(3), 46–53.

Begeny, J. C., Krouse, H. E., Groce, M. K., & Mann, C. M. (2011). Teacher judgments of students' reading abilities across a continuum of rating methods and achievement measures. *School Psychology Review, 40,* 23–38.

Bhattacharya, A., & Ehri, L. C. (2006). Graphosyllabic analysis helps adolescent struggling readers read and spell words. *Journal of Learning Disabilities, 37*(4), 331–348.

Biancarosa, G., & Snow, C. (2004). *Reading next: A vision for action and research in middle and high school literacy* (A report to Carnegie Corporation of New York). Washington, DC: Alliance for Excellent Education.

Bisland, A. (2005). Using learning-strategies instruction with students who are gifted and learning disabled. In S. Johnsen & J. Kendrick (Eds.), *Teaching gifted students with disabilities* (Gifted Child Today Reader Series; pp. 161–178). Waco, TX: Prufrock Press.

Blachowicz, C., & Fisher, P. (2011). A word for the words. *Educational Leadership, 68*(6), 6669.

Black, P., Harrison, C., Lee, C., Marshall, B., & Wiliam, D. (2003). *Assessment for learning: Putting it into practice.* Maidenhead, England: Open University Press.

Black, P., Harrison, C., Lee, C., Marshall, B., & Wiliam, D. (2004). Working inside the black box: Assessment for learning in the classroom. *Phi Delta Kappan, 86*(1), 8–21.

Black, P., & Wiliam, D. (1998). *Inside the black box: Raising standards through classroom assessment.* London, England: GL Assessment.

Black, P., & Wiliam, D. (2005). *Assessment for learning.* Buckingham, England: Open University Press.

Bloom, B. S., & Krathwohl, D. R. (1956). *Taxonomy of educational objectives: The classification of educational goals, by a committee of college and university examiners* (Handbook 1: Cognitive domain). New York, NY: Longman.

Bowers, P., Kirby, J., & Deacon, S. (2010). The effects of morphological instruction on literacy skills: A systematic review of the literature. *Review of Educational Research, 80*(2), 144–179.

Brooks, J. G., & Brooks, M. G. (1999). *In search of understanding: The case for constructivist classrooms* (Rev. ed.). Retrieved from http://www.ascd.org/readingroom/books/brooks99book.html#intro

Brooks, S. R., Freiburger, S. M., & Grotheer, D. R. (1998). *Improving elementary student engagement in the learning process through integrated thematic instruction* (Master's thesis). Retrieved from ERIC database. (ED421274)

Brown, A. L., & Day, J. D. (1983). Macrorules for summarizing texts: The development of expertise. *Journal of Verbal Learning and Verbal Behavior, 22,* 1–14.

Brulles, D., Cohn, S. J., & Saunders, R. (2010, Winter). Improving performance for gifted students in a cluster grouping model. *Journal for the Education of the Gifted, 34*(2), 327–350.

Bryan, T., & Burstein, K. (2004). Improving homework completion and academic performance: Lessons from special education. *Theory Into Practice, 43*(3), 213–219.

Budhos, M. T. (2006). *Ask me no questions.* New York, NY: Atheneum Books for Young Readers.

Burns, M. K. (2007). Reading at the instructional level with children identified as learning disabled: Potential implications for response-to-intervention. *School Psychology Quarterly, 22,* 297–313.

Caldwell, L., & Leslie, L. (2010). Thinking aloud in expository text: Processes and outcomes. *Journal of Literacy Research, 42*(3), 308–340.

Canney, G., & Schreiner, R. (1976–1977). A study of the effectiveness of selected syllabication rules and phonogram patterns for word attack. *Reading Research Quarterly, 12*(2), 102–124.

Castillo, L. C. (1998). The effect of analogy instruction on young children's metaphor comprehension. *Roeper Review, 21*, 27–31.

Catone, W., & Brady, S. (2005). The inadequacy of individual educational program (IEP) goals for high school students with word-level reading difficulties. *Annals of Dyslexia, 55*(1), 53–78.

Cho, K., Schunn, C. D., & Charney, D. (2006). Commenting on writing: Typology and perceived helpfulness of comments from novice peer reviewers and subject matter experts. *Written Communication, 23*(3), 260–294.

Collins, J. L., & Madigan, T. P. (2010). Using writing to develop struggling learners' higher level reading comprehension. In J. L. Collins & T. G. Gunning (Eds.), *Building struggling students' higher level literacy: Practical ideas, powerful solutions*. Retrieved from http://www.utdanacenter.org/udln/downloads/2011-may-retreat/7d-collins-writing-struggling-learners.pdf

Collins, S. (2004). *Gregor the overlander*. New York, NY: Scholastic.

Common Core State Standards Initiative. (n.d.). *The standards*. Retrieved from http://www.corestandards.org/the-standards

Cooper, H. (1989). *Homework*. White Plains, NY: Longman.

Cooper, H. (2007). *The battle over homework* (3rd ed.). Thousand Oaks, CA: Corwin.

Cowie, B. (2005). Pupil commentary on assessment for learning. *Curriculum Journal, 16*(2), 137–151.

Crinon J., & Legros D. (2002). The semantic effects of consulting a textual database on rewriting. *Learning and Instruction, 12*, 605–626.

Cross, T. (2002). Competing with myths about the social and emotional development of gifted students. *Gifted Child Today, 25*(3), 44–48.

Csikszentmihalyi, M. (1990). *Flow: The psychology of optimal experience*. New York, NY: HarperCollins.

Curtis, C. P. (1995). *The Watsons go to Birmingham—1963: A novel*. New York, NY: Delacorte Press.

Daane, M. C., Campbell, J. R., Grigg, W. S., Goodman, M. J., & Oranje, A. (2005). *Fourth grade students reading aloud: NAEP 2002 Special Study of Oral Reading* (NCES No. 2006-469). Retrieved April 1, 2007, from U.S. Department of Education, National Center for Education Statistics website: http://nces.ed.gov/nationsreportcard/pdf/studies/2006469.pdf

Daiker, D. A., Kerek, A., & Morenberg, M. (1990). *The writer's options: Combining to composing* (4th ed.). New York, NY: Harper & Row.

Daniels, H. (2006). What's the next big thing with literature circles? *Voices From the Middle, 13*(1), 10–15.

Dantonio, M., & Paradise, L. V. (1988). Teacher question-answer strategy and the cognitive correspondence between teacher questions and learner responses. *Journal of Research and Development in Education, 21*, 71–76.

Delisle, J., & Galbraith, J. (2002). *When gifted kids don't have all the answers*. Minneapolis, MN: Free Spirit.

Denton, C. A., Barth, A. E., Fletcher, J. M., Wexler, J., Vaughn, S., Cirino, P. T., . . . Francis, D. J. (2011). The relations among oral and silent reading fluency and comprehension in middle school: Implications for identification and instruction of students with reading difficulties. *Scientific Studies of Reading, 15*(2), 109–135.

Diab, M. (2010). Effects of peer- versus self-editing on students' revision of language errors in revised drafts. *System, 38,* 85–95.

Dinnen, J. L. D., & Collopy, R. M. B. (2009). An analysis of feedback given to strong and weak student writers. *Reading Horizons, 49*(3). Retrieved from http://scholarworks.wmich.edu/reading_horizons/vol49/iss3/5

Duke, N. K. (2004). The case for informational text. *Educational Leadership, 61*(6), 40–44.

Dunn, R., Dunn, K., & Price, G. E. (1984). *Learning style inventory.* Lawrence, KS: Price Systems.

Eckert, T. L., Dunn, E. K., Codding, R. S., Begeny, J. C., & Kleinmann, A. E. (2006). Assessment of mathematics and reading performance: An examination of the correspondence between direct assessment of student performance and teacher report. *Psychology in the Schools, 43,* 247–265.

Edwards, R. A., Jr. (2005*). Differentiating instruction for gifted students in the English/ language arts classroom.* University of Georgia Theses and Dissertations. Retrieved from http://hdl.handle.net/10724/9776

Ehri, L., Nunes, S., Stahl, S., & Willows, D. M. (2001). Systematic phonics instruction helps students learn to read. *Review of Educational Research, 71,* 393–447.

Elleman, A., Lindo, E., Morphy, P., & Compton, D. (2009). The impact of vocabulary instruction on passage-level comprehension of school-age children: A meta-analysis. *Journal of Educational Effectiveness, 2,* 1–44.

Elwar, M. C., & Corno, L. (1985). A factorial experiment in teachers' written feedback on student homework: Changing teacher behavior a little rather than a lot. *Journal of Educational Psychology, 77*(2), 162–173.

Esteves, K. J., & Whitten, E. (2011). Assisted reading with digital audiobooks for students with reading disabilities. *Reading Horizons, 51*(1). Retrieved from http://scholarworks.wmich.edu/reading_horizons/vol51/iss1/4

Evslin, B. (1984). Heroes, gods and monsters of the Greek myths. New York, NY: Laurel-Leaf.

Fetzer, E. A. (2000). The gifted/learning-disabled child. *Gifted Child Today, 23,* 44–50.

Fisher, D., Frey, N., & Lapp, D. (2008). Shared readings: Modeling comprehension, vocabulary, text structures, and text features for older readers. *The Reading Teacher, 61,* 548–557.

Ford, M. P. (2005). *Differentiation through flexible grouping: Successfully reaching all readers.* Naperville, IL: Learning Points Associates.

Fuchs, L. S., Fuchs, D., & Deno, S. L. (1982). Reliability and validity of curriculum-based informal reading inventories. *Reading Research Quarterly, 18,* 6–26.

Gagné, F. (2003). Transforming gifts into talents: The DMGT as a developmental theory. In N. Colangelo & G. A. Davis (Eds.), *Handbook of gifted education* (3rd ed., pp. 60–75). Boston, MA: Allyn & Bacon.

Gajria, M., & Salvia, J. (1992). The effects of summarization instruction on text comprehension of students with learning disabilities. *Exceptional Children, 58,* 506–516.

Gansle, K. A., Noell, G. H., VanDerHeyden, A. M., Naquin, G. M., & Slider, N. J. (2002). Moving beyond total words written: The reliability, criterion validity, and time cost of alternate measures for curriculum-based measurement in writing. *School Psychology Review, 31*, 477–498.

Gardner, H. (2003). *Frames of mind: The theory of multiple intelligences.* New York, NY: Basic Books. Original work published 1983

Gaskins, I. W. (1998). There's more to teaching at-risk and delayed readers than good reading instruction. *The Reading Teacher, 51*(7), 534–547.

Gentry, M. L. (1999). *Promoting student achievement and exemplary classroom practices through cluster grouping: A research-based alternative to heterogeneous elementary classrooms* (RM99138). Storrs, CT: National Research Center for the Gifted and Talented.

Gentry, M., & Kielty, W. (2001). Rural and suburban cluster grouping: Reflections of staff development as a component of program success. *Roeper Review, 26*, 147–155.

Gill, B. P., & Schlossman, S. L. (2000). The lost cause of homework reform. *American Journal of Education, 109*, 27–62.

Graham, S., & Harris, K. R. (1989). A components analysis of cognitive strategy instruction: Effects on learning disabled students' compositions and self-efficacy. *Journal of Educational Psychology, 81*, 353–361.

Graham, S., & Hebert, M. A. (2010). *Writing to read: Evidence for how writing can improve reading* (A Carnegie Corporation Time to Act Report). Washington, DC: Alliance for Excellent Education.

Graham, S., & Perin, D. (2007). *Writing next: Effective strategies to improve writing of adolescents in middle and high schools: A report to Carnegie Corporation of New York.* Washington, DC: Alliance for Excellent Education.

Grant, H., & Dweck, C. S. (2003). Clarifying achievement goals and their impact. *Journal of Personality and Social Psychology, 85*, 541–553.

Grant, M. M., & Branch, R. M. (2005). Project-based learning in a middle school: Tracing abilities through the artifacts of learning. *Journal of Research on Technology in Education, 38*(1), 65–98.

Graves, M. F. (2006). *The vocabulary book.* New York, NY: Teachers College Press.

Green, S., Smith, J., III, & Brown, K. (2007). Using quick writes as a classroom assessment tool: Prospects and problems. *Journal of Educational Research and Policy Studies, 7*(2), 38–52.

Hadaway, N. L., Vardell, S. M., & Young, T. A. (2001). Scaffolding oral language development through poetry for students learning English. *The Reading Teacher, 54*, 796–806.

Hagaman, J. L., & Reid, R. (2008). The effects of the paraphrasing strategy on the reading comprehension of middle school students at risk for failure. *Remedial and Special Education, 29*(4), 222–234.

Hammill, D. D., & Larsen, S. C. (2009). *Test of written language—fourth edition (TOWL-4).* Austin, TX: Pro-Ed.

Hannel, C. L., & Hannel, L. (2005). *Highly effective questioning* (4th ed.). Phoenix, AZ: Hannel Educational Consulting.

Harris, K. R., Graham, S., & Mason, L. (2006). Improving the writing performance, knowledge, and motivation of young struggling writers in second grade. *American Educational Research Journal, 43*(2), 234–253.

Hasbrouck, J., & Tindal, G. A. (2006). Oral reading fluency norms: A valuable assessment tool for reading teachers. *The Reading Teacher, 59*(7), 636–644.

Hattie, J. C. (2009). *Visible learning: A synthesis of over 800 meta-analyses relating to achievement.* New York, NY: Routledge.

Hattie, J., & Timperley, H. (2007). The power of feedback. *Review of Education Research, 77*, 81–112.

Heacox, D. (2002). *Differentiating instruction in the regular classroom.* Minneapolis, MN: Free Spirit.

Helsel, L., & Greenberg, D. (2007). Helping struggling writers succeed: A self-regulated strategy instruction program. *The Reading Teacher, 60*(8), 752–760.

Hmelo-Silver, C. E., & Barrows, H. S. (2008). Facilitating collaborative knowledge building. *Cognition and Instruction, 26*(1), 48–94.

Hmelo-Silver, C. E., Duncan, R. G., & Chinn, C. A. (2007). Scaffolding and achievement in problem-based and inquiry learning: A response to Kirschner, Sweller, and Clark (2006). *Educational Psychologist, 42*(2), 99–107.

Horowitz, A. (2006). *Stormbreaker.* United Kingdom: Walter Books.

Hudson, R. F., Lane, H. B., Arriaza-Allen, S., Isakson, C., & Richman, T. (2011). An examination of small group decoding intervention with struggling readers: Comparing accuracy and automaticity criteria. *Learning Disabilities Research and Practice, 26*(1), 15–27.

Huebner, T. A. (2010, February). Differentiated instruction. *Educational Leadership, 67*(5), 79–81.

Irvin, J., Meltzer, J., & Dukes, M. (2007). *Taking action on adolescent literacy.* Alexandria, VA: ASCD.

Ivey, G., & Baker, M. (2004). Phonics instruction for older students? Just say no. *Educational Leadership, 61*(6), 35–39.

Jacobs, V. (2002). Reading, writing, and understanding. *Educational Leadership, 60*(3), 58–61.

Jainta, S., & Kapoula, Z. (2011). Dyslexic children are confronted with unstable binocular fixation while reading. *Plus One, 6*(4). doi: 10.1371/journal.pone.0018694

Jenkins, J. R., Fuchs, L. S., Van den Broek, P., Espin, C., & Deno, S. L. (2003). Sources of individual differences in reading comprehension and reading fluency. *Journal of Educational Psychology, 95*(4), 719–729.

Johnsen, S. (2004). *Identifying gifted students: A practical guide.* Waco, TX: Prufrock Press.

Johnston, A. M., Barnes, M. A., & Desrochers, A. (2008). Reading comprehension: Developmental processes, individual differences, and interventions. *Canadian Psychology, 49*, 125–132.

Jonsson, A., & Svingby, G. (2007). The use of scoring rubrics: Reliability, validity and educational consequences. *Educational Research Review, 2*(2), 130–144.

Joseph, L. M. (2002). Facilitating word recognition and spelling using word boxes and word sort phonic procedures. *School Psychology Review, 31*, 122–129.

Joseph, L. M., & Eveleigh, E. L. (2011). A review of the effects of self-monitoring on reading performance of students with disabilities. *The Journal of Special Education, 45*(1), 43–53.

Kamil, M. L. (2003). *Adolescents and literacy: Reading for the 21st century.* Washington, DC: Alliance for Excellent Education.

Kamil, M. L., Borman, G. D., Dole, J., Kral, C. C., Salinger, T., & Torgesen, J. (2008). *Improving adolescent literacy: Effective classroom and intervention practices: A practice guide* (NCEE No. 2008–4027). Washington, DC: U.S. Department of Education, Institute of Education Sciences, National Center for Education Evaluation and Regional Assistance.

Katzir, T. (2009). How research in the cognitive neuroscience sheds lights on sub-types of children with dyslexia: Implications for teachers. *Cortex, 45,* 558–559.

Keenan, J. M., Betjemann, R. S., & Olson, R. K. (2008). Reading comprehension tests vary in the skills they assess: Differential dependence on decoding and oral comprehension. *Scientific Studies of Reading, 12,* 281–300.

Keyes, D. (1987). *Flowers for Algernon.* Orlando, FL: Harcourt Brace.

Keys to Literacy. (2012a). *Research supporting keys to literacy programs.* Retrieved from http://www.keystoliteracy.com/reading-comprehension/professional -development/consulting-services.htm

Keys to Literacy. (2012b). *Results matter.* Retrieved from http://www.keystoliteracy .com/reading-comprehension/professional-development/consulting-services.htm/

Kingore, B. (2004). *Differentiation: Simplified, realistic, and effective.* Austin, TX: Professional Associates.

Kingore, B. (2006). Voice from the field: Recognizing and nurturing gifted poten-tial. In G. Morrison (Ed.), *Early childhood education today* (10th ed.). Upper Saddle River, NJ: Pearson Education.

Koga, N., & Hall, T. (n.d.). *Curriculum modification.* Retrieved from http://www .cast.org/publications/ncac/ncac_curriculummod.html

L'Engle, M. (1973). *A wrinkle in time.* New York, NY: Dell.

Lenz, B. K., Ellis, E. S., & Scanlon, D. (1996). *Teaching learning strategies to adoles-cents and adults with learning disabilities.* Austin, TX: Pro-Ed.

Lindblom, K., & Dunn, P. (2006). Analyzing grammar rants: An alternative to tra-ditional grammar instruction. *English Journal, 95*(5), 71–79.

Lindemann, E., & Anderson, D. (2001). *A rhetoric for writing teachers.* New York, NY: Oxford Press.

Lovett, M. W., Lacerenza, L., Borden, S. L., Frijters, J. C., & Steinbach, K. A. (2000). Components of effective remediation for developmental reading disabilities: Combining phonological and strategy-based instruction to improve out-comes. *Journal of Educational Psychology, 92*(2), 263–283.

Lovett, M. W., & Steinbach, K. A. (1997). The effectiveness of remedial programs for reading disabled children of different ages: Does the benefit decrease for older children? *Learning Disability Quarterly, 20,* 189–210.

Lowry, L. (1989). *Number the stars.* Boston, MA: Houghton Mifflin.

Macbeth, K. (2010). Deliberate false provisions: The use and usefulness of models in learning academic writing. *Journal of Second Language Writing, 19,* 33–48.

Many, J. E., Taylor, D. L., Wang, Y., Sachs, G. T., & Schreiber, H. (2007). An exami-nation of preservice literacy teachers' initial attempts to provide instructional scaffolding. *Reading Horizons, 48*(1), 19-40.

Marzano, R. J. (Ed.). (2009). *Leading edge anthology: On excellence in teaching.* Bloomington, IN: Solution Tree.

Marzano, R. J., & Pickering, D. J. (2007). The case for and against homework. *Educational Leadership, 64*(6), 74–79.

Mason, L. H., Kubina, R. M., & Taft, R. A. (2009). Developing quick writing skills of middle school students with disabilities. *Journal of Special Education, 44,* 205–220.

Masters, G., & Forster, M., (1996). *Progress maps.* Melbourne, Australia: Australian Council for Educational Research.

Mather, N., Hammil, D. D., Allen, E. A., & Roberts, R. (2004). *Test of silent word reading fluency.* Austin, TX: Pro-Ed.

Matsumura, L. C., Patthey-Chavez, G. G., Valdés, R., & Garnier, H. (2002). Teacher feedback, writing assignment quality, and third-grade students' revision in lower- and higher- achieving urban schools. *Elementary School Journal, 103*(1), 3–25.

McCutchen, D. (2006). Cognitive factors in the development of children's writing. In C. MacArthur, S. Graham, & J. Fitzgerald (Eds.), *Handbook of writing research* (pp. 115–130). New York, NY: Guilford Press.

McEachern, A. G., & Bornot, J. (2001). Gifted students with learning disabilities: Implications and strategies for school counselors. *Professional School Counseling, 5,* 24–31.

McGrail, L. (1998). Modifying regular classroom curricula for high-ability students [Electronic version]. *Gifted Child Today, 21*(2), 36.

Meltzer, J., Cook Smith, N., & Clark, H. (2002). *Adolescent literacy resources: Linking research and practice.* Providence, RI: Northeast and Islands Regional Educational Laboratory at Brown University.

Mokhtari, K., & Reichard, C. (2002). Assessing students' metacognitive awareness of reading strategies. *Journal of Educational Psychology, 94*(2), 249–259.

Morris, R. J., & Mather, M. (2008). *Evidence-based interventions for students with learning and behavioral challenges.* Mahwah, NJ: Lawrence Erlbaum.

Mowat, F. (2001). *Never cry wolf.* Boston, MA: Back Bay Books.

National Council for Curriculum and Assessment. (2006). *Strategic Plan 2006–2008.* Dublin, Ireland: Tom Collins.

National Council of Teachers of English. (2009). *Standards for the assessment of reading and writing* (Rev. ed.). Retrieved from http://www.ncte.org/standards/assessmentstandards

National Council of Teachers of English, Commission on Reading. (2004). *A call to action: What we know about adolescent literacy and ways to support teachers in meeting students' needs.* Retrieved from http://www.ncte.org/positions/statements/adolescentliteracy

National Institute of Child Health and Human Development. (2000). *Report of the National Reading Panel. Teaching children to read: An evidence-based assessment of the scientific research literature on reading and its implications for reading instruction: Reports of the subgroups* (NIH No. 00–4754). Washington, DC: U.S. Government Printing Office.

Nazzal, A. (2011). Differentiation in practice: An exploration of first year teacher implementation of differentiation strategies as expected outcomes of teacher preparation program. *Current Issues in Middle Level Education, 16*(1), 17–27.

Nelson, S. M., Gallagher, J. J., & Coleman, M. R. (1993). Cooperative learning from two different perspectives. *Roeper Review, 16,* 117–121.

Nicolson, R. I., & Fawcett, A. J. (2009). Dyslexia, dysgraphia, procedural learning and the cerebellum. *Cortex, 47*(1), 117–127.

Nokes, J. D., & Dole, J. A. (2004). Helping adolescent readers through explicit strategy instruction. In T. L. Jetton & J. A. Dole (Eds.), *Adolescent literacy research and practice* (pp. 162–182). New York, NY: Guilford Press.

Nova Scotia Department of Education. (2010). *Gifted education and talent development.* Retrieved from http://studentservices.ednet.ns.ca/sites/default/files/Gifted%20Education%20and%20Talent%20Development.pdf

Nuthall, G. (2007). *The hidden lives of learners.* Wellington, New Zealand: NZCER Press.

Nystrand, M. (2006). Research on the role of classroom discourse as it affects reading comprehension. *Research in the Teaching of English, 40*(4), 392–412.

Nystrand, M., Wu, L., Gamoran, A., Zeiser, S., & Long, D. (2003). Questions in time: Investigating the structure and dynamics of unfolding classroom discourse. *Discourse Processes, 35*(2), 135–198.

Orwell, G. (1996). *Animal farm.* New York, NY: Penguin Group. Original work published 1945

Parr, J., & Timperley, H. (2008). Teachers, schools and using evidence: Considerations of preparedness. *Assessment in Education: Principles, Policy & Practice, 15*(1), 57–71.

Parr, J., & Timperley, H. (2010). Feedback to writing: Assessment for teaching and learning and student progress. *Assessing Writing, 15*(2), 68–85.

Patel, P., & Laud, L. (2007a). Integrating a story writing strategy into a resource curriculum. *Teaching Exceptional Children, 39*(4), 34.

Patel, P., & Laud, L. (2007b). Using songs to strengthen reading fluency. *Teaching Exceptional Children Plus, 4*(2). Retrieved from http://journals.cec.sped.org/cgi/viewcontent.cgi?article=1463&context=tecplus

Patel, P., & Laud, L. (2009). Using goal-setting in "P(paw)LANS" to improve writing. *Teaching Exceptional Children Plus, 5*(4), Article 3.

Paulsen, G. (2006). *Hatchet.* New York, NY: Simon Pulse.

Porter, L. (1999). *Gifted young children.* Buckingham, England: Open University Press.

Pressley, M. (2000). What should comprehension instruction be the instruction of? In M. Kamil, P. Mosenthal, P. D. Pearson, & R. Barr (Eds.), *Handbook of reading research, 3,* 545–561. Hillsdale, NJ: Erlbaum.

Pullen, P. C., Tuckwiller, E. D., Konold, T. R., Maynard, K. L., & Coyne, M. D. (2010). A tiered intervention model for early vocabulary instruction: The effects of tiered instruction for young students at risk for reading disability. *Learning Disabilities Research and Practice, 25,* 110–123.

Radencich, M. C., & McKay, L. J. (1995). *Flexible grouping for literacy in the elementary grades.* Boston, MA: Allyn & Bacon.

Rasinski, T. (2004). Creating fluent readers. *Educational Leadership, 61*(6), 46–61.

Reardon, R. M. (2009). Instructional leadership and blended learning: Confronting the knowledge gap in practice. In Y. Inoue (Ed.), *Cases on blended learning and online learning in higher education: Concepts and practices* (pp. 44–62). Hershey, PA: IGI Global.

Reeves, D. (2003). High performance in high poverty schools: 90/90/90 and beyond. *Center for Performance Assessment Newsletter.* Retrieved from http://www.sjboces.org/nisl/high%20performance%2090%2090%2090%20and%20beyond.pdf

Reeves, D. (2005). Questions and answers from the real world. *Center for Performance Assessment Newsletter.* Retrieved from http://www.marshallmemo.com/articles/Interim%20Assmt%20Report%20Apr.%2012,%2006.pdf

Reeves, D. B. (2009). *Leading change in your school: How to conquer myths, build commitment, and get results.* Alexandria, VA: Association for Supervision and Curriculum Development.

Richards, M. R. E., & Omdal, S. N. (2007). Effects of tiered instruction on academic performance in a secondary science course. *Journal of Advanced Academics, 18*(3), 424–453.

Robinson, A. (2003). Cooperative learning and high ability students. In N. Colangelo & G. Davis (Eds.), *Handbook of gifted education* (3rd ed., pp. 282–292). Boston, MA: Allyn & Bacon.

Robinson, A., Shore, B., & Enerson, D. (2007). *Best practices in gifted education: An evidence-based guide.* Waco, TX: Prufrock Press.

Roets, L. (1993). *Modifying standard curriculum for high ability students.* New Sharon, IA: Leadership.

Rogers, K. B. (2007). Lessons learned about educating the gifted and talented: A synthesis of the research on educational practice. *Gifted Child Quarterly, 51*(4), 382–396.

Rolheiser, C., & Ross, J. A. (2001). *Student self-evaluation: What research says and what practice shows.* Retrieved from http://www.cdl.org/resource-library/articles/self_eval.php/

Rosenblatt, L. M. (2005). *Making meaning with texts: Selected essays.* Portsmouth, NH: Heinemann.

Roundy, A. A., & Roundy, P. T. (2009). The effect of repeated reading on student fluency: Does practice always make perfect? *International Journal of Social Sciences, 4,* 54–59.

Ruiz-Primo, M. A., & Furtak, E. M. (2006). Informal formative assessment and scientific inquiry: Exploring teachers' practices and student learning. *Educational Assessment, 11*(3/4), 205–235.

Sachar, L. (1998). *Holes.* New York, NY: Random House.

Saddler, B. (2005). Sentence combining: A sentence-level writing intervention. *The Reading Teacher, 58,* 468–471.

Saddler, B., Behforooz, B., & Asaro, K. (2008). The effects of sentence combining instruction on the writing of fourth grade students with learning disabilities. *Journal of Special Education, 42,* 79–90.

Sadler, R. (1989). Formative assessment and the design of instructional systems. *Instructional Science, 18,* 119–144.

Salinger, J. D. (2001). *Catcher in the rye.* New York, NY: Back Bay Books.

Samuels, S. J., & Farstrup, A. E. (2007). *What research has to say about reading instruction.* Upper Saddle River, NJ: Pearson Education.

Sandmel, K., Brindle, M., Harris, K., Lane, K., Graham, S., Nackel, J., . . . Little, A. (2009). Making it work: Differentiating tier two self-regulated strategies development in writing in tandem with schoolwide positive behavioral support. *Teaching Exceptional Children, 42,* 22–33.

Schunk, D. (1990). Goal setting and self-efficacy during self-regulated learning. *Educational Psychologist, 25,* 71–86.

Schunk, D. H., & Zimmerman, B. J. (2007). Influencing children's self-efficacy and self-regulation of reading and writing through modeling. *Reading and Writing Quarterly, 23,* 7–25.

Scruggs, T. E., & Mastropieri, M. A. (2000). The effectiveness of mnemonic instruction for students with learning and behavior problems: An update and research synthesis. *Journal of Behavioral Education, 10,* 163–173.

Shakespeare, W. (1992). *Romeo and Juliet* (Folger Shakespeare Library Series). New York, NY: Washington Square Press. Original work published 1597

Shaywitz, S. (2003). *Overcoming dyslexia: A new and complete science-based program for reading problems at any level.* New York, NY: Alfred A. Knopf.

Shepard, L. A. (2005). Linking formative assessment to scaffolding. *Educational Leadership, 63*(3), 66.

Sheth, K. (2007). *Keeping corner.* New York, NY: Hyperion.

Shippen, M. E., Houchins, D. E., Steventon, C., & Sartor, D. (2005). A comparison of two direct instruction reading programs for urban middle school students. *Remedial and Special Education, 26,* 175–182.

Smutny, J. (2000). *Teaching young gifted children in the regular classroom.* Retrieved from the ERIC database. (ERIC Digest 595)

Snow, C. (Chair). (2002). *RAND reading study group: Reading for understanding: Toward an R&D program in reading comprehension.* Santa Monica, CA: RAND.

Snowling, M., Cain, K., Nation, K., & Oakhill, J. (2009). *Reading comprehension: Nature, assessment and teaching.* Economic and Social Research Council.

Solis, M., Cuillo, S., Vaughn, S., Pyle, N., Hassaram, B., & Leroux, A. (2011). Reading comprehension interventions for middle school students with learning disabilities: A synthesis of 30 years of research. *Journal of Special Education* (Advance online publication). doi: 10.1177/0022219411402691

Soto, G. (2003). *Taking sides.* New York, NY: Harcourt.

Stahl, S., & Heubach, K. M. (2005). Fluency-oriented reading instruction. *Journal of Literacy Research, 37,* 25–60.

Stanley, T. (2012). *Project-based learning for gifted students: A handbook for the 21st century classroom.* Waco, TX: Prufrock Press.

Stecker, P. M., Fuchs, L. S., & Fuchs, D. (2005). Using curriculum-based measurement to improve student achievement: Review of research. *Psychology in the Schools, 42*(8), 795-819.

Stetter, M., & Hughes, M. (2010). Using story grammar to assist students with learning disabilities and reading difficulties improve their comprehension. *Education and Treatment of Children, 33*(1), 115–151.

Stiggins, R. J. (2005). *Student-involved assessment FOR learning* (4th ed.). Columbus, OH: Merrill Prentice Hall.

Stiggins, R. (2007). Assessment through the student's eye. *Educational Leadership, 64*(8), 22–26.

Stone, C. A., & May, A. L. (2002). The accuracy of academic self-evaluations in adolescents with learning disabilities. *Journal of Learning Disabilities, 35,* 370–383.

Stone-Harris, S. (2008). *The benefit of utilizing audiobooks with students who are struggling readers* (Unpublished doctoral dissertation). Walden University, MN.

Sung, Y. T., Chang, K. E., Chang, T. H., & Yu, W. C. (2010). How many heads are better than one? The reliability and validity of teenagers' self- and peer assessments. *Journal of Adolescence, 33*(1), 135–145.

Swicord, B. (2011). *Problem-based learning: A promising strategy for gifted students.* Retrieved November 11, 2011, from http://www.nsgt.org/resources/articles/problem_based_learning.asp

Talbert, J. E. (2010). Professional learning communities at the crossroads: How systems hinder or engender change. In A. Hargreaves, A. Lieberman, M. Fullan, & D. Hopkins (Eds.), *The second international handbook of educational change* (Springer International Handbooks of Education, Vol. 23, pp. 555–571). Dordrecht, Netherlands: Springer.

Taylor, B. M., Pearson, P. D., Clark, K., & Walpole, S. (2000). Effective schools and accomplished teachers: Lessons about primary grade reading instruction in low-income schools. *Elementary School Journal, 101*(2), 121–166.

Taylor, B. M., Pearson, P. D., Peterson, D. S., & Rodriguez, M. C. (2003). Reading growth in high-poverty classrooms: The influence of teacher practices that encourage cognitive engagement in literacy learning. *The Elementary School Journal, 104*(1), 3–28. doi: 10.1086/499740

Thomas, J. W. (2000). *A review of research on project-based learning.* Retrieved November 11, 2011, from http://www.bobpearlman.org/BestPractices/PBL_Research.pdf

Tomlinson, C. A. (1999). *The differentiated classroom: Responding to the needs of all learners.* Alexandria, VA: Association for Supervision and Curriculum Development.

Tomlinson, C. A. (2001). *How to differentiate in mixed-ability classrooms* (2nd ed.). Alexandria, VA: Association for Supervision and Curriculum Development.

Tomlinson, C. A., & Eidson, C. C. (2003). *Differentiation in practice: A resource guide for differentiating curriculum, Grades 5–9.* Alexandria, VA: Association for Supervision and Curriculum Development.

Tomlinson, C. A., Kaplan, S. N., Purcell, J., Leppien, J., Burns, D. E., & Strickland, C. (2005). *The parallel curriculum in the classroom* (Vols. 1 & 2). Thousand Oaks, CA: Sage.

Topping, K. J., Samuels, J., & Paul, T. (2008). Independent reading: The relationship of challenge, non-fiction and gender to achievement. *British Educational Research Journal, 34*(4), 505–524.

Torgesen, J. K. (2005). Recent discoveries from research on remedial interventions for children with dyslexia. In M. Snowling & C. Hulme (Eds.), *The science of reading: A handbook.* 521–537. Oxford, England: Blackwell.

Vadasy, P. F., & Sanders, E. A. (2008). Benefits of repeated reading intervention for low achieving fourth- and fifth-grade students. *Remedial and Special Education, 29,* 235–249.

Van Tassel-Baska, J. (2003). Differentiating the language arts for high ability learners. *Gifted Education Digests,* Arlington,VA: Council For Exceptional Children.

Van Tassel-Baska, J. (2005). Gifted programs and services: What are the non-negotiables? *Theory Into Practice, 44,* 90–97.

Van Tassel-Baska, J., & Brown, E. F. (2007). Toward best practice: An analysis of the efficacy of curriculum models in gifted education. *Gifted Child Quarterly, 51*(4), 342–358.

Vaughn, L. A., Childs, K. E., Maschinski, C., Paul Niño, N., & Ellsworth, R. (2010). Regulatory fit, processing fluency, and narrative persuasion. *Social and Personality Psychology Compass, 4,* 1181–1192.

Vaughn, S., Cirino, P. T., Wanzek, J., Wexler, J., Fletcher, J. M., Denton, C. A., . . . Francis, D. J. (2010). Response to intervention for middle school students with reading difficulties: Effects of a primary and secondary intervention. *School Psychology Review, 39*(1), 3–21.

Wanzek, J., Vaughn, S., Roberts, G., & Fletcher, J. (2011). Efficacy of a reading intervention for middle school students identified with learning disabilities. *Exceptional Children, 78,* 73–87.

Westberg, K. L. (1995). Meeting the needs of the gifted in the regular classroom: The practices of exemplary teachers and schools. *Gifted Child Today Magazine, 18*(1), 27–29, 41.

Whelan, G. (2001), *Homeless bird.* New York, NY: HarperTrophy.

Whitener, E. M. (1989). A meta-analytic review of the effect on learning of the interaction between prior achievement and instructional support. *Review of Educational Research, 59*(1), 65–86.

Wiggins, G. (1998). *Educative assessment: Designing assessments to inform and improve student performance.* San Francisco, CA: Jossey-Bass.

Wiggins, G. (2005). *Understanding by design.* Alexandria, VA: Association for Supervision and Curriculum Development.

Wiggins, G., & McTighe, J. (2005). *Understanding by design* (Expanded 2nd ed.). Upper Saddle River, NJ: Prentice Hall.

Wiliam, D. (2010). Standardized testing and school accountability. *Educational Psychologist, 45*(2), 107–122.

Williams, J. P., Hall, K. M., Lauer, K. D., Stafford, K. B., DeSisto, L. A., & deCani, J. S. (2005). Informational text comprehension in the primary grade classroom. *Journal of Educational Psychology, 97*(4), 538–550.

Williams, J. P., Lauer, K. D., Hall, K. M., Lord, K. M., Gugga, S. S., Bak, S. J., . . . deCani, J. S. (2002). Teaching elementary school students to identify story themes. *Journal of Educational Psychology, 94,* 235–248.

Williams, J. P., & Pao, L. (2011). Teaching narrative and expository text structure to improve comprehension. In R. O'Connor & P. Vadasy (Eds.), *Handbook of reading interventions.* New York, NY: Guilford Press.

Wilson, M., & Bertenthal, M. (Eds.). (2005). *Systems for state science assessment.* Washington, DC: National Academies Press.

Wilson, V. (2002). *Feeling the strain: An overview of literature on teacher's stress.* Glasgow, Scotland: University of Glasgow, Scottish Council for Research in Education.

Winebrenner, S. (2009). *Teaching gifted kids in the regular classroom: Strategies and techniques every teacher can use to meet the academic needs of the gifted and talented.* Minneapolis, MN: Free Spirit.

Wipprecht, C. (2007). *Dyslexia: The problem of proper reading.* GRIN Verlag.

Wixson, K. K., & Lipson, M. Y. (1991). *Reading diagnosis and remediation.* Glenview, IL: Scott Foresman.

Wolgemuth, J. R., Cobb, R. B., & Alwell, M. (2008). The effects of mnemonic interventions on academic outcomes for youth with disabilities: A systematic review. *Learning Disabilities Research and Practice, 23,* 1–10.

Wylie, E. C., & Wiliam, D. (2006, April). *Diagnostic questions: Is there value in just one?* Paper presented at the annual meeting of the American Educational Research Association (AERA) and the National Council on Measurement in Education (NCME), San Francisco, CA.

Yang, J.-C., Ko, H. W., & Chung, I. L. (2005). Web-based interactive writing environment: Development and evaluation. *Educational Technology and Society, 8*(2), 214–229.

Yep, L. (1977). *Dragonwings.* New York, NY: HarperTrophy.

Index

CORWIN

A SAGE Company

The Corwin logo—a raven striding across an open book—represents the union of courage and learning. Corwin is committed to improving education for all learners by publishing books and other professional development resources for those serving the field of PreK–12 education. By providing practical, hands-on materials, Corwin continues to carry out the promise of its motto: **"Helping Educators Do Their Work Better."**

Printed in Dunstable, United Kingdom

70702315R00132